P9-DIB-396

# The Joyful Community

Benjamin David Zablocki
# THE JOYFUL COMMUNITY

AN ACCOUNT OF THE BRUDERHOF,
A COMMUNAL MOVEMENT NOW IN ITS
THIRD GENERATION

THE UNIVERSITY OF CHICAGO PRESS

CHICAGO AND LONDON

To Elaine and Abraham and the farmers of Magic
Forest, and to farmers, builders, hunters, gatherers,
minstrels, and toymakers everywhere.

The University of Chicago Press, Chicago 60637
The University of Chicago Press, Ltd., London

© 1971, 1980 by Benjamin Zablocki
All rights reserved. Published 1971
Phoenix Edition 1980
Printed in the United States of America

84 83 82 81 80      5 4 3 2 1

ISBN: 0-226-97749-8
LCN:

The Publisher acknowledges that *The Joyful Community* presents a
sociological view of the Bruderhof and does not constitute a definitive
statement or evaluation of the aims and practices of the community.

# □ CONTENTS

# ☐ PREFACE TO THE PHOENIX EDITION

When a book about communal living written at the beginning of the 1970s is reissued at the beginning of the 1980s, it is reasonable to ask whether the perspective taken then is still relevant to the events as we understand them today. This book describes the evolution and organizational dynamics of the Bruderhof, a commune whose men and women require of themselves the absolute surrender of their self-interests. This radical organizing principle seemed at that time to be an anomaly within American society, even among communes. By now, however, it has proved itself to be the goal and destiny of many hundreds of thousands of contemporary youths and older persons in America and throughout the secularized regions of the world. Some of the more well-known products of this pattern of choice—the Moonies, the Manson Family, the Jesus Freaks, and the inhabitants of Synanon and Jonestown—have convinced many people of the need to know more about this mysterious and sometimes terrifying phenomenon.

Response to the first edition of *The Joyful Community* was, if anything, too uniformly positive. It is not that I object to praise, but rather I suspect that too many readers have been enchanted with the story of the Bruderhof as history and ethnography, and are therefore unwilling to pay much attention to what must have seemed a set of interesting but rare social processes. The sociological idea of the Bruderhof is that a stable society can be structured around the capacity to love. Whether true or false, this is too important an idea—and in the light of our knowledge of the rapidity with which undiscriminating love can become undiscriminating hate, too fateful an idea—to be accepted uncritically as the premise of an interesting and inspiring story. I want, therefore, in this brief preface, to try to locate this study within a larger corpus of unfinished sociological business.

If I were rewriting this book today, there are several things that I would change but many more I would leave alone. The argument of the book is built upon four theoretical concepts: charisma, communion, collective behavior, and thought reform. Of these, only collective behavior has not withstood the test of time. It is not that it is wrong necessarily to describe the joyous communion of the Bruderhof decision-making circle as a controlled collective behavior experience, just that there is so much more that can and should be said. The use of the concept of collective behavior, by giving a name to a pattern of interrelationships, puts an end to inquiry just at the point where it really ought to begin. Recent advances in our ability to trace subtle changes in networks of relationships have made it possible to view as structural what formerly could be detected only at a cognitive level.

The concept of charisma should perhaps have had a larger place in the analysis. Although the critical role of the charismatic leader comes through clearly in the book, the notion that entire patterns of social structure can themselves be charismatic is not explored. To the extent, however, that the book provides evidence that charismatic influence is potentially widespread within any collectivity and that it can be evoked by both the needs of the followers and the intention of the leader, the ideas presented are those which have continued to shape my more recent work.

The rapidly rising tide of charismatic movements in America makes it urgent that we remember what has been too quickly forgotten about this potent but dangerous social force and that we learn more about its actual dynamics. Sociologists have been right in following Weber's lead in attempting to trace the origin of many social forms to the routinization of charisma. But a consequence of this preoccupation is that we know little about the circumstances which give rise to charismatic patterns of interaction in the first place. It seems likely that the 1980s will be a time in which both the religious and the political thirst for charismatic intervention will intensify in our society. Building upon our knowledge of the Bruderhof and other charismatic communities, can we begin to formulate testable propositions about the genesis of charisma in the larger society?

The concept of communion is closely related to the concept of charisma. In the last few years, the work of Herman Schmallenbach, whose theory of communion greatly influenced me during the writing of *The Joyful Community*, has become more widely available in English.* One hopes this will have the effect of stimulating more research on communion as a form of social organization. It is questionable, however, whether it will stimulate this work along the lines laid out by Schmallenbach, lines which require the recognition that unconscious human dispositions have a central role in the formation of social bonds. Sociology, at the present, seems to be in retreat from its brief flirtation with the unconscious as a source of knowledge about society. I doubt that this book itself can do much to turn the tide. Although I sympathize with the great difficulties the concept of the unconscious has presented to sociological measurement, I cannot sympathize with the tendency to ignore fruitful lines of inquiry on the grounds of convenience.

We come finally to the concept of thought reform, which is used to account for the radical and dramatic experiences of resocialization and personality change which accompany the conversion crises of most Bruderhof members. Many more recent studies have corroborated my findings in this area since this book was first published. From a practical point of view, the success of the so-called deprogrammers in reversing the permanent effects of such total resocialization strengthens our confidence in the essential validity of the concept. Of course much more is now known about the technical intricacies of

---

* *See* Gunther Luschen and Gregory P. Stone eds., *Herman Schmalenbach: On Society and Experience* (Chicago: University of Chicago Press, 1977).

thought reform, and we may be at the threshold of finally understanding how to arm people psychologically against its assaults.

Overall, I think it is fair to say that the first six chapters of this book, those dealing with the Bruderhof itself, have stood up well to subsequent investigations. The same cannot be said for the final chapter on contemporary communes. This chapter has been completely superseded by subsequent research,† and is included here only for its historical interest. A comparison of this chapter with my more recent treatment of the subject may also be interesting from the point of view of highlighting the difficulties of studying a social movement while it is still going on.

And what of the Bruderhof itself? How has it endured these nine years? As predicted in the book, the Bruderhof has moved to reincorporate itself within the Hutterian Church. This is seen within the community as the most significant event of the decade. Aside from this renewed identification with something larger than itself, the Bruderhof has undergone very little change. No new "hofs" have been built in America and the one in England has simply regrouped at a new location. A trickle of apostate or exiled members continues to be reinstated as the wounds of the great crisis slowly heal. New members continue to be drawn from both *sabra* and outside stock. The daily life of the Bruderhof continues to flow along pretty much unchanged. This pattern of life, as exemplified in cults, has attracted much recent attention, almost all of it negative. Alongside all of this the Bruderhof continues to bear quiet witness to a beautiful and life-affirming version of the same form of social organization which has elsewhere—as in Jonestown—caused so much death and suffering.

† *See* Benjamin Zablocki, *Alienation and Charisma: A Study of Contemporary American Communes* (New York: The Free Press, 1980). This is a systematic comparative study of 120 communes conducted over the period from 1965 to 1978.

# SONG FOR THE PRESENT DAY

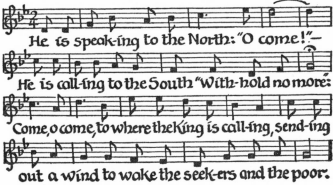

He is speak-ing to the North: "O come!"—

He is call-ing to the South "With-hold no more:

Come, o come, to where the King is call-ing, send-ing

out a wind to wake the seek-ers and the poor.

There is nothing that can bar your way,
Though the breaking may be blood upon the sand:
Lift your hearts, for hark, the wind is calling,
Breaking down the barriers, however high
they stand.

There are rivers running strong between,
There are watches where the stars are never still,
Come, though come, to where the King is calling,
Calling for a people in a city on a hill.

In the Tumult of a world of steel,
There's a whisper of a wind upon the street:
Rise, and come, though long and hard the journey,
Yonder is the city, where the South and North
shall meet.

Philip Britts.

*Bruderhof poet*

# □ ACKNOWLEDGMENTS

Many people helped me with this book. I am all the more grateful to the members of the Bruderhof for their help and hospitality, considering their often-stated contempt for 'studies'. I want to thank the ex-members, especially, for their courage in talking openly and freely to a stranger about an intimate and often very painful subject. All of them contributed, not only information, but important ideas. However, through their wishes, they must remain anonymous.

My wife Elaine worked with me at every stage of the project. Every idea in the book comes out of long discussions between us. Much of the material on Bruderhof women is her contribution alone and, because of the sex-segregated character of much of Bruderhof life, would not have been otherwise obtainable.

Within the academic community, Professor Daniel Bell and Professor Staughton Lynd helped me to get started in my search for contemporary intentional communities at a time when I was groping blindly. Professor John Markoff, Professor Robert Friedmann, Professor Neville Dyson-Hudson, and Professor Sasha Weitman made many valuable suggestions during the planning stage of this research. I am particularly indebted to Professor Weitman for calling my attention to the work of Herman Schmalenbach on communion. Professor Philip Selznick and Professor Neal Smelser read an early version of the manuscript and offered important criticisms which have been incorporated into the book.

This research was originally carried out and presented as a Ph.D. thesis in the Department of Social Relations, at the Johns

Hopkins University, in Baltimore, Maryland. I cannot begin to express my gratitude to my two mentors at Hopkins, Professor James Coleman and Professor Arthur Stinchcombe. Both of them had the faith in me to allow me to follow my own leading, even at times when it was incomprehensible to them. At the same time, both were constant sources of inspiration to me. Professor Coleman taught me to seek answers to the 'important questions' of sociology, and not to get sidetracked by anything less. Professor Stinchcombe taught me how to pursue an argument that is more than three steps long without getting lost. I hope that they will be pleased with the way I have incorporated these lessons into this book.

In chapter seven, I mention that I have visited close to a hundred contemporary communes in the last five years. I was a founder or a member of a few of them. At most of them, I was merely a guest. All of them are a part of my family. It would be impossible to acknowledge each act of help, hospitality, and love that I have experienced in my commune journeys. But some communitarians have taught me so much, that I must mention them by name. Mildred Loomis, editor of the *Green Revolution*, doesn't know anything that isn't known by thousands of communitarians across the country; she just figured it all out a generation before anyone else did, and was busy teaching it when people finally decided it was time to listen. I consider Calvino De Filipis, Steve Durkee, and Lou Gottlieb the three wise men of the communitarian movement. I have been privileged to work and talk with all of them. My friends, David and Kitty Stephens, have taught me more about the emotional side of community than anyone else.

I was lucky in having as an editor of this book, my old friend and fellow communitarian, Abigail Grafton. I'm one of those sociologists who doesn't write 'to gud', and she performed the miracle of transforming my manuscript into a comprehensible book. Sometimes she had to beat me over the head before I would allow this to happen.

This book required money and typing. The former was supplied by the National Institute of Mental Health, first in the form of a doctoral fellowship and later as part of a grant to the Haight Ashbury Research Project. The latter was supplied by Virginia Bailey, Lynn Turner, Genevieve Tsaconis, Karen Muhonen, Linda Woita, and Peggy Atkin.

Susan Margolis, Albert Duvall, and Abraham Zablocki also helped, and so did Lisa.

University of California
Berkeley
1966 – 70

# □ INTRODUCTION

Community is an idea whose time has come. America is currently experiencing a flowering of communitarian experiments unequalled even by the great utopian movements of the early nineteenth century. It almost seems as if the post-industrial Western world, having solved (theoretically at least) the problems of *liberté* and *égalité*, has turned its energies toward that last and most elusive item on the French Revolutionary agenda – *fraternité*: brotherhood, tribalism, community. This rapidly awakening interest can be seen not only in the thousand or more currently existing rural communes of the hippies and in the even more numerous urban communes, but also in the widespread participation in encounter groups by the older middle class, and in the movement away from integration and toward the development of ethnic solidarity on the part of many racial minority groups. Communitarianism in America today is still primarily a movement of the young, but a movement in which portents for the future of our entire society can be read.

The Bruderhof is a community unlike any I have ever seen. When I first visited it in the winter of 1965, I felt as if I had wandered in a dream into a medieval village, or into a world outside of history where neither time nor space existed. Never before or since have I felt the presence of brotherly love so permeating a place that I felt I was breathing it. I have visited close to a hundred contemporary communes and studied the history of those of the last century. The Bruderhof can be classified with neither the new nor the old. It is not at all a typical case. I present this study not as a key to the understanding of some larger social movement, but because I feel that the problems that it raises and the solutions that it offers are fundamentally related to our society's quest for *fraternité*.

In 1947, in a cave near Qumran at the northern end of the Dead Sea, an Arab boy made a discovery which was to bring to the world a knowledge of one of the most fascinating social experiments of the ancient Near East. This discovery of the so-called 'Dead Sea Scrolls' has thrown light on the beliefs and daily life of the Essenes, a communitarian sect within ancient Judaism whose members lived approximately two thousand years ago. The Roman occupation of Palestine had posed a grave crisis to the Jewish religion. The ancient traditions were crumbling upon contact with modern Hellenistic influences. Various movements arose in response to this crisis. The Zealot revolutionaries were working to expel the Roman conquerors by force. The Pharisees were reformers, choosing to work within the system, modifying a bit here, reinterpreting a bit there. The Essenes chose a completely different strategy. Rather than attacking or trying to modify the Roman Empire, they ignored it. Reasoning that Roman authority could not be omnipresent, they chose to live within the interstices of occupied Palestine. They chose a rather austere and remote habitat on the banks of the Dead Sea and there set up a microcosm of life as they believed it should be lived. Those who would call this the strategy of the ostrich must argue with the many scholars who believe that Jesus and the early Christians were profoundly influenced by their early contacts with the Essenes.

The Essenes represent the first known instance, in the Western world, of a phenomenon which has recurred periodically throughout subsequent history, and of which the Bruderhof is a contemporary example – the phenomenon of the communitarian response. Arthur Bestor, in his brilliant study of early American utopian communities, defines it as one of four methods for implementing change:

Communitarianism was, in fact, one among four ... alternative programs. Today we are apt to think of but three. Individualism, now largely associated with conservative thinking, we can recognize as an authentic philosophy of reform in the hands of an Adam Smith or a

Jefferson, and in the ringing words of Emerson's Phi Beta Kappa Address of 1837, 'If the single man plant himself indomitably on his instincts, and there abide, the huge world will come round to him.' Revolution, too, is a possible path to social change, as present to our experience as it was to the eighteenth or nineteenth century. In between we recognize, as a third alternative, the multitude of reform movements, best described as gradualistic, which employ collective action but aim at an amelioration of particular conditions, not a total reconstruction of society.

Communitarianism does not correspond exactly to any of these. It is collectivistic not individualistic, it is resolutely opposed to revolution, and it is impatient with gradualism. Such a position may seem no more than an elaborate and self-defeating paradox. To the communitarian it was not. The small, voluntary, experimental community was capable, he believed, of reconciling his apparently divergent aims: an immediate root and branch reform, and a peaceable, non-revolutionary accomplishment thereof. A microcosm of society, he felt, could undergo drastic change in complete harmony and order, and the great world outside could be relied on to imitate a successful experiment without coercion or conflict.[1]

Many writers on the subject have referred to communitarian experiments as 'utopian communities'. I have chosen to use the term 'intentional community' instead. This term is Quaker in origin. Its use avoids the value loadings of such alternatives as 'utopian community', 'communistic society', or 'cooperative colony'. The Fellowship of Intentional Communities, a federation of communities, that existed during the 1950s, formulated an operational definition of the term that will serve well enough for our purposes:

An intentional community is a group of persons associated together [voluntarily] for the purpose of establishing a whole way of life. As such, it shall display to some degree, each of the following characteristics: common geographical location; economic interdependence; social, cultural, educational, and spiritual inter-exchange of uplift and development. A minimum of three families or five adult members is required to constitute an intentional community.

Communitarian movements seem to arise in waves at particular times in particular places. America during the nineteenth century experienced several waves of intentional-community building, many of them originally European movements transplanted to the New World. Europe after World War I experienced a wave of communitarianism, as did America and Japan after World War II; and, of course, the same phenomenon is occurring in America at the present time. Israel's kibbutz movement was begun after World War I and experienced its greatest expansion in the years following World War II.

It would seem that the rise of communitarianism has something to do with wars, but the relationship is not simple. This disruption of normal life patterns and the upheaval of moral and social norms brought about by war often precede the appearance of intentional communities. The Fourieristic communities which arose in America in the 1840s constitute the most striking exception to this rule. It is interesting that England and Europe, having sprouted so many communal experiments after World War I, were unreceptive to such movements after World War II. The crucial difference seems to be the feeling that a new age was dawning, which was prevalent in Europe in 1920 but decidedly not in 1945.

The myth of a new age dawning often stimulates the rise of communitarian movements. We can well imagine that the messianic fever that swept through Palestine in the century preceding the birth of Jesus was instrumental in motivating the Essenes to make the sacrifices necessary for their communitarian retreat. Again, during and after the Protestant Reformation, more than 1500 years later, we can see that a feeling that the dead hand of the past had been removed and that a new and better life was on the horizon stimulated the birth of innumerable intentional communities. The Hutterians, one group of communitarian experiments spawned by the Reformation, have kept their structure intact to the present day.

Turning to more recent times, widespread belief in the coming of a new age certainly helps to explain the impetus behind many of the communitarian experiments of nineteenth century America. The virginity of the frontier combined with the pragmatic philosophy of the new American republic fostered the belief that man was free to create his own forms of social organization. Precisely this attitude was most bitterly criticized by Karl Marx in his famous attack on the 'utopian socialists' in the *Communist Manifesto*:

> Historical action is to yield to their personal inventive action, historically created conditions of emancipation to fantastic ones, and the gradual, spontaneous class-organization of the proletariat to an organization of society especially contrived by these inventors. Future history resolves itself, in their eyes, into the propaganda and the practical carrying out of their social plans.[2]

Karl Marx and his nineteenth century revolutionary followers also believed that the coming of a new age was imminent. To understand why they turned to revolution where others turned to communitarianism we must ask what forces these groups saw as impeding the arrival of the new age. Revolutionaries characteristically see the problem as a power struggle. Their vision of a new society is clear and unambiguous, but certain segments of society prevent its realization. The problem thus becomes one of gaining and using sufficient power to remove the obstacles to the coming of the new age.

Exactly the contrary is true for communitarians. They picture a society in which the means for ushering in a new age are readily at hand but in which men's hearts have not been stirred by the vision of this new age. While Marxists see men as historically determined, communitarians believe that men are essentially free to choose their own destinies. Some communitarians would agree with Marx that society is based on conflict. They seek not to transform the world but to separate themselves from it. Other communitarians believe that ignorance is the only barrier to global peace and harmony. They seek to educate the world by the power of their example. The Bruderhof falls into this latter category.

## *Chapter One* □ THE LIVING CHURCH

I first met the Bruderhof almost by accident. I had been staying at the Catholic Worker Farm in nearby Tivoli, New York, when one day a friend said, 'There's another intentional community right near here called the Bruderhof. Would you like to go see them?' I had heard vaguely of the Bruderhof, a large old community of toymakers, and I was curious. So, even though it was snowing hard and the highway patrol was advising people to stay home, we got into my friend's Volkswagen and started out.

The Woodcrest colony of the Society of Brothers is built on a hill. The Volkswagen made it halfway up the hill, where some Brothers met us and brought us the rest of the way. The little village was full of movement – effortless movement, it seemed to me. It was midmorning, and children were running everywhere. Men were clearing the roads with a snowplow, unloading a big truck, patching a leaky roof. It was near lunchtime, and I saw women bustling in the kitchen. I stayed only a day and went away, remembering the joy in all of the faces and the indescribable sound of the entire community singing, determined to come back and find out more.

The Bruderhof is a federation of three colonies located in New York State, Pennsylvania, and Connecticut. The colonies are known as *hofs* (rhyming with the English word 'loaf'), which is German for 'dwelling place', and Bruderhof means 'dwelling place of brothers'. The total population of the community numbers about 750 men, women, and children holding all goods and property in common. The Bruderhof supports itself through a communal industry – the manufacture and sale of high-quality and expensive wooden toys, most of which are bought by schools. In 1970 the community is celebrating its fiftieth birthday. It was founded in Germany in 1920, and has since undergone migrations to England, Paraguay, and finally, in 1954, to the United States. It is held together by its common religion – a radical, fundamental Anabaptist Christianity.

A most striking thing about the Bruderhof is the people. Here are no rugged, bearded Amish peasants transplanted from another age but, for the most part, sophisticated, middle-class, college-educated individuals. The population is highly diversified in background – ex-millionaires and ex-tramps, holders of post-graduate degrees and grade-school dropouts, a dozen nationalities, and as many religions. Unlike the Hutterians and Amish, the Bruderhof has never become a blood-related ethnic group. The community still has some of its original members and is beginning to raise a fourth generation of '*sabra*' children but it has remained constantly open to a stream of new members from the outside world. At the time of this study, the majority of Bruderhof members were converts who had joined within the past ten years. This combination of survival through at least three generations with a continually open membership policy is a major accomplishment, often striven for but rarely achieved among communitarian groups.

There is complete economic sharing between Woodcrest and its two sister *hofs* – Oak Lake, six hours to the west, and Evergreen, two hours to the east. Much visiting takes place among the three *hofs*, and individuals or families often move from one colony to another. Members are considered to belong to the Bruderhof as a whole, not to any particular *hof*.

Woodcrest is located on a hundred-acre estate about two hours' drive from New York City. It is the oldest and the largest of the three currently existing *hofs*. Of the Bruderhof's current population of approximately 750, close to three hundred live at Woodcrest. It is, in a sense, the main *hof* – it is the largest, it contains the central office of Community Playthings, and it is the residence of the *Vorsteher* (bishop) for all three *hofs*.

The colony is located in an area of great natural beauty – rolling, hilly, partially forested countryside with the Catskills visible in the distance. A visitor turns off the highway running along the Walkill River and drives half a mile up a private road to reach the buildings. The first thing he sees is 'the shop' – three large buildings which house production and shipping departments for Community Playthings. A little farther up the road, he comes to a small village with many buildings dotted on the hillside. There is a winding drive running through them, and no building is more than a few minutes' walk from any other (see map, page 25). The whole place is clean, neat, and cheerful. Flowers are planted everywhere.

The central building of the community is the Carriage House, occasionally called the Main House. The kitchen and dining room are located on its ground floor. In the dining room, there are over twenty community-made tables, each seating ten. This provides adequate space, since the youngest children have their meals separately. The Carriage House is built out over the hillside, and from the large windows on three sides of the dining room there is a view of the valley, the next hill, mountains in the distance, and, when the hour is right, the setting sun. The dining room is the hub of the communal life. It is used for all meetings of the whole community, as well as for meals, dances, and celebrations.

The large Victorian house across the lawn from the Carriage House contains a school for grades one to eight. The large high-ceilinged rooms are admirable classrooms; there are pottery, woodworking, and arts-and-crafts rooms in the basement. All the other buildings that were on the property when the Brothers bought it have been remodeled into living quarters. Four large residential buildings have been constructed. The lower floors of some of these buildings house work departments – laundry in Sinntal House, sewing rooms in Rhön House, preschool in Sannerz House and, oddly enough, baby nursery in Baby House. The first three of these buildings are named after previous Bruderhof settlements in Germany, England, and Paraguay. These two- and three-storey buildings each house five families or

## 1. *Woodcrest*

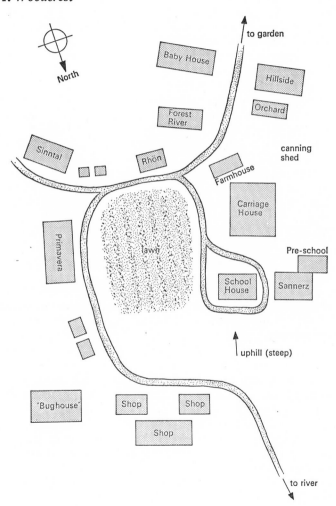

North

to garden

Baby House

Hillside

Orchard

Forest River

canning shed

Sinntal

Rhön

Farmhouse

Carriage House

Primavera

lawn

Pre-school

School House

Sannerz

uphill (steep)

'Bughouse'

Shop

Shop

Shop

to river

more. The remodeled farm buildings and the cottages have room for only a family or two each.

Many single women live on the upper floor of Primavera House, while others are scattered over the *hof*, one or two to a room. Most of the single men live in a building located near the shop, named Periwinkle Lodge but called the Bughouse in tribute to its disorder.

The quality of the living quarters necessarily varies, since some of the residential buildings were not originally built for this purpose. Some families are always more crowded than others. The Housemothers try to assign the available housing in the best way, keeping many different considerations in mind. Often people are shifted around in a complicated pattern reminiscent of musical chairs.

In the new buildings, each hallway has a refrigerator, stove, sink, and ironing board for everyone's use, as well as toilets, bathrooms, and showers. Each family is given a large common room which serves as living room, dining room, and kitchen. The Bruderhof believes that it is important for each family to be able to eat some meals together in its own living quarters, even though it costs a considerable amount to set things up so that this is possible. Sometimes the common room is also used as a bedroom for the parents or for some of the children. Additional bedrooms are assigned, according to family need, adjacent to or near the common room. Two, three, or four children share the same bedroom, often using double-decker beds.

A Bruderhof family common room is typically a very pleasant room to be in, although not in middle-class American style. There are drawings hanging on the walls, or perhaps a copy in fine script of a favorite song, or a picture made of wood veneers. These have been made by Bruderhof members and exchanged as birthday or Christmas presents. The quality of Bruderhof arts-and-crafts work is outstanding. Over the table there may hang an air castle made of shining straws. On the table for special occasions there is a cross-stitched tablecloth. On the shelves there are some books, a candle in a wooden candlestick, perhaps some of the fine wooden bowls the community made in Paraguay, or a clay bowl or candlestick made by a child in school. The room is simple, cheerful, homely. One family has a guinea pig and a caged bird in a corner of their room. Many have bird-feeders just outside their windows.

South of the cluster of buildings is a large garden which produces a substantial amount of fresh vegetables and fruit – enough to eat fresh and to can for the winter. The children's rabbit hutches are behind the Baby House, and the stable for Eeyore the donkey, which the schoolchildren built themselves, is over near the schoolhouse. Southwest of the house, the ground rises to a ridge, the highest ground on the property, on top of which the community has its reservoir. From here, there is a fine view of the whole community and of the Catskills, and this is a favorite location for a Sunday afternoon walk or a picnic tea. On warm Sunday mornings, the adults and older children meet on the hillside near the reservoir for the weekly household meeting, a gathering for silence and songs.

## 2. *Bearing Witness: The Religious Ideology*

Life at Woodcrest flows on with such apparent harmony that the casual observer can easily believe himself within the narrow confines of a medieval village. Quite the opposite is the case. The Bruderhof is a social movement whose members are deeply concerned with world problems and totally committed to bringing about radical social change. Its social program, however, is not as visible as it might be because it is based on the precepts of Christianity.

Non-Christians tend to dismiss the Bruderhof as other-worldly; Christians tend to be interested in the intricacies of its ideology. Actually, the Bruderhof is neither other-worldly nor theological. It has as definite a social program as does any political party. The reader need not take a stand as to the truth or the untruth of the Bruderhof's brand of Christianity. But he must have an understanding of this Christianity, not as a theological system, but as the mythic basis of a social movement, in the sense of Georges

Sorel, who speaks of a unifying central myth underlying every significant social movement.

Sorel defines myth as a segment of a world-view that attempts to explain *why* certain phenomena were, are, or shall be.[3] The literal truth or untruth of a myth, according to Sorel, is relatively unimportant. It speaks directly to the heart, activating its still unarticulated hopes and needs. A myth must be internally consistent within the framework it creates but it need not necessarily conform to standards that others call reality. One does not 'understand' a myth. One directly feels (or fails to feel) its truth. In this perspective, the sociological significance of (e.g.) Christianity, or Marxism, or Zen-Macrobiotics is not in its predictive or explicative power, but in its ability to stir men's hearts.

The Bruderhof myth is a cosmic myth. The universe is involved in a death-struggle between good and evil. God is at the head of the forces of good, which, therefore, must ultimately triumph. Man can help by emptying himself of ego and allowing himself to be filled with the Holy Spirit. God calls man to aid him in the struggle, but not as a hero and not as an isolated individual. God calls man to serve by *bearing witness* to the spirit of goodness, peace, love, and truth in all of the simple everyday acts of living, and to do so as part of a *separate people*, separated from the world but intimately involved with it.

The idea of a cosmic war between good and evil is, of course, far older even than Christianity. Its most powerful expression is Milton's *Paradise Lost*. But the Bruderhof finds it in the writings of a late-nineteenth-century prophet named Christoph Blumhardt:

There must have been a rebellion in heaven. As a result a portion of heaven was lost to God and came under the control of the daemonic forces. God created the earth right in the middle of this lost territory. Man's task was to win this land back for God, but he failed. (Paraphrased by an ex-member.)[4]

The cosmic perspective is a feature of many social movement myths. For instance, the Communist Party identifies its political activities with the working-out of an inevitable Hegelian dialectic process whereby the *kairos* of history will eventually be attained through the class struggle and the victory of the proletariat.

Gabriel Almond and many others have documented the power of such a perspective in engendering loyalty and commitment.[5] In the Bruderhof, this function is illustrated by the following statement of a member:

> I feel that if I have overcome my tendency to return an angry word when a Brother has spoken to me, I have resisted the evil spirit. I have struck a blow for winning back part of the universe for God Almighty.

Another recurrent theme found in the myths of successful social movements is the combination of the necessity for struggle and the certainty of ultimate victory. According to the Bruderhof, good will triumph, but only through the uttermost efforts of men. A physician at Woodcrest spoke to me about two diverse groups that he admired: the Quakers and the Freudians. Both, he felt, were impotent in the world, despite the glimmerings of truth that both possessed:

> Quakers know that all men have an inner goodness. But this often becomes, all men have a goodness which you can rely upon, which is absolutely false. Freudians, on the other hand, are so impressed with the destructive tendencies which they uncovered that they see little else. The Bruderhof is mid-way. We see a struggle between good and evil, but we're confident that good is going to win out [paraphrased].

Commitment to the Bruderhof cause is thus engendered in two ways: through the desire to be on the winning side, and through the feeling that one's services are desperately needed.

According to the Bruderhof, participation in the struggle is only possible if one is willing to pay the price, which is the renunciation of one's own ego:

> Man is given the task of serving in the army of God. But he is also given the riddle to solve of how he may effectively serve. He finds that any action taken on his own strength is ineffective. Then he discovers why. Individual action implies an ego, and ego boundaries, and thus separation. Strong action is made possible by strong boundaries. But God is unity, the breaking down of boundaries. So any action taken by man under his own leadership, whatever its intent, cannot further God's

purposes. Man must first strive to give up his own ego. Then he can be open to the love of God and to the will of God which are streaming down upon him all the time, though he fails to recognize them.

Many Bruderhof members have taken part in other communitarian experiments before coming to the Bruderhof. Their belief in the necessity of ego-renunciation is buttressed by experiences of failure in communities that did not demand it. Some speak of themselves as pragmatic Christians, who joined a Christian community, not because they were originally Christians, but because they had tried every other method of community living and found that this was the only one that worked. A Bruderhof pamphlet alludes to these experiences:

... Men, as their nature is now constituted, are incapable of community. The changing moods of the disposition, the possessive impulses craving for happiness of body and soul, the powerful mental currents of touchiness and ambition, the urge to have personal influence on men, indeed, human privileges of all kinds – all of these place a humanly insurmountable barrier in the way of actual and real community building. Faith does not succumb to the delusion that these factual realities of the covetous impulses and weaknesses of character are decisive. In actual fact, they are of no significance in the face of the power of God and His all-conquering love. The energy of His Spirit, which builds community, overcomes everything.

Once a man or woman succeeds in becoming an empty vessel, and is filled with the Holy Spirit, then his sensory and motor functions, his mind, and his strength can be put to use, not under his own direction, but following the will of God. This to the Bruderhof is the symbolic meaning of the story of the crucifixion and the resurrection: each human ego first must die, and then the person is reborn in the spirit of Christ. His every act, however commonplace, then becomes an act for the Kingdom of God. This is what the Bruderhof calls 'bearing witness'.

Bearing witness means living in such a way that other people see evidence for God in one's actions. Thus it is an important part of the Bruderhof ideology, not only to live a particular style of life, but to make this life visible to the rest of the world. In this respect, it is symbolically important that Woodcrest is on a hill.

Reference is often made to the 'city on a hill' spoken of in the Sermon on the Mount:

Ye are the light of the world. A city that is set on a hill cannot be hid.

Neither do men light a candle, and put it under a bushel, but on a candlestick; and it giveth light unto all that are in the house.

Let your light so shine before men, that they may see your good works, and glorify your Father which is in heaven.[6]

Many people besides the Bruderhofs have sought to bear witness. For some this has meant heroism, saintliness, or even martyrdom. The Bruderhof, in contrast, is concerned with bearing witness in the simple, everyday acts of living – thus showing the average man what his life could be like if it were permeated with the same spirit. 'We are not trying to imitate Christ, but to follow him; not to do as he did, but to do as he said,' one Bruderhof woman told me. For this reason, the Bruderhof de-emphasizes sacraments and rituals. Visitors are often struck by the fact that, in a community that calls itself a Church, there is no church building. One member explained this to me:

We have no gestures or forms. What's inside is what's important. The spirit of life is trying to get in all the time, and when we let it, can either be in a meeting or digging potatoes.

This attitude also helps to overcome the dichotomy of God 'up there' and man 'down here'. It is interesting to note a similar sentiment expressed in a Zen Buddhist monastery in California:

Every activity at Zen Mountain is held to be of equal importance. All is an aspect of the practice of Zen. There is no distinction between zazen and peeling onions. Nothing is preparation for anything else. Everything is what it is.[7]

The Bruderhof and the Zen monastery have quite different purposes. What they have in common is a desire to destroy the notion of a secular sphere of life. The message is that there are no activities, however trivial, that cannot be permeated by the divine spirit.

Bruderhof members do not believe that the path of bearing witness in everyday life is any easier than those chosen by heroes, saints and martyrs. Eberhard Arnold, the founder, has said:

Just as the fellowship of the body can only be maintained by the constantly renewed sacrifice of the cells of the body, so fellowship of life can only come into being in the growing organism of the church-community through heroic sacrifice. . . . In the common life every kind of softness, every pampering arising from weakness, is overcome by the glowing sharpness of love.

When I was at Woodcrest, we heard a news report that a young Quaker had made himself into a human torch and killed himself as a protest against the Vietnam War. That evening, a member said to me, 'I also want my life to be a burning torch for the world, not in suicide, but in the life I lead.' This is put succinctly in a Bruderhof expression: 'We're prepared to die for each other, but to live for each other is something much harder.'

The unifying myth of the Bruderhof movement specifies not only that its members bear witness, but that they do so as a separate people, removed from the world. It is this part of the myth which distinguishes between the Bruderhof and other 'witnessing' denominations such as the Quakers, Mennonites, and Brethren. This idea is expressed in an article by a Bruderhof member entitled, 'The Spirit of Prophecy':

The demand of the prophetic spirit is distinguished by its call for a *people*: the Hebrew people of God of the Old Covenant, and the Christian people of the New Covenant and its conscious revivals. 'The Holy People' are to be set apart from the Surrounding World. The peace-minded Anabaptists of the sixteenth and the Quakers of the seventeenth century saw themselves as the revival of the all-inclusive prophetic demand to form the core of the future people of God and to take up the battle with the world in new and changing forms. That was a tremendous demand. It is no wonder that later generations were not equal to its greatness, and turned off into the domain of personal salvation; that they attempted to reinterpret the words of prophecy in philosophic or pietistic terms and in other respects adjusted themselves to the evil world to the best of their ability. . . . The visible people of God became one religious group among others and the salt lost its savour.

The communal society at Woodcrest is an attempt at a concrete expression of the Bruderhof myth. The primary manifestation of the life of bearing witness is the breaking down of barriers among people. One of the most important barriers is ownership of private property. Another is the psychological boundary around the individual ego. It is almost impossible for an isolated individual, surrounded by other individuals who do not feel as he does, to break down these barriers. But in a community of individuals pledged to the same goals, this can begin to happen. When it does, the individual begins to decrease in importance, and the 'separate people' begins to emerge.

The ideology of bearing witness has practical consequences in every area of Bruderhof life. In the economic life of the community, it finds expression in the classification of all work as service. Here the Bruderhof sharply differs from the kibbutz. In the kibbutz work is glorified and esteem is dependent upon ability and effort at work. In the Bruderhof, work is considered important but it is not exalted. Many songs are sung of the *Wandervogel* – free adventurers of the German youth-movement days. There are jokes (rarely carried through) about sneaking off for the day to hike and loaf and be free. Tramps are admired and envied.

Esteem is never given for proficiency at work. In the kitchen, when someone thoughtlessly complimented Kathy for the delicious pies she had baked, that person was quickly and firmly reminded that Sue and Elaine had also helped in the baking. Elaine, my wife, had performed the humble but necessary service of peeling and slicing the apples.

There are two reasons for this extreme emphasis on work as service. Both have to do with the communal need to deny the value of individual achievement. It is essential to the ideology of bearing witness that the achievements of the Bruderhof in creating an intentional community not be perceived by the world as the achievements of exceptional men. The witness to community is a witness that this way of life is possible for all men. The limitations of individual achievement are thus emphasized, and the virtues of sheer cooperation, regardless of who is doing the cooperating, are proclaimed.

The second reason is more important, although perhaps less conscious. The Bruderhof needs to maintain a feeling of the dependency of the individual upon the group. As we shall see more fully in chapter six, in order for an individual's ego to go through the process of symbolic death and rebirth, it must be stripped of external means of identification. In our society, one of the major ways in which an individual defines himself is as a producer of wealth. This must be taken from him. He must come to feel that all material goods come to him from the grace of God. Yet it is necessary for the community to have some justification for imposing a work discipline. The notion of work as service accomplishes both of these aims.

The definition of work as service (i.e., as bearing witness) creates an extraordinary high work morale. If one's job is dull or tiring, one can always be refreshed by contemplating the cosmic significance of one's actions. The energy liberated by a sense of creativity, which in our society is tapped only by a small minority of productive workers, in the Bruderhof is available to every person.

I was especially impressed by the loving care with which the most routine jobs were done. For instance, I once helped a group of men move chairs and tables in preparation for a meeting. We moved the tables to the side of the room and then arrranged the chairs in several concentric circles. Each member of the crew took great pains to see that the chairs were arranged at the proper distance from each other and that benches were facing at the proper angle. These people were bearing witness in the act of arranging chairs.

In the regular work, bearing witness is manifested in many ways. During the last half hour of any day the pace of work in an ordinary shop (unless under time pressure) will usually slacken. In the Bruderhof toy factory and the other work departments, it usually increases. One time there was a large truck delivery of toys produced at another *hof* to be stored at Woodcrest. It arrived around lunchtime. After the foreman and most of the workers had gone up to lunch, the sky began to darken and it looked as if it might rain. Some of the younger men were still there and they decided, quite matter-of-factly, to put the shipment away so that it wouldn't get wet, giving up part of their lunch hour to do this.

On a more dramatic level, the community as a whole recently decided unanimously to cut back on its production of some products out of fear of growing too rich. 'We don't live in community to get rich – this we can do in outside life,' said the shop foreman. Another Brother told me:

We've faced the problem of poverty and come through it. Now we face the problem of affluence, which may be even more difficult. . . . The Bruderhof will never reach the stage when it starts enjoying its surplus no matter how well Community Playthings does.

Economics, of course, is not the only sphere in which the Bruderhof bears witness. Even a sign on the public telephone (on which incoming calls are received after the office switchboard closes) reminds people to 'be prepared to do a service' if they answer the phone. People spend a great deal of time making gifts and doing little thoughtful favors for each other. Once a couple had taken a group of children camping by the river, when a fierce thunderstorm broke out. Another couple drove to a nearby place on the road and waited there till dawn, just in case the campers should decide that they wanted to go back home. (It was expected that the campers would probably stick it out, however, and they did.)

No action can bear witness if it is not visible to the world. Accordingly, the Bruderhof practices an open-door policy. Visitors are always welcomed except during times of communal crises. Even long-term visitors (those who stay for a month or more) never pay anything for their room and board, but anyone staying longer than a day is expected to participate fully in the communal work and to fit in with the Bruderhof style of life. Membership is open to anyone who asks for it. A prospective member is never judged according to his ability to contribute wealth, skills, or even youth and strength. However, he must undergo a lengthy novitiate, at which time his willingness to give up his ego and dedicate himself totally to the life is thoroughly tested.

Although the Bruderhof has always had an open-door policy, it has wavered on the question of whether the bearing-witness ideology also demands missionary activity. At times the Bruderhof has pursued new members aggressively. At other times, known in the community as periods of 'creative withdrawal', it has waited for people to seek it out.

The ideology of bearing witness is certainly not unique to the Bruderhof, or even to Christianity. The Hassidic Jews are an example of another witnessing sect. In their early days, the Hassidim fasted on Orthodox Jewish feast days, and feasted on fast days, to emphasize their scorn for specific sacraments, and their belief that one's entire life should be a sacrament. The Hassidim also felt the call to be a separate chosen people (within a chosen people). In both Bruderhof and Hassidic communities, the bearing-witness ideology has given rise to a specific style of life – a relaxed, homey, familial style, emphasizing simplicity and earthiness. The Bruderhof frequently uses a German word, *gemütlich*, to indicate this style of life.

## 3. *The Gemutlich Tenor of Life*

The Bruderhof frequently gives the appearance of being one big family. Many observers have noted this, both about the Bruderhof and about various communities of the nineteenth century. One informant said:

They [the Bruderhof] try to run their whole community of a thousand people like a family of seven – and they get away with it. They spend fortunes on long-distance telephone calls and airline bills so that the various branches of the family won't drift apart.

Each age and sex group has its unique place in the family, although, as in the traditional extended family, these places, or statuses, are unequal. Parent-child roles are particularly important. Adults are children with respect to the Servants of the Word (ministers) and the Housemothers. Novices are children with respect to members. Guests are children with respect to members and novices. Bruderhof children are considered to be the children of all the adults in the community.

Grandparents (*omas* and *opas*) perform many of the roles performed by grandparents in traditional societies. One girl spoke of how hard it must be on the outside for grandparents to stay in a room by themselves most of the time. 'Here grandparents give advice. We all go wrong sometimes, and they help put us back on the track.' There is no problem of the aging at the Bruderhof. Old people participate as fully in the life as their health and strength permit. They are bearers of community tradition, and their voices are given weight in communal decision-making.

Bruderhof young people spend quite a bit of time with one another. There are few opportunities for outside friendships to develop and, if he expects to remain a part of the community, the young person will have to marry within the Bruderhof. But there is no individual dating. Boys and girls interact in school, on work projects, and on frequent trips and outings. However, these are always group activities. Courtship can be a subtle art at the Bruderhof, as the following story, told by an ex-member, illustrates:

There was never a breath of scandal about the youth going off together camping overnight (boys and girls) without any adults. And so far as I know, NOTHING ever happened. If anything ever happened it was sort of outside the context of a formal youth meeting as such. I remember one time a friend of mine had been wildly in love with this girl for about two years. And he had already asked the Servants if he could marry her. And they said, 'Wait a little bit. She's only 18. She's kind of young.' They went on a youth trip together. They went down to the river. And he went so far as to take her for a little boat ride about a hundred yards down and back. Just her and him and the boat you know. Of course, the other kids were around all over the place, but he was very worried about what he had done. He thought, 'Have I gone too far?' They didn't say anything to each other. God forbid that they should hold hands or anything. This never entered their heads. But just being alone with her. Maybe he'd gone too far, you know.

[Q: Did they both know that they were interested in each other?] Well, I don't think that she did. But he sort of thought that, after that, she must have twigged it.

It is in keeping with the *gemütlich* tenor of life that the children be kept natural and innocent. Sometimes this creates difficulties in assimilating the children of new members, who have been partly raised in the outside world. A woman whose family visited the Bruderhof with intentions of joining told the following anecdote:

My husband and I were called in and told that Naomi had used the word 'equilibrium'. The Servant sat there, very serious, and he said that they were very surprised that Naomi had used the word equilibrium, and that a three-year-old shouldn't use that kind of word. We both sat there absolutely stunned.

You know at first I almost burst out laughing. I was going to say, 'Yeah, ain't she cute?' Then I realized, play it cool, 'cause this was a very very serious thing to them. But I really felt like laughing and saying, 'Smart kid, huh, for a three-year-old?' She had said to some-body who was annoying her that they were disturbing her equilibrium. This brought up the whole thing about the innocence of childhood. They quoted that thing about anyone who disturbs the innocence of children should have a mortar tied around his neck [paraphrased].

Watching television, going to movies, concerts, or other entertainments are not generally part of the Bruderhof life. There are no rigid prohibitions against these activities. (The community watches an occasional T.V. program on a set that they keep locked up most of the time, and goes to see an occasional movie – for instance, *The Sound of Music*.) But members rely on each other for most entertainment and recreation. Anyone who has an artistic, literary, or musical talent is encouraged to develop it and given opportunity to express it. When I admired the art work in the dining room, one member (who had had only a sixth-grade education himself) told me proudly that it ought to be good since they had three high-school girls majoring in art.

There are many people in the larger society who have some talent that they never get the opportunity to develop. In the Bruderhof, where proficiency with the cello is considered just as important a contribution to the communal effort as proficiency with the chain saw, almost everybody paints, dances, mimes, writes poetry, composes music, or plays an instrument. When a celebration occurs, everybody, from the youngest to the oldest, participates and, as the communal joke goes, hardly anybody is left sitting down to be an audience.

All important occasions in the Bruderhof are marked by a love meal. This is one of the most important Bruderhof institutions. The simple act of eating food together holds much inner meaning for the Brothers. A love meal lasts an hour and a half or two hours – much longer than an ordinary meal – and there are special presentations suited to the occasion: different groups sing, play music, or act in skits; there may be serious reading or extemporaneous speaking.

A day that is to end in a love meal has an aura of expectation and preparation about it. The girls in the kitchen bake bread. The dining room tables are arranged in a horseshoe, spread with white tablecloths and specially decorated; the dining room is lit by candles. Instead of walking into the dining room by ones and twos, as they usually do, everyone gathers outside before the meal. They sing a song and walk into the room together. The love meal has many moods, because it takes place on so many different occasions – to celebrate an engagement or a wedding, to commemorate a death, to welcome or say good-bye to a guest from another *hof*.

When a member of the community dies, he is buried in silence, but at the love meal in his honor afterwards everyone speaks about their experience of him. The tone is solemn but joyful, that the soul of a Brother or Sister has returned to God. His qualities are extolled in sacred or mythic terms. If he was able-bodied in life, he is spoken of as a tireless soldier in God's Army. If he was intelligent, this is spoken of as clarity. If the death was unexpected, the speeches emphasize childlike faith in God's arbitrary wisdom. If expected, the speakers may call attention to the light of eternity that had already begun to shine in the ailing person, even before his death. The following is an example of such a reminiscence:

During the night she sometimes awakened, opened her eyes wide with a clear look and placed her raised hands together in prayer. And once she said, 'My spirit is already far away, but also completely with all of you. I have a foretaste of eternity. I feel as though I were standing between time and eternity, as though I were connecting you with eternity.'[8]

While I was at Woodcrest I observed two engagement cele-brations. One was for Stanleigh, Eberhard Arnold's grandson, and Martha. Stanleigh's father had been in England, and the engagement was announced soon after his return. Our next-door neighbors returned from the Brotherhood meeting one night and invited us to visit them, as they had some news to share. Over popcorn and homemade wine, they told us about the engagement. Only the upper hierarchy had known, but a few ordinary members had guessed that Stanleigh and Martha were interested in each other. After the serious business meet-ing, Stanleigh spoke, reaffirming his dedication to the life, and saying he wanted to continue along this way with Martha. Then Martha spoke, saying she was called to live this life with Stanleigh. The Brotherhood approved the engagement amid an air of excitement and bubbling joy. There was much teasing about who had had his suspicions, and much excited planning for the love meal the next evening.

Stanleigh and Martha went off to spend the next day to-gether – the first time they'd ever been alone for long – while the *hof* buzzed with preparations. Everyone was involved in the quiet frenzy. The sewing room made a shirt for Stanleigh and a dress for Martha from the same piece of brightly colored cloth. At the love meal a skit written by the Woodcrest Servant of the Word was performed. The Servant unbent and played Stanleigh: Stanleigh daydreaming over his work, Stanleigh dashing to the mail room for a letter from Martha, Stanleigh trying to get his father to come home sooner so the engage-ment could be announced. Everyone went home beaming and laughing.

In the spring of 1965, Bob and Julia were engaged to be married. Bob was a Hutterian convert from North Dakota. Julia was a *sabra* child. The entertainment in their honor began with a presentation by a serious and accomplished string trio. This was followed by the school choir singing some songs from 'The Peasant Wedding'. Then the 'Rifton Troubadors' played and sang a few numbers. The critic for the school newspaper had this comment: 'Dwight called it chamber music. It was actually not.'

There was the inevitable funny skit with all parts taken by men. The skit was about an evening that the couple spent at the Steward's house and arrangements to take Julia back to Poughkeepsie where she was attending nursing school. The Steward was played by a man who had been in jail during World War II for his anti-war activities. His wife was played by a former influential Philadelphia lawyer. Bob was played by a recent Bruderhof convert from England. Julia was played by a former millionaire steel tycoon. The Steward's three daughters were played by the school physician and another Bruderhof member and his teenage son. In one of the subtle touches that the Bruderhof delights in, the son played the older daughter and his father the younger. A minor character in the skit was played by a former member of the Wisconsin state legislature.

The visual setting was described by two eighth graders in an article in the Woodcrest school newspaper:

There were very nice decorations. On the table were real daisies and daffodils with ferns and pussy willows. Also on the table were little mobiles. Behind Bob and Julia was a big wooden heart covered with greens. There were two big yellow candles on the heart, along with wooden stars. The heart was on the west side of the dining room. On the east side was a big heart-shaped picture. It was a picture of Bob and Julia in the middle with flowers all around them.

One of the most immediately striking things about the Bruderhof to the casual observer is the dignity accorded to simple pleasures: lighting a candle, wearing a garland, dancing, singing, hiking, visiting, greeting visitors. Simplicity is an indication that one is like a little child. A childlike spirit is valued highly in the Bruderhof as an aspect of bearing witness. A person reborn in the holy spirit has a childlike sense of expectation that God will provide for him. He will be simple and innocent like a child, not complex and self-sufficient like an adult. One manifestation of this spirit is in the Bruderhof love of surprises, jokes, and trips. The following are the news notes from an issue of the Oak Lake school newspaper:

March 13    Art and Mary left for Evergreen to be at Jane and Jerry's wedding. Then Jane and Jerry went to Niagra Falls for a honeymoon and, on the way back, came to Oak Lake.
March 16    The M.s arrived from Bullstrode.
March 30    Mike, Shirley, and Judith went to Woodcrest to greet Dick who had just come back from Europe.
March 31    Herman went to Bullstrode.
April 1
to June 2   The adventures of Mike's Beard.
April 1     April Fools' Day: Pink, green, and yellow milk. Merrill played Surprise Symphony, interrupted by the Tar Baby.
April 10    The A.s had a baby. Also, Moni's birthday.
April 25    Heini, Annemarie, and Milton and Sandy, and Georg came to visit. First visit for Milton and Sandy.
April 27    Milt, Fritzie, and Jorge went swimming. Then Milt and Jorge threw Mike in the water. Terrifically funny.
May 4       Hans Herman and family arrived at Oak Lake.
May 4–11    Oma and Rosewith arrived. Oma visited all the classes one morning and brought chocolate. [Oma is the nickname of Emmy Arnold, widow of Eberhard. Rosewith is her grandchild.]

Another manifestation of the childlike spirit is the tendency to exalt the commonplace. A woman who wanders into the kitchen just when an extra hand is needed for a moment feels that she was 'sent' to the kitchen for just this purpose. A man who has committed some trivial transgression gets up to confess it in meeting and goes into a long speech about how he was seduced by the devil. As long as such thoughts don't occupy too much of a Brother's mind, they are likely to be tolerated with amusement by the other members. Such behavior is not considered delusion, but merely the tendency to carry to extremes the idea of bearing witness in every aspect of life.

## 4. *A Circular Sense of History*

Earlier, I mentioned that the Bruderhof first struck me as existing somehow outside of time and space. Woodcrest, at first sight, has an air almost of an enchanted village. I learned later that this had been noticed by many other visitors. It is a manifestation of a part of the bearing-witness ideology: the call for a chosen people of God, standing in the world, but not of it.

Time, to the Bruderhof, is not cyclical because it is inexorably progressing toward the day of the Last Judgment, and Christ's triumph over the forces of evil. But history, the record of the affairs of men, is cyclical. It is not going anywhere. Men must wait, trapped within an eternally recurring story, until the Spirit of God breaks through.

In the Bruderhof year, the emphasis is on cycles, rather than on the linear progress of time. Great emphasis is placed on the 'eternal return' of certain events – springtime, autumn, birthdays, Christmas, etc.

It is a Bruderhof saying that 'the days seem long, but the years seem short.' This is a characteristic phenomenon of total institutions (places such as prisons, monasteries, nursing homes where the residents spend virtually all of their time interacting with the same group of people).[9] The day is long as the immediate present is experienced by the organism. This may be an indication of boredom. But the year cannot be experienced in this direct way, but only through memory. The year is short because the memory finds little content in it. Content is perceived in change – in progress toward a goal. The constant repetition of a cycle, however, means that the same day or week is experienced over and over again.

The circular time sense is functional for the maintenance of the bearing-witness ideology, particularly the necessity for ego loss. One ex-member illustrated this point with this observation:

> In ordinary society, one can and must plan one's actions, have hopes, and expectations. If one does not plan a career, one at least cherishes the expectation of a stable continuation of present circumstances.
>
> At the Bruderhof, in the service of restricting autonomy, this sketching of the future is prevented. Of course, anything like occupational or power-structure ambition is taboo. It is also bad to want anything too much – in my case, marriage to a particular girl.

As will be seen later, crises are common in Bruderhof life. Crises are unplanned and unexpected interruptions of the community routine. In one sense, they are a great handicap to efficient work. But from the point of view of the maintenance of the larger structure, crises are functional. They teach the ego that it hasn't the power to provide for the future by conscious planning. They inculcate the sense that whatever you are doing is not so important, and you'd better be prepared to accept interruptions calmly and with good grace.

It is important to emphasize that, according to the Bruderhof, the struggle between good and evil takes place in time but not through the medium of history. The attitude recalls the famous quotation from James Joyce, 'History is a nightmare from which we struggle to escape.' This concept is difficult to understand. Perhaps the following quotation, taken from an interview with a rather scholarly ex-member of the Bruderhof, will help clarify the distinction:

The Bruderhof talks a lot about history, about all its own history. But in another sense, this is an a-historical existence. The individual has no career that can be planned, nor indeed any other series of life-choices at his own discretion, except entering and leaving the community. The community, although it may be building, planning, etc., is essentially not following a line of Getting Better, but *striving to stay close to a static Good*.

We always used to talk about New Beginnings (*Neuanfang*). Both the individual and the community undergo them after an experience marked as a Fall, or sin. But in a more petty sense, every day is a fall, or falling short, and every morning requires a new beginning.

One cannot *get somewhere*. Spiritually, there is no such thing as achievement, and to think so is one of the typical traps of Pride. One can only keep starting over again, and in a sense, one is never better, safer, more of the good self in the arms of the Good Mother, than at the instant of the New Beginning. This is one way to see the compulsion to confess – it wipes the slate clean and leaves one the pristine Good Child.

Mircea Eliade says that, in the life of the primitives, the goal or ideal is not a future target, but the object of repeated actualization – of *entering into* the archetypal images.[10] The experience intervening since the last celebration or event is wiped off, the deviance or progress, like dirt, is washed away. The same is true in the life of the Bruderhof.

One way of maintaining this a-historical existence, which has been found effective by many monastic orders, is to break up the daily life into small segments. An extreme example of this policy is practiced at the previously mentioned Zen monastery in California:

> Our way of training is to limit students in time and space so that their entire day is reduced to essentials. There is no opportunity for personal time. The student doesn't have to think about anything and we try to make it so he can't. If he starts to think he can't keep up with the schedule. This forces the student to deal with himself and his relationships with other people. He is confronted with the immediacy of the situation and gets his identity from it. He ceases to be Chris or John and becomes a man getting up, a man getting a meal. Then he sees that all objects exist only in relationship.
>
> 'It's a kind of liberating totalitarianism,' one student said. 'You have to go inside to find freedom.'[11]

The Bruderhof schedule too, forces one to go inside to find freedom.

## 5. *The Bruderhof Day*

A Bruderhof day is a patterned day, divided into small segments, each with its planned activity. Bells ring for lunch, for supper, for the evening activity, for the morning and afternoon sessions of work and school. But there is none of the frantic rushing to be on time that is so familiar on a city street. A Brother who is late once, or twice, will not be reproved by anyone. A Brother who is late frequently will find himself having a little talk with one of the spiritual leaders of the community, the Servant or a Witness Brother. Perhaps there is some problem at home that he needs help with – the community may ask a 'single' to help out at breakfast in a very large family. Or perhaps his lateness is a problem of inner attitude . . . .

The Bruderhof has a forty-eight-hour work week – Monday through Saturday from eight to six, with two hours off for lunch. Women with families go to work an hour later in the morning and an hour later in the afternoon, but this is not free time. The morning hour is for house-cleaning in the woman's own apartment, and the afternoon hour is for the children. From two to three each afternoon, the children come home from school or Baby House to have a quiet time in the middle of the day with their mothers. Mothers also leave work a half hour earlier in the evening to prepare for the family's evening homecoming.

This routine varies but little throughout the week. On Wednesdays and Saturdays, work ends at five instead of six. On Saturdays, all women's work departments, the school, and the Baby House close at noon. The women and children spend Saturday afternoon together. One favorite Saturday occupation is baking. Young children roll out cookies, and a teenage girl makes sweet yeast rolls for Sunday breakfast. When the baking is finished, everyone takes some to a friend, to share.

Sometimes the Bruderhof day is marked by a bell at an unusual hour, to gather the community because a special guest from another *hof* has arrived or is leaving – a newly married couple, a busload of schoolchildren, or some member of the hierarchy come to exchange views on a serious Brotherhood problem. There is a pattern for these greetings. The bell rings, the community gathers from all over the *hof*, a song is sung. The guests shake hands with each person. Sometimes one detects a special warmth in a particular handshake, as if these two people would like to hug each other with joy upon meeting; but the communal life is no place for particular likings, and emotion stays within the proper channels.

The day of a typical Bruderhof family begins early in the morning. The mother, or perhaps someone else, cooks breakfast – usually hot cereal or pancakes or eggs. Cold cereal is a special treat. Before the meal the family may sing a song together. The unmarried members of the community eat together in their group meeting room. At 7:50, the first bell of the day rings, warning the children that it's time to be at the communal school.

The Bruderhof follows the German custom of frequent mealtimes throughout the day. At ten o'clock in the morning, work stops for around twenty minutes for what is known as second breakfast. This is not a mere coffee break. A table in the work area is spread with generous amounts of coffee, tea, Kool-Aid, bread, margarine, peanut butter, jam, and sometimes fruit. For many, second breakfast is a bigger meal than first breakfast. A similar 'snack' is served in the middle of the afternoon work period.

Lunch and supper are the two main meals of the day. The entire community, except for the smallest children and their supervisors, gathers in the dining room. The tables are set with unbreakable plastic dinnerware, and often there is a bouquet or other decoration on each table. People come into the dining room and sit right down, since the meal will be served to them by *austeilers*. Austeiling is a rotating chore, assigned to different people each week. At a specified time, the dining room doors are closed; there is a moment of silence, a communal song, and then the meal is served. Latecomers must wait outside during the silence and the singing, and come in as the meal is beginning.

Perhaps the most memorable thing about the Bruderhof is the singing. It is one of the crucial activities of Bruderhof life for which there is no parallel in the outside world. Two fat songbooks are found by each seat in the communal dining room, although quite a few of the members know many of the songs by heart. There is a song for every mood, every event, every season. There are winter songs, summer songs, morning songs, evening songs, folk songs, love songs, birthday songs, and wandering songs. Some of these were the songs of the German Youth Movement, others were written by Bruderhof members, and others are folk songs from many different lands which the Bruderhof has adopted. The singing itself is beautiful and moving, with effortless three- or four-part harmony on every song. Anyone may start a song that he feels is appropriate, and occasionally, when no song is given, the community sits together in silence for a few minutes before beginning its meal. Many of the songs have an inner meaning, in one way or another reminding the individual of his commitment to the life.

During the communal meal there is only a minimum of casual conversation. One person reads aloud through a microphone – a light book such as *The Wind in the Willows* during lunch, something of a more serious nature at the evening meal. Once a week at supper someone reads excerpts from the week's news, mostly from the *New York Times*, emphasizing (in 1965) civil rights and foreign policy from an anti-war viewpoint. In addition to the reading, guests are introduced at mealtimes, and miscellaneous announcements are made. After about half an hour, the meal is closed with another song. Following each meal there is some unstructured time – an hour in the afternoon and a shorter period in the evening.

Wednesday is family supper night, and there is no communal meal. Work ends an hour early. The kitchen puts out supplies which people take home with them. Each family eats as a unit, either in its own house or visiting another family.

Most evenings at the Bruderhof are occupied by meetings. After supper, there is a 'pause' for resting, chatting, or putting children to bed. Then a bell rings, calling the full members of the community together for the Brotherhood meeting, at which all communal business is decided. These generally last two or three hours. On nights when there is no Brotherhood meeting, there may be a program of organized games or a homemade puppet show. Sometimes there is an evening of folk dancing. Generally an attempt is made to leave one or two nights a week free.

Sunday is a special day. There is no work, except for the necessary kitchen work and some baby watching; and these jobs are rotated. Breakfast and lunch are a bit later than usual. Sunday breakfast is especially good, with eggs or something special baked on Saturday afternoon. Most families invite people or are invited to share Sunday breakfast.

At 9:30, the whole *hof*, from two-week infants up, gathers in the main dining room for Family Meeting. The chairs or benches are arranged in a big circle. Songs celebrate the events of the past week – a birthday, a welcome for a baby's first communal appearance. Someone reads a story, or a children's group presents a play.

Family Meeting is short, not to tire the little children. It is followed by a short period of free time. People walk about and greet each other, and the youngest children gather in their age groups and are taken for a walk or other activity. Then the adults (and the older children who wish to attend) gather for Household Meeting. The purpose of Household Meeting is to reflect the serious inner meaning of Bruderhof life. It begins and ends with a period of silence. There are serious songs. A Brother may speak about how he originally decided to join the Bruderhof. A novice or a guest considering membership may speak about his spiritual progress.

Lunch is the only communal meal on Sunday. Sunday afternoon is the only long stretch of free time in the Bruderhof week. It is often used for special projects, hikes, or family outings. Sunday supper is a family meal of food put out by the kitchen.

In the evening, the adults gather in the dining room for *Gemeindestunde*, the Bruderhof's only formal religious service. Unlike Household Meeting, which is open to anyone, *Gemeindestunde* is attended only by Brotherhood members and novices in good standing, and guests upon special invitation. *Gemeindestunde* usually ends earlier than a Brotherhood Meeting, leaving some free time on Sunday evening, perhaps to be spent visiting neighbors. Then the day ends; on Monday the week starts again.

## 6. *The Sacred Year*

The themes of the Bruderhof year are eternal return and surprise. Eternal return manifests itself in a cyclical Church Year, with recurrent myth-activating festivals. Christmas and Easter mark the eternal return to archetypal situations. Even the unscheduled events – exclusion, baptism, hearing someone confess or ask for the novitiate, death, and burial – are significant to people as renewals of their own root self-images and situation-definitions.

Surprise manifests itself in the expectation of the second coming of Christ. Never get so engrossed in what you are doing that you're not prepared to leave it at a moment's notice, should you hear the call. The Bruderhof takes seriously the words of Jesus as reported in the Gospel of Mark:

Take ye heed, watch and pray: for ye know not when the time is. For the Son of man is a man taking a far journey, who left his house, and gave authority to his servants, and to every man his work, and commanded the porter to watch. Watch ye therefore: for ye know not when the master of the house cometh, at evening, or at midnight, or at the cockcrowing, or in the morning: Lest coming suddenly he find you sleeping. And what I say unto you I say unto all, Watch.[12]

Unlike many other Christians, Bruderhof members do not defer the coming of the Kingdom of God to the indefinite future. They try to keep alive a real sense that it could happen tomorrow, or even today. Once a novice, coming up for baptism, was asked if he literally believed that the Kingdom of God was coming to earth. He replied, 'Yes, but not this year.' For this answer, his baptism was withheld and he was sent back to the novitiate.

The four special seasonal holidays of the Bruderhof are Christmas, Easter, Pentecost (Whitsunday), and the Lantern Festival. The first three of these festivals correspond to what the Bruderhof believes to be the three greatest events in history: the birth of Christ, his death and resurrection, and the first outpouring of the Holy Spirit to the assembled church-brotherhood. The Lantern Festival does not commemorate an historical event, but is roughly comparable to the secular Halloween.

Christmas and Easter are each preceded by several weeks of excited preparation and expectation. The time before Christmas is the Advent season. During Advent, the living quarters and communal rooms are decorated with wreaths and candles, and each family puts an Advent calendar on its door. In the middle of the night before the first Sunday in Advent, some of the schoolchildren dressed as angels come singing to each family. You wake up. There is an angel standing at the foot of your bed. You can hear children singing as they walk through the *hof*, waking everyone up, carrying candy and small gifts. The next morning there is a breakfast love meal, with appropriate songs and readings.

The Christmas celebration is simple. There is a silent Nativity scene, with a real baby and real animals. Emmy Arnold, widow of the community's founder, has written a book (*Torches Together*) describing the Bruderhof's early years. In it she writes:

This nativity scene has become well known in our Bruderhof communities. As often as possible we chose the simplest cattle shed for it. At times we had nothing but this silent crib scene on Christmas Eve; the sharing of the presents and all the joy for the children followed the next day.[13]

Christmas reminds the Bruderhof of the poverty and helplessness of God's birth into the world. A plaque above the door of the Woodcrest dining room reads: 'He who would to be born of God must be mindful of how Christ's birth took place.' The message of Christmas is that Bruderhof members must put aside pride and self-reliance and be reborn in a state of childlike dependency.

Christmas is generally a happy time in the Bruderhof. The community eschews commercialism, but many simple gifts are made and exchanged. More than a month before Christmas, the mood of the community changes. People go off in their free time, busy with secret projects. Children are full of anxious anticipation. The community gets out its special Christmas songbooks, and the song selections for the month are taken from the huge variety of Christmas songs in the Bruderhof repertoire.

The time before Easter is a time of forgiveness and repentance. There is no formal period of Lenten penance, however. One girl at Woodcrest was asked if the Bruderhof observed Lent. First she said, 'What's Lent?' Then she remembered it from public high school, where some girls gave up smoking for Lent. She didn't think much of the sacrifice because they continued to desire cigarettes. 'What's the good of that?' she said. 'If they could have stopped wanting them, that would have been worthwhile.' The sort of personal changes to which the Bruderhof aspires during the Easter season are the deeper ones of ego-death and psychic resurrection.

In some years, when all the members of each *hof*, and all the *hofs* together, are in perfect unity, a ceremony called 'the Lord's Supper' is held around Easter time. The Lord's Supper is the holiest and most profound of the Bruderhof festivals. It is always

preceded by a period of several weeks of intense spiritual preparation. The Brothers delve deep into themselves looking for hidden
sins. At the time of this writing, there had been no celebration of
the Lord's Supper in the Bruderhof for five or six years, so
seriously do the Brothers take the requirement that absolute
unity must first prevail.

Concerning the observance of Easter, Emmy Arnold writes:

Easter was always a special time for us. During Holy Week we would
gather around the events of two thousand years ago, and on Holy
Thursday we usually held a meal together for which a lamb (actually a
kid goat) would be prepared. Probably many know the songs, 'Bei
stiller Nacht' ('By quiet night') and 'Da Jesus in den Garten ging'
('When Jesus went into the garden'). Good Friday was observed for
the most part as a quiet day for each one individually, after the story of
Good Friday had been read to us in the morning. On Saturday we
would assemble in silence only at the hour of Jesus' burial . . . .

Easter Sunday was a very special day of celebration, because the evil
power, sin, separation and death are overcome through the resurrection
of Christ! Often we would climb up to the Weiperz Cross before day-
break, at three o'clock in the morning. Here a fire was prepared beforehand. After we had kindled it we walked around its flames, silently and
slowly. Everyone to whom it was given would say a brief word. At the
rising of the sun we sang all our beautiful Easter songs and the Easter
message was read aloud.[14]

Pentecost, or Whitsun, is especially important to the Bruderhof, 'for it was through Pentecost and the first church in Jerusalem
that we were called to this life.' A huge fire is lit which is a symbol
of the burning up of the old and the hope of the coming of the
new. Emmy Arnold writes: 'We were thinking of the fire of which
Jesus said, "I came to cast fire upon the earth; and would that it
were already kindled!" '.

The symbolic meaning of Pentecost to the Bruderhof lies in its
emphasis of the insufficiency of human effort. The followers of
Jesus had gathered together after His death. They had the teachings, belief, goodwill, and good works. Yet they were impotent
until something broke in on them from outside. Eberhard
Arnold writes:

Because we find our first real fulfilment in the flame from the other world, we can say that it is not enough to realize that our wills are directed toward the same objective, nor to realize a common, mutual emotional experience in the currents of our feelings. But we sense rather that something else must come over to us to lift us off this purely human level, to fill this human sphere, this human level, with the powers of an entirely different world. Just as the rays of the sun constantly stream on to our earth, as the lightning brings light and fire down from the clouds above, an element must burst into our midst which does not originate from us. It does not come even from our highest thoughts, endeavors and feelings, not even from the holiest part of our being nor from our noblest special traits. It really comes over us and cannot come from us.[15]

I observed a Lantern Festival at Woodcrest. This is held about the time of Halloween, which the Bruderhof does not celebrate. When the weather started to get cold, the community began to sing Lantern songs, of which the Bruderhof has a large selection, as it does for Christmas and Easter. Some are simple and childlike: 'I walk with my little lantern, it lights the way for me.' Others point to an inner meaning, like the one that ends 'brothers of one light are we'. The Lantern Festival symbolizes the necessity of community life, that each person is given only a tiny part of the light and that the lights of many different men and women must be brought together in order to see the truth.

As the time for the Lantern Festival drew near, lanterns were brought out of storage and the school children got busy making more, each with a place for a short candle inside. I particularly remember one made by a high school student. It was made of black construction paper mounted on a wooden frame, with silhouettes cut out and colored tissue paper pasted over. When the candle was lit you saw stars and a crescent moon and harvest fruits, all glowingly silhouetted by the black frame.

On the night chosen for the Lantern Festival, everyone gathered in two groups, bringing their lighted lanterns. Even quite young children were there. Both groups formed into lines, and each walked through the *hof*, singing lantern songs and enjoying their own light, and the lights twinkling from the other hillside. After an hour, we all met on the lawn in front of the school house, sang together, and had punch and cookies.

Birthdays are the most important personal celebrations of the Bruderhof year. One's birthday is the one day on which the individual ego is allowed to come out and play. Adults, as well as children, eagerly look forward to the coming of their birthdays, which are celebrated both on the actual date and on the Sunday following. The family and the community sing birthday songs. I never heard 'Happy Birthday to You' at the Bruderhof, but, as for every other occasion, they have many of their own unique birthday songs.

A person receives gifts from his family and friends, and also from the community at large. The communal kitchen bakes a cake for each person. Presents are simple, often homemade. One seven-year-old boy showed me the presents he'd received; they included a puzzle made out of wood by his father, a box of sixteen large crayons, mittens, socks, a new shirt, homemade candy, cocoa mix, Hi-Ho crackers, vienna sausages, two jars of jam, Hershey bars. Adult birthdays are celebrated just as much as children's. One woman remarked that on her birthday she had asked for beef and dry wine, to cook something special; and another woman said she had specially asked for olive oil. But presents are not over-emphasized; it is the love and brotherhood that matters, and a child who refused to share his candy would be reprimanded.

National holidays are observed casually at the Bruderhof. On Thanksgiving, for example, there is turkey, but people work a normal day.

Bruderhof members have a taste for elaborate surprises. For example, I heard the eighth graders report in the dining room at lunch about a trip they had just returned from. The adults had decided two months before where the trip was going, and kept it a secret till the very last minute. The bus started to go in the direction of the Adirondacks. They all started to sing mountain songs – and then they noticed that the bus had turned around and was heading south. Even then the adults were teasing the kids, saying that maybe they were going to Cape May or Washington. When at last they admitted that the trip was headed for Oak Lake, a shout went up.

Most of the Oak Lake community didn't know that the group was coming, and they entered the community by a roundabout way to surprise them. The high schoolers enjoyed reminiscing about the ice cream and candy and thirty bottles of soda that celebrated their arrival. When they left, the Oak Lake fifth and sixth grades were lined up by the road, to wave good-by to them. They were pleased. Further along the road, the seventh grade was lined up to wave good-by – great surprise and enjoyment! *Everyone* in the community seemed to get a great deal of enjoyment out of this story; we heard them talking and laughing about it again at tea.

I once remarked to a Bruderhof member that it must be hard to give up forever the pleasure of suddenly deciding, 'This is such a beautiful day I won't work, I'll go on a picnic instead.' She said that the Bruderhof enjoys things like that, but 'the decision is a communal, not an individual, decision'. A few days later an engagement was announced at Oak Lake, and this particular Sister was chosen to be one of the representatives from Woodcrest, the first time she had ever had a trip to another *hof*.

Surprises are symbolic of the ephemeral nature of Bruderhof life. One never knows if the next day will be an ordinary day, or bring a visitation of the highest joy, or the deepest gloom. As the visitor becomes more familiar with Bruderhof life, he soon becomes very sensitive to these periodic ups and downs of spiritual/emotional life which always occur, and which are as much a part of the community as the changing of the seasons. The Bruderhof as a living church, attempting to be a vessel for the effervescent Holy Spirit, is particularly prone to this periodic cycling of crisis and euphoria.

## 7. *The Moral Basis*

The moral basis of any religious system has to do with the dichotomy between sacred things and profane things and with the necessity of keeping the sacred pure from contamination by the profane. On the basis of his study of primitive religions, Emile Durkheim defines religion as

a unified system of beliefs and practices relative to sacred things, that is to say, things set apart and forbidden – beliefs and practices which unite into one single moral community called a church, all those who adhere to them.[16]

What is unusual about the Bruderhof is that its chief sacred object is not a mountain, or a stone, or a book, but the community itself. To keep the community free from contact with profane objects, from without and within, is thus one of the major goals of the Bruderhof.

Perhaps the distinction between sacred and profane, which is so crucial for understanding the dynamics of the Bruderhof system, can be clarified by noting that profane objects possess only attributes while sacred objects (although they may possess attributes as well) are distinguished by the possession of spirit.[17] Attributes are real properties of the object and cannot be modified without modifying the nature of the object itself. For example, a chair possesses attributes of size, shape, and color. We can paint this chair a different color, thus modifying its color in a specific predictable way. People possess attributes, but we also recognize a different sort of property in a person when we speak of mood, or spiritual state, or, perhaps most clearly, when we speak of the relational quality of being in love. These properties of 'spirit' are not constant attributes of the person. Neither do they seem to fluctuate according to any regular pattern. And likewise, religious objects also possess a spiritual property: holiness. The good spirit, or holiness, is not a real attribute of the person or the religious object; rather it is an ephemeral property that enters and leaves the person or religious object according to a pattern that we cannot recognize.

Any object – tree, book, picture – may become endowed with holiness. A person endowed with holiness possesses a form of charisma. Charisma is not a personal attribute – it may enter or leave a person according to a pattern he doesn't understand. It is important that the relevant viewpoint here is phenomenological rather than empirical. A later generation of psychologists and sociologists may be able to measure and predict charisma as its laws come to be understood. Similarly, in the past, some people regarded a lunar eclipse as a loss of spirit by a holy object, a spirit that gave the moon an ephemeral sacred property. Today we recognize an eclipse as a predictable event in an orderly and understandable (and therefore profane) solar system. An object is sacred, then, to the extent that its importance is its *seemingly* ephemeral spirit. An object is profane when laws explaining it deal with its attributes in a predictable manner.

The Bible is a sacred object, but its sacredness is not ephemeral – although the Old Testament affords a recurring discussion of the ephemeral nature of holiness. The Bible represents an attempt to transform spirit into attribute. It illustrates the desire to make permanent the ephemeral spirit, a desire which is responsible for the institutionalization of the sacred. We find a similar attempt by South Sea Island tribes to preserve a sacred property – mana – through institutionalized means for retaining it. The history of religion illustrates attempts to build elaborate institutions to make the spirit permanent, and the opposition to such attempts.

When a religion is successful in containing individual spiritual experience a church emerges. Durkheim uses the term 'church' to denote the fellowship of those who believe in common. The word can also be used to denote the profane house which is built to hold the sacred spirit. In both senses it is important to bear in mind that the Bruderhof regards itself as a church – a structure for the preservation of the Holy Spirit on Earth.

The moral basis of the Bruderhof consists in whatever enables the community to contain the Holy Spirit. Thus the normative system is open and flexible. What is right for one person and at one time may well be considered wrong for another person or for the same person at a different time. The Bruderhof goes very much by feeling and intuition in discerning what is right and what is wrong. Nevertheless, certain rudimentary codes of proper attitude do exist.

In the private sphere of life good attitudes consist of joy (above all), openness, eagerness to participate in communal activities, and, of course, a childlike spirit. Aloofness, grumpiness, and a desire for solitude are frowned upon. Very much required are willingness to seek help with internal problems and openness to admonishment.

In the interpersonal sphere cooperation and friendliness are the correct feelings. Judgmentalism, formalism, and unwillingness to work will generally be considered wrong attitudes. But by far the most important moral requirement in interpersonal relationships is that absolutely under no conditions for any reason whatsoever shall there ever be any gossiping about a person behind his back. This rule, known as 'The First Law in Sannerz', is the cornerstone of the Bruderhof moral system, and the tenacity with which the community holds to this rule is, I believe, one of the major contributions to the Bruderhof's survival and success. The no-gossip rule is the only codified Bruderhof rule; copies of it are posted in many places in each *hof*.

## THE FIRST LAW IN SANNERZ*

There is no law but that of love. Love is joy in others. What then is anger at them?

Passing on the joy that the presence of the others brings us means words of love. Thus words of anger and worry about members of the brotherhood are out of the question. In Sannerz there must never be talk, either open or hidden, against a brother or sister, against their individual characteristics – under no circumstances behind their back. Talking in one's own family is no exception to this either.

Without the commandment of silence there is no faithfulness and thus no community. The only possible way is direct address as the spontaneous brotherly service to the one whose weaknesses cause something in us to react negatively. The open word of direct address brings a deepening of friendship and it is not resented. Only when one does not find the way together immediately in this direct manner is it necessary to talk together with a third person whom one can trust to lead to a solution and uniting in the highest and deepest.

> Each one in the household should hang this admonition up at his place of work where he always has it before his eyes.

* Sannerz: The first Bruderhof settlement.

In the decision-making sphere one has a responsibility to speak up and express one's opinion. It is wrong to conceal misgivings, even if nobody else agrees with you. But it is wrong to 'bring in a disturbance'. This means that disagreement, if necessary, must be made in a tentative, humble, and questioning way. An image from the Lantern Festival is relevant here. Each person brings his own unique light to a decision-making meeting. His unique vision is necessary, but he must never fall into the error of thinking it sufficient. Only all the candles shining together bring enough light to reveal the truth.

Finally, in the inter-*hof* sphere, it is important to avoid 'local patriotism'. One must not consider the needs of one's own *hof* out of perspective to the needs of the Bruderhof as a whole. One should be generous in allocating money and manpower to weaker or poorer *hofs*. One should remember that one belongs to the entire Bruderhof, not merely to the *hof* of residence, and one should be ready and willing to move to a different *hof*, should the need arise, without regret or attachment.

Behavioral norms, of necessity, cover only a finite portion of possible behavior. The joke about totalitarian societies – *everything not forbidden is compulsory* – points up the absurdity of trying to establish norms covering all possible actions. The sparseness of specific behavioral norms at the Bruderhof indicates an attempt to go beyond norms to a system of total control of the system and of individuals in the system. Note the similarity to the Taoist advice to ancient Chinese monarchs: 'When the Way is lost, then come laws . . . '.

The problem of *how* Bruderhof attitudes become internalized in the individual will be discussed in chapters five and six. Here I only want to mention one such mechanism which is important for an understanding of the system of social control. The Bruderhof does not try to make its members morally perfect. In fact, any Brother who thought himself perfect would be guilty of the grave sin of pride. The community instead relies on the mechanism of repentance and forgiveness. All misdeeds, however serious, may be forgiven upon adequate repentance. Everyone sins. Only the community has the power to forgive these sins. At the same time that the Bruderhof chastises a Brother, it holds out the assurance of faithful, dependable group support. One respondent remarked wryly that he never was so much aware of the community's love and concern for him as when it was helping him to struggle with his sin. Admonishment is the stick and forgiveness is the carrot. The rule is that under no circumstances is a person's past to be held against him once he has been forgiven. An ex-member said:

You must never, never, never mention somebody's past troubles. This is one of the worst things you could do in the Bruderhof. It is far better to talk about sex or blow a noisy fart than to talk about anybody's past troubles once they've been taken back.

The repentance-forgiveness relationship leads to a childlike dependence of the individual on the community, the all-nurturing mother (*Die Gemeinde ist unserer aller Mutter*). Only the little child without a sense of the 'I' is capable of true identification with, as opposed to merely compliance to, the communal norms.

Total identification by all the members with the community norms is, of course, an ideal which is never even approximated in the Bruderhof. But this is not necessary. It's enough to have created a situation in which members feel guilty for any deviation from communal expectations, even when this deviation is in the area of attitude rather than behavior.

Since the Bruderhof is much more concerned with its members' attitudes than with their behavior, sanctions are almost always concerned with a person's pride, or wilfulness, or selfishness, rather than directly with anything a person has done. Through the mechanism of confession, repentance, and forgiveness the community is then able to anticipate behavioral deviance through analysis of attitudinal deviance. Thus appropriate preventive techniques such as counselling, isolation, or a change of work assignment can be used to reform the person before he actually does something wrong.

Bruderhof counselling and guidance is the responsibility of every community member, but it lies particularly in the hands of certain executive officers. The male executives are called Servants of the Word. The female executives are called Housemothers. There are also intermediate executives (male) called Witness

Brothers, who do not do this work full time, but are employed in the ordinary community labor force, and called upon only when needed. The functions of these various offices will be discussed in much greater detail later.

Bruderhof solidarity rests very heavily on the certainty that individuals have internalized a certain set of attitudes. However, it is necessary to infer a member's internal state largely from his external behavior. Thus great importance is attached to the phrases people use, their gestures, and their mannerisms, all as clues to how the individual really stands. This can sometimes be carried to absurd lengths, as can be seen by the following story told by a woman who had visited the Bruderhof with her husband and children for six months but had never become a member:

One time I went into the Housemother's room because I needed some shampoo. And so I asked if I could have some shampoo. And they said I couldn't. They said they didn't have any.

I said, 'Oh, there's some on the shelf.' They said, 'Well, that's for somebody's birthday. It's a present for somebody . . . .'

Well I went to the Housemother . . . . I was sort of puzzled about it, and as I was standing there thinking this was sort of goofy, D. walked in and said, 'We've decided to give you this shampoo.' I said, 'Thank you. Well, that's great,' but then I said I was uneasy about the situation. She said, 'Well, Alice will talk to you about it!' She was one of the women in there at the time.

And so I talked to her about it. And she said that she resented very much my coming in and asking for the shampoo as though I expected to get it. She said, 'There was something in your voice. You expected to get it.' I said, 'Well it was on the shelf, so I expected to get it.' She said, 'Well you don't understand, when you ask for something, you don't ask as if you're entitled to it. When you ask for something you ask in a really humble way. You acted as though you walked into a store.' So I said, 'Well I'm sorry, but it does look like a store in here, and I just didn't think about it.' She said, 'Well, something has to happen within you; you think about it.'

So I thought about it, and was more watchful and attentive as other people asked for things. I noticed that when my husband went in to ask for toothpaste or something, he always got it. I listened to his voice and noticed that he always asked in a sort of tentative way, like 'is it possible for me to have some toothpaste?'. . . .

So I listened and other people would ask, 'Is it possible?' or they would say, 'I wonder if there is some honey today for the little honey lovers on the third floor.' In other words, you're wondering, is it possible, is there any possibility, etc. But you just don't go in and say 'gimme'.

Now the best way I discovered is to go in and say, 'Dear Housemother, I have a problem. My hair is dirty. What should I do?' And then the Housemother, you see, she would say, 'Well, I think you ought to wash your hair. Here is some shampoo for you.' Then you have solved this problem in an open honest way, and the Housemother has been of help to you.

I have said that the Bruderhof normative system emphasizes attitudes rather than behavior. In the Bruderhof, the word 'attitude' is used as an English translation of the German word '*haltung*' (meaning 'the way one holds oneself'). Thus 'attitude' has the connotation of *willed* feeling. It is not possible to say, for instance, 'That's just my attitude. I can't help it.' When a person is being admonished he is not told that he has a 'bad' attitude. One formula, used frequently in Paraguay, was to say, ' *Das ist ja gar keine Haltung*' ('that's no kind of attitude at all'). In North America, more frequently it will be said, 'You are not standing right,' with connotations that the person is not 'holding himself' right, or, 'That is not a "proper" attitude,' (not a 'real' attitude). 'Go and develop an attitude for yourself.'

The entire Bruderhof moral system is pervaded with a very German emphasis on individual responsibility. The modern American attitude, which sees the individual as a more or less helpless pawn of social forces, is completely foreign to the Bruderhof. It is possible to pick oneself up by one's own bootstraps. True love is not coddling; true love is sharp. Very likely, this moral basis stems from the origins and historical development of the community. At the beginning, a bunch of bourgeois intellectuals in Germany had to shake themselves loose of all their traditions, and put themselves firmly down in the alien and unknown communitarian path. Communitarianism is not natural to modern Western man, and the first thing that every new member is required to do is to pick himself up by his own bootstraps and make a sharp and radical break with all of his old habits and assumptions about the world and about himself.

## Chapter Two □ FROM COMMUNION TO TRUE COMMUNITY

German sociologists have traditionally distinguished between two basic forms of association: *gemeinschaft* and *gesellschaft*.[18] These can be roughly translated as community and society. Community is defined as that form of association based on natural bonds. People are involved in a relatively stable network of relationships based on factors such as kinship and geographical proximity – factors which seem to the participants to be rooted in the natural order of things. Society, in contradistinction, is thought to be based on rational bonds. People enter into constantly changing sets of relationships in order to exchange with other people such things as food, tools, services, protection, and loyalty. Communal relationships are based on tradition; social relationships are based on reciprocity.

Community was once the overwhelmingly dominant form of association for mankind. But Western civilization during the last few centuries has tended to evolve in the direction of the disintegration of communities and the formation of ever more complex and inclusive societies. The Bruderhof constitutes a remarkable exception to this trend. Its members have made the opposite transition, from society to community. This bucks the tide of Western civilization so strongly that one could call it a reversal of social entropy. Bruderhof members are remarkable, less because of the way they live, than because they can live this way after having grown up in sophisticated modern society.

As Herman Schmalenbach has pointed out, one cannot set about purposely to create a community:

... community implies the recognition of something taken for granted and the assertion of the self-evident. Generally speaking, one will not expressly sanction or condemn those communities to which one belongs. One is not likely to be fully aware of them. They are given. They simply exist .... As a rule we are not likely to take much notice of our membership in them ....[19]

In this sense, the idea of an intentional community is almost a contradiction in terms. But not quite. It is true that a group of people cannot will themselves directly into a state of community. But it is possible, though rare, that a group of people can put themselves into a collective situation in which changes will be worked upon them which will eventually bring about a state of true community. This is the meaning behind the Bruderhof statement that, for community to be possible, the old self must be left behind, something in the person must die and something new be born.

The state of non-communal preparation for future community is recognized, by Schmalenbach, as a third discrete form of association, different from both community and society. This form is called communion.[20] Communion is based on emotional feelings; for example, a friendship is a communion relationship. Communion differs from society in that the members are committed to one another as whole people. Utilitarian considerations, if present, are always secondary. Also, people are important to each other in a communion for what they are, rather than what they can do.

The difference between communion and community is less easy to see. In fact, since communion formation is often accompanied by the desire for community, the one is often mistaken for the other. For instance, many hippie communes are thought of by their members as communities although they are actually communions. Schmalenbach discusses the difference as follows:

Often feelings are construed as the basis of community relations, because they are erroneously thought to be deeper or nearer the unconscious than rational thought .... Now, it is precisely in this context that the fundamental differences between community and communion may be established. The reality and basis of community do not consist in feeling. Nevertheless, a community does exhibit quite specific emotions, some of them directed toward itself, even if the community does not owe its reality or its basis to these feelings. Such sentiments include the sense of tenderness for the other members of the community, or for the community as such, the feeling of happiness in knowing of one's belonging, or even a sense of pride. The essence of community is association constituted in the unconscious. Community, as an organic and natural coalescence, precedes emotional recognition of it by its members. Feelings are simply subsequent forms of experience at the level of consciousness. They are products of community . . . .

In the case of human communion this is radically different. Emotional experiences are the very stuff of the relationship . . . . Jubilant followers who swarm around a leader chosen in an inspired flood of passion do not intend . . . to be bound up with him and one another on the basis of characteristics they naturally have in common. They are bound together by the feeling actually experienced. Indeed, each one is *en rapport* . . . .

It may seem questionable that feelings are in fact constitutive of communions. Some may argue that a religious congregation, for instance, is kept together not so much by the several feelings of its individual members as by the god to whom they pray . . . . And yet the noumenal must . . . be received with some kind of religious feeling. Then the religious congregation becomes, in fact a communion . . . .[21]

The Bruderhof began as a communion, coalescing around the charismatic leadership of Eberhard Arnold, and, under his guidance, starting along the path of evolution toward true community. After fifty years of existence, this evolution has not yet been completed. Perhaps it never will be. In fact, it can be argued that an intentional community can only become a true community by undergoing a devolution to the state of ethnic subculture – such as was experienced by the Hutterians. But a fundamental value of the Bruderhof is that membership be based, not upon the accident of birth, but upon free choice available to insiders and outsiders alike. As long as this value is cherished, it is unlikely that the Bruderhof will ever become a community based on tradition, and it is likely that there will always remain a latent conflict between freedom of choice and the absolute nature of one's commitment to the life.

The Bruderhof dates its formal beginnings to the renting of Sannerz Farm by Eberhard Arnold in the summer of 1920. Since that time, the community has evolved through a number of different forms (see accompanying Table). But the origins of the Bruderhof go further back in time to the meeting of two forces: the visionary and revolutionary Christianity of Eberhard Arnold and the German Youth Movement of the years after World War I.

Eberhard Arnold and his wife, Emmy, were both born in the 1880s. Both came from Christian upper-middle-class German academic backgrounds, and both had felt stirrings early in life of a desire for dedication to something beyond themselves. Eberhard had had a powerful direct experience of Christ at the age of sixteen after which he had put aside any thought of a respectable career. In 1907, Eberhard and Emmy met, at one of the revival meetings which were popular in Germany at that time. Emmy Arnold describes this meeting in *Torches Together*:

After some profound and earnest talks together about the nature of Christian discipleship we were engaged, though we had known each other only a few days. From then on we went our way together.[22]

Their families did not want them to get married until Eberhard had gotten his Ph.D. This he did in 1909 'with a thesis that found Nietzche's assaults on the church vindicated to an extent by the practice of the first Christians.' Eberhard and Emmy were married three weeks later. The parents were still not pleased, feeling that they should have waited until Eberhard had become economically established. Emmy writes:

We, however, wanted to put our common life entirely on the basis of faith. This faith has never let us down in any sphere of our lives.[23]

During the next ten years, Eberhard Arnold was involved in lecturing and Christian socialist publishing. He became a speaker and organizer for the Student Christian Movement, and later its General Secretary. This brought him into contact with many young people in Germany who were searching for new ideas and a new way of living:

Germany in those inflation-ridden postwar years, amid the fragments of Wilhelminian pomp and ambition, was a vast California of cults, crusades, causes, and movements. The younger generation, almost in a body, rejected the bourgeois ways of its elders, and hiked out into the country with rucksacks and short pants, a little like coeducational senior Scouts, but with a messianic mission. This was the German Youth Movement. Howard Becker (*German Youth: Bond or Free*; New York, Oxford University Press, 1946) describes its positive values as 'a revolt against tradition; love of nature; a love of nation, which seemed to consist in a vague mystique of the "folk"; self-expression; emphasis on the emotional aspect of life; the gospel of "joy in work".'

Eberhard Arnold was searching for a more basic way to bring Christianity into practical life. The Youth Movement, with its 'bands' of twenty or so, joining in hikes and singing sessions in the 'hest' or clubhouse, already involved, Becker says, 'a sense of belonging to a band of dissenters, to a conventicle of the elect'.[24]

Many of these people were disillusioned with the political and social order, disillusioned by the war and the results of the war. Over a million young people were loosely associated with the German Youth Movement.

The Arnolds held weekly open-house meetings which were attended by a wide variety of people. Emmy Arnold writes:

> We were waiting and open for any kind of helpful word; and it came to us, too. Oftentimes we sat up together until after midnight, until finally, after a prolonged struggle, a word of help was given.[25]

Conferences were held in the countryside. 'Interested and seeking friends' from the Youth Movement met and discussed such topics as ways to start a folk school, returning to the land, founding a social work center; Eberhard Arnold spoke on the need for radical Christianity, a Christianity that followed the way of the Sermon on the Mount. They cooked their meals on open fires, wore simple peasant clothes, sang folk songs, and danced together. Emmy Arnold says, of those days:

> There was a spirit of joy, a spirit of true comradeship alive among us. This kind of thing one must experience personally. Our dances were, I must say, a truly religious experience.[26]

Bruderhof girls still wear the simple bright dresses, braided

## THE PHASES OF BRUDERHOF HISTORY

| Years | Type of Organization | Location | Leadership |
|-------|----------------------|----------|------------|
| 1920–26 | Communion | Sannerz, Germany | Eberhard Arnold |
| 1926–35 | Charismatic community | Rhön, Germany | Eberhard Arnold |
| 1935–40 | Transitional community | Germany, England | Emerging collective leadership |
| 1941–50 | Isolated sect | Paraguay, England | Collective leadership (authoritarian) |
| 1950–58 | Communitarian social movement | Paraguay, Uruguay, England, Germany, United States | Limited democracy |
| 1959–62 | Years of crisis and schism | | |
| 1962– | Church community | United States, England | Democratic centralism under authority of David Arnold |

| Major Events and Characteristics | Basis of Solidarity |
|---|---|
| (1) Eberhard Arnold rents farm at Sannerz, 1920<br>(2) First major crisis, 'Faith vs. Economics,' 1922<br>*Time of joy, miracles, spontaneous brotherhood* | Emotional feelings of belonging together; Eberhard Arnold's charismatic guidance |
| (1) Founding of first Bruderhof, 1926<br>(2) Merger with Hutterians, 1931<br>*Groping toward communal forms* | Attempt at formal structure but major reliance still on Eberhard Arnold |
| (1) Death of Eberhard Arnold, 1935<br>(2) Expulsion from Germany and relocation in England, 1937<br>(3) Many new English members<br>(4) Exodus from England, 1940<br>*Transition from Germanic to International Character* | Living from Crisis to Crisis with aid of Hutterian forms of structure; commitment heightened by external pressures |
| (1) Settlement in Paraguay, 1940<br>(2) Another English Colony, 1942<br>(3) Split with Hutterians, 1950<br>*Isolation and authoritarianism* | The Hutterian forms; isolation from external influences |
| (1) Founding of Woodcrest in New York State, 1954<br>(2) Founding of Community Playthings, 1954<br>(3) The Nine-*Hof* Conference, 1957<br>*The big thaw; De-Hutterization, trend away from patriarchal authoritarianism, expansionism* | Missionary enthusiasm; relative affluence; residue of Hutterian forms |

Constant trouble leading eventually to about half the membership leaving either through expulsion or voluntary departure. All South American *hofs* disbanded. The European branch reduced to one short-lived colony in England. The Bruderhof consolidated in North America. Revivalism, reaction to democracy, and to the new prosperity, purification.

| | |
|---|---|
| (1) 200 exiles return, 1963; Year of the harvest<br>(2) Bulstrode disbanded, 1966<br>*Prosperity, puritanism, stability* | Mixture of Hutterian authoritarianism, democracy, and charismatic leadership of David Arnold |

hair, and flowery garlands of the Youth Movement of those days, and the community today often sings the songs of the Youth Movement:

> When we're marching side by side
> And together old songs singing,
> Echoes from the deep woods bringing,
> Then we feel the cause goes forward –
> With us moves the great new time![27]

or:

> And deep in the wood there is blooming
> The tiny flower blue;
> And just to win this flower
> We'll travel the wide world through.
> The trees are a-rustle, the stream murmurs slow
> And he who to seek the flower blue would go
> Must be a wanderer too,
> Must be a wanderer too![28]

## 1. *Communion (1920–26)*

The Arnolds themselves were searching for the right path. They felt the need for an active Christianity more radical than Communism. They knew they were called to live the life of the Sermon on the Mount – but what exactly did that mean, in practical terms? They wanted to live a life of service, but how could they serve best? At one time they thought of buying a gyspy trailer and traveling from village to village, rebuilding homes destroyed by the war, making music and spreading joy as they went.

Another Bruderhof historian describes what happened next:

Then one night before Easter in 1920, the creative moment came. A young group gathered with Arnold and read together the ethical commands of the Sermon on the Mount; they read the passage in Acts: 'The multitude of them that believed were of one heart and one soul. Neither said any of them that aught of the things which he possessed was his own; but they had all things common .... Neither was any among them that lacked.'

They felt that God had spoken to their hearts, had answered their searching with a direct challenge to pool all their belongings, buy a farm, and live and work together, sharing property, work, and faith. They did so, because they could do nothing else. Bruderhof life was conceived not as an 'experiment', to see what would happen; it was an obedience to what God said had to happen.[29]

In 1920 the Arnolds rented a large house, with an orchard and some fields for farming, in the village of Sannerz. There was no financial basis for the proposed community, but friends had donated enough money to pay the first year's rent, and the Arnolds believed in trusting to God and acting in faith. They started to work on small-scale farming and on publishing. Emmy Arnold writes:

Our kitchen was of the simplest kind imaginable. It sometimes happened that the cook (though in fact we did not have anyone who could properly be called a cook) was sitting outside in the open, doing a landscape painting or writing poetry, while the soup or the potatoes boiled over onto the fire. Naturally the wood fire was put out or the soup was burned. Nobody worried about it . . . . [30]

Many guests visited. In the fall of 1920, there were seven adults, having all things in common, living at Sannerz. Emmy Arnold gives a description of that time in *Torches Together*:

Our life in the community was a very joyful one, filled with the expectation of a new future. This was especially so during the first two years. Every day that we were able to live together in community was a great day of celebrating, truly a festive day! Everything that happened was used as an occasion to celebrate. When we had bought a cow or a goat, for instance, we would decorate it with wreaths of wild flowers and lead it through the village, singing together. Whether we picked up stones and rocks from the fields we had rented, whether we hoed beans, peas or potatoes, or whether we preserved fruit and vegetables or stirred jam – all of these occasions were opportunities for celebrating and for experiencing fellowship together. Everbody joined in, even those who were overburdened with work in the office because of the many books we published during those first years. Everybody wanted to share in the common work.

. . . . When I think back to these times and their movements, during this period following the first World War, I feel it was a foretaste of what we can expect in a much greater and more perfect measure in the future of the kingdom of God. This was so in our life in Sannerz, and perhaps just as much at the Rhön Bruderhof. Often, I almost shiver, but also feel a sense of deep joy and thankfulness when I remember those days. Something that came from eternity was living among us, something that made us oblivious of the limits of time and space. Thus miracles, as one may perhaps call them, were experienced among us in a quite natural way. All this happened in spite of us, as it were, in spite of our insufficiencies and incapabilities.

It is difficult to tell about such events. Often it happened quite simply and unobtrusively in our meetings that demonic powers had to retreat; that sick people became well again, almost unnoticed; that things happened which simply cannot be explained by men. In those times, times of expectation, we did not regard such occurrences as unusual at all.[31]

A controversy within the Christian Youth Movement developed in 1921 and 1922. Some wanted to develop new ways of life; others wanted to return to the established ways, and be the leaven in the old loaf. Many long evening discussions were held at Sannerz, with people taking one side or the other. There were the original seven members, and then many guests and helpers had decided to stay on, so there were about sixty people at Sannerz. Emmy writes:

At that time the group was not closely knit and welded together in such a way that one could speak of a group belonging together for life. Among the guests the first circle was called 'the holy seven'. We all wore the open ring of the early Church, which was also worn by other friends of the movement. We were a fighting band, in the process of growth. We talked everything over together and fought everything through together.[32]

The years at Sannerz represent the communion phase of the Bruderhof's history. Miracles abounded. Spontaneity rather than structure characterized group relationships. There was a great deal of anarchism in the life as a residue of the Youth Movement. In the beginning, freedom was taken to mean that one worked only when one felt the urge. Gradually, this was replaced by the more practical principle: 'Work is love made visible.'

There was a certain funky quality about this early life which Emmy Arnold describes with amusement:

Oh yes, there were many fanatics too, who wanted to eat nothing but raw vegetables or fully ripened fruit. A certain young friend of the movement would not eat anything at all any more, and in the end died of starvation . . . .

Eberhard had won an old friend . . . to help us with the farming . . . . He was a very nice fellow, a true idealist, but he knew hardly anything about farming. First, he wanted to let the villagers remove the dung heap from the *Hof* free of charge, because it was such an eyesore! . . . To the great amusement of the villagers he would sit under the cow, with his big, horn-rimmed glasses, milking and making verses at the same time . . . .

The guest who most impressed us was Hans Fiehler, who called himself Hans-in-Luck. He wore a red woolen peaked cap, a red waistcoat, and shorts. On his back was written in bold letters, Hans-in-Luck. He traveled through the country with two violins . . . . He also had four ocarinas which he called the 'great-grandmother', the 'grandmother', the 'mother' and the 'child' . . . .

Our house was full to overflowing with guests – up to two thousand during the first year! There were strange characters among them.[33]

Eberhard's personal magnetism was the important factor holding the community together at this point, and he was absent much of the time. In the summer of 1922 the severe inflation in the German economy magnified the strains within the community, and there was a crisis. The Arnolds felt that trust in God must be stronger than economic necessity, while most of the community felt that faith and economics didn't go together. More than forty people decided to leave, and seven remained to begin building up again slowly.

One gets the impression, from reading Emmy Arnold's book, that she regards the Sannerz period as the happiest Bruderhof time. Despite the crises, it was a honeymoon before settling down to the serious hard work of making the marriage. It is not surprising that many intentional communities never attempt to go beyond this communion phase. As we shall see in chapter seven, Sannerz is very similar to many contemporary hippie communes.

## 2. *Charismatic Community (1926–35)*

In 1926, the community, once again numbering about forty or fifty people, including many highly educated men and women, bought a larger farm in the Rhön mountains, which was known as the Rhön Bruderhof. The contract was signed without any idea where the ten-thousand-mark down payment, which was due ten days later, was to come from. But a day or two before the payment was due, a friend gave the money.

The move to Rhön did not signal any radical changes in Bruderhof life. Yet important changes had been occurring gradually which reached fruition during the years there. For one thing, the community had gathered a stable and growing population beyond the original Arnold circle. The distinction between member and guest became sharper, and business meetings, which originally had been open to all, were now restricted to those who had made a lifetime commitment to the community. Increased population also brought about the beginnings of a division of labor. A person was needed to serve as storekeeper, another as work coordinator. The increasing number of children made it necessary to build a baby house. Some women worked there, freeing others for different work.

Along with these changes in structure came a change in the tone of Bruderhof life. Life at Rhön was quieter, more serious, more subdued, than it had been at Sannerz. Given such a short lapse of time, this cannot be satisfactorily explained in terms of the members' growing older. It rather has to do with the Bruderhof's movement away from the communion phase of its history. Schmalenbach says:

> We must distinguish between ... the inclination of unconscious attitudes and the establishment, within the unconscious, of social structures. Where we have the former, feelings are likely to appear and reappear. Only where periodic excitement calms down once more – perhaps even dies out – and is then replaced by a kind of coalescence between emotion and unconscious disposition, can one speak of community. It is for this reason that, in the case of younger religions,

the meetings of similarly excited persons are more likely to lead to communion than to community.[34]

As the Bruderhof grew out of the communion phase, the emotional excess which had been the charm of Sannerz was also left behind. Eberhard Arnold waged a constant battle against emotionalism in Bruderhof life, not always with success. Emmy Arnold writes:

What pained [Eberhard] in particular was certain emotional, all-too-human relationships between members at the Rhön Bruderhof. There was very little listening or feeling for God's speaking in our time. Eberhard tried to impress this on us through the history of the martyrs of the sixteenth century . . . . But at that moment people did not have a listening ear . . . . They loved human goodness, and so sometimes they coddled one another instead of correcting one another.

So it naturally came about that there was also talking about others behind their backs. All values were much too emotional, too human.[35]

The community at Rhön revolved around Eberhard Arnold, as had the one at Sannerz. He was a good deal older than most of the other members. He was a highly charismatic and saintly man, gifted not only with unusual grandeur of vision, but with the ability to communicate with other people and to inspire them with his visions. Emmy writes:

In the fall of 1928, Eberhard said in a talk to the brotherhood . . . that one day our movement would grow considerably. Eberhard said that he could visualize all manner of people coming – men of industry, professional people, workers, teachers, washerwomen and the very poorest of every description. All of them would want to live in community, and he could see a great procession of people approaching; it was our task to make room for them and to build for them.[36]

To the extent that Arnold brought the Bruderhof away from emotions to a cosmic perspective, he brought it from communion to community. It was community in that it stressed the intrinsic nature of brotherhood. In the beginning of this chapter I defined community as association based on natural bonds, and gave as examples kinship and geographical proximity. The Bruderhof, of course, is not a kinship group, and having assembled together from all over in order to build a community, the members could hardly turn around and make their proximity the reason for community. Arnold was able to make them see that they really were a kinship group, and, what is more important, to feel in their bones the 'givenness' of their brotherhood streaming out from their common Father in Heaven. This must be what religious people mean when they say that the brotherhood of man is not possible without the fatherhood of God. For brotherhood to become an unconscious disposition, and not merely a mental and emotional attitude, one must really come to experience the cosmic interrelatedness of the family of man.

In a communion, the members say to one another, 'You are my brother because I love you.' This kind of love is emotional and is called *eros*. In a community, the members say to one another, 'I love you because you are my brother.' This kind of love is called *agapē*. Eberhard Arnold took the erotic love that was already present in the German Youth Movement and, by deepening his followers' perspectives, transmuted it into *agapē*. Thus he created a community. But it was not yet a true community. As long as Arnold lived, the Bruderhof remained a charismatic community, continually dependent on him to remind the Brothers how they were related.

The Rhön years were lean economically. The community was very short of food and money. One of the Arnold children didn't learn to walk till he was three, because the food was so poor. At one point the sheriff seemed to come every Friday, to impound community property for nonpayment of bills; Eberhard joked that the sheriff would not need to wait a year to become a member of the Brotherhood, since he had been visiting every Friday. Even in these circumstances, homeless children were taken in by the community. A sign hung in the kitchen:

TEN WERE INVITED AND TWENTY HAVE COME
PUT WATER IN THE SOUP AND BID THEM
ALL WELCOME

and this was the custom the community followed.

During the years at Rhön, the community started to read the writings of the sixteenth-century Anabaptists, particularly the

Hutterians. They were amazed to discover that people in the sixteenth century seem to have been called by the same Spirit as they, and had developed a similar communal life. Many of the Hutterian writings about the organization of communal life illuminated the customs which had slowly developed in Sannerz and the Rhön. Emmy writes:

We were very much interested also in the kind of outward form in which their life was expressed. Not that we wanted to copy or imitate anything. Yet the larger our circle had grown, the more we felt that we were moving in the same direction. Essentially we already had the functions of the various services in our own midst. We already had a Servant of the Word, though not by that name; a brother to represent the business and economic side; another to oversee the work; and still another to keep things in good order everywhere. We had a house-mother, a nurse, a sister who helped out in all matters, a school principal and several teachers. These services, however, had grown out of the life, without having been designated or recognized as such.[37]

It was even more exciting to learn that the Hutterians were still in existence, living in the United States and Canada. In 1930 and 1931, Eberhard Arnold spent a year visiting the Hutterians. The Brothers felt isolated in Germany, and they were interested in uniting with the Hutterian movement; they also hoped for financial aid from the Hutterians.

From the Hutterian point of view, the Bruderhof seemed to offer a very necessary fresh perspective for a movement which was, after all, four hundred years old, and excessively encumbered by medieval forms of dress and behavior. The Hutterians were particularly impressed with the serious scholarship of the Society of Brothers (the Bruderhof publishing company had reprinted many old Hutterian writings), and with Eberhard Arnold's qualities of charismatic Christian leadership.

The Bruderhof was disturbed by the traditionalism of much of Hutterian life. The Hutterians wore an antiquated costume, with long skirts and head scarves for the women, and beards and dark jackets for the men. They rejected music, pictures, and smoking. Emmy Arnold writes:

We especially did not want to place ourselves under laws that were not born out of our living experience. We cherished the hope that new life would break through in the Hutterian movement as it had often done already.[38]

But, on the whole, the Bruderhof felt that the advantages of union outweighed the disadvantages. In December of 1930, in a ceremony at Stand-Off Colony, in Alberta, the Bruderhof was admitted to the Hutterian Church and Eberhard Arnold was ordained as a Hutterian minister. This was officially confirmed three months later in a letter to all Hutterian settlements:

> The Hutterian Brethren
> Stand-Off Colony
> Macleod, Alberta
> March 20, 1931.

To the Bruederhoefe:

Information to the Hutterian Congregations

1. On December 9, 1930, Eberhard Arnold of the German Bruderhof of the church of God, was incorporated into the Brotherhood who are called the Hutterians, at the Stand-Off Colony, with the teaching of Matthew 28, by Elias Walter, Christian Waldner, Johannes Kleinsasser, and Johannes Entz, in the presence of the Stand-Off Colony and Joseph Wipf and Jerg Waldner.

2. On December 19, 1930, Eberhard Arnold was confirmed in the service of the Word with laying on of hands by the elders Christian Waldner, Elias Walter, Johannes Kleinsasser, and Johannes Entz. It took place in the Stand-Off Colony with the teaching of Titus I, and was delivered by Johannes Kleinsasser of the Buck Ranch Bruderhof. Thereby the commission of the brotherhood was given to Eberhard Arnold for Germany, there to proclaim the Word of God, gather the zealous, and establish in the best order the Bruderhof existing in Neuhof (Fulda) in Hesse-Nassau.

> (Signed) *Elias Walter.*[39]

Meanwhile, Eberhard's prolonged visit gave the Bruderhof at Rhön a chance to see how it could do without him. Although it is doubtful that the community could have sustained the permanent loss of its leader at this point, it was able, at least according to the account of Emmy Arnold, to manage fairly well during his temporary absence:

Now, how did things go otherwise during Eberhard's trip to America? Seen as a whole, it went really very well. It had been given over to Hans, then twenty-three years old, to represent Eberhard; those who did the other services – housemother, steward, work distributor and store-keeper – tried to stand by him in a special way in the daily life. Of course, the whole brotherhood supported him! The life was not without struggles. Ambition, arrogance, the perpetual enemies of the community life, came to the fore soon after Eberhard's departure. Again and again we had to occupy ourselves with our own and others' weaknesses. But it was good that these things were repeatedly taken in hand and overcome by the entire brotherhood. It was given to Hans at that time to see the way and the direction and to hold to it in a very loving but clear way.[40]

When Eberhard returned, many customs and forms of communal organization were adopted from the Hutterians:

All the men grew Hutterian beards .... The women's costume became a uniform – long skirts with a waist-to-ankle apron, long-sleeved bodices, and a head kerchief, an ensemble that was retained even in subtropical Paraguay.

... The practice of a yearly Lord's Supper, preceded by confession and reconciliation, was moulded on Hutterite lines, using Hutterite texts as ritual. The Youth Movement's feminist equality of man and woman gave way to a sex segregation in the communal dining room, and the feeling that women should participate in decisions only when asked to. The natural dominance of Eberhard Arnold in the religious, economic, and cultural life of the community was reinforced in the office of the Servant of the Word (Minister), which among the Hutterians carried more a paternalistic emphasis than a democratic one .... Until 1950, the community was officially called the 'Society of Brothers, known as Hutterians'.[41]

· The strict austerity of the Hutterian forms served well to counterpoise the spontaneity of the Youth Movement, and these forms were of inestimable value in preserving the community after Eberhard's death. But, as many of the forms were just arbitrary rules, they also had a very detrimental effect. For about twenty years there was great fighting about the rules. The community was split into two factions: one wanted to follow the rules as exactly as possible; the other felt that the life had to grow out of experience and inspiration.

The Hutterian merger was the crowning achievement of Eberhard Arnold's life. It is a tribute both to his power and his wisdom. His power is demonstrated in the remarkable achievement of persuading his freedom-loving ex-Youth Movement followers to accept the sudden imposition of an alien authoritarian system with hardly a serious protest. His wisdom is illustrated in his doing what few other charismatic community leaders have ever done – preparing his community to survive his death.

In 1933, when the Nazis came to power in Germany, the Bruderhof of course entered a time of great trouble. The *hof* was searched by the SS, SA and Gestapo, and books and papers were carried away. Severe restrictions were placed on visitors. The Bruderhof school was closed, and the Brothers were told that their children would have to have Nazi teachers. The children were quickly spirited away to a place of refuge, first in Switzerland, later to a new *hof* in Lichtenstein, called the Alm Bruderhof. When word came that a law had been passed requiring young men to register for military service, the Brotherhood had a long meeting:

Had the hour come for us to suffer for the resistance? Or did we feel our task was to continue building up, on the Alm Bruderhof for instance, where men were very much needed for the work? After a time of silence to ask God for the right guidance in this hour, we decided to send the young men in question to the Alm Bruderhof that same night – by rail, bicycle, or on foot, by different routes, since we did not have the means to send them all by railroad.[42]

All of them got through safely, and their families later joined them.

The Alm Bruderhof could not be expanded much beyond this. Missionaries were sent to Switzerland, Holland and England, looking for a place for a new *hof*. Peter Arnold, the Arnolds' son, had made contacts in England while studying there, and four English people had already joined the Bruderhof.

During all these events, from 1933 on, Eberhard Arnold was troubled with a complicated fracture of the leg, which never completely healed. It was in a walking cast, and Eberhard walked on it a good deal while looking for a place to found a new *hof*; he did not spare himself. In November 1935, another operation was necessary. The operation was unsuccessful, and on November 22 he died.[43]

## 3. *Transitional Community (1935–40)*

The death of the founder and leader of a movement is always a blow to it. For the Bruderhof, this came at a time of crisis, both external (the rise of Naziism in Germany) and internal (the spiritual struggle at the Rhön Bruderhof). The situation was so desperate that Eberhard's death did not have the disastrous effect it might have had in better times; the necessity for struggle helped to unify the community. An ex-member described the situation in this way:

For about seven years there was not much unity but mainly struggles between the leaders in connection with the Hutterian rules and regulations. What kept the community going was an astonishing loyalty of the members without precise responsibilities – the younger people. Very few left in that first seven years after Eberhard's death.

Early in 1936, the Cotswold Bruderhof was founded in England. The young men were no longer safe in Lichtenstein, and they traveled to England as a group of strolling players. Their passports were not quite in order, but they were allowed in. Emmy writes, about the beginning days in England:

Meanwhile the number of those of us arriving from Germany and Lichtenstein had grown, so that there seemed no way out other than to occupy a cottage – the grey cottage, as it was called – before so much as a penny had been paid! And wasn't the owner of the farm astonished on finding people there! He said, 'This is not usually done in England.' (Nor in other countries, I think.)[44]

In 1937 the German government ordered the Rhön Bruderhof dissolved, and all the residents were ordered to leave within twenty-four hours. They could take none of the communal property with them – just small bundles of personal property. The three chief Brothers were imprisoned (for three months, and then released, as it turned out). The government permitted the community to leave the country together, and go to the *hof* in England.

In 1938 the Alm Bruderhof was closed, and a new *hof* in England, at Oaksey, was founded. A new publishing house was started. Refugee children were cared for. The farm work was very successful. The Bruderhof in England rapidly grew to a population of over three hundred. In a time of growing preparation for war, many British conscientious objectors were drawn to the life. One such man who joined at this time told me that he felt challenged by the war to make a commitment that went beyond passive nonviolence to the creation of a viable nonviolent life style. The Bruderhof seemed to him to represent such a commitment. He was particularly impressed by the way in which members of German and of English backgrounds were able to live together, within the Bruderhof, in love and harmony.

Not everyone responded favorably to the Bruderhof. Especially after 1939, the rise in anti-German sentiment brought attacks and boycotts from Cotswold neighbors. One man stayed with the community for a while and then reported in a newspaper article that the majority were simply slaves to an inner circle who were mostly Germans. He said that this élite used Gestapo surveillance tactics, and solitary confinement, and that the doors locked only from the inside so that rooms could be searched while the occupants were away. This was denied in a letter from the Bruderhof, but there probably was at least a grain of truth in the charges. Punishment by isolation from the social life of the community (not solitary confinement) was certainly practiced as this was an integral part of the Hutterian orders.

The English period was an interlude in Bruderhof history. The mood was simply one of holding together in the face of Arnold's sudden death, the sudden expulsion from the homeland, and growing local hostility due to the heightened emotions of war. The rapid influx of English members paved the way for the transformation of the Bruderhof from a German to an international movement, but curiously the English members themselves did not bring about this change:

In the years that followed, the English contingent was thoroughly digested. Most of them managed to learn German, which remained the dominant language. Their English was bent to the German Bruderhof vocabulary. They added some religious literature and songs, but contributed no new ideas, made no innovations. Most had been somewhat churchly, few had any social-revolutionary notions beyond the narrow point of pacifism, and in all, their impact on Bruderhof belief and practice was nil.[22]

Leadership positions, during this period, were largely in the hands of Eberhard Arnold's original circle of lieutenants and, increasingly, of his sons. The five years after the death of Arnold can be described as a time of emerging collective leadership. No one, as yet, quite knew how to lead a community like the Bruderhof, and the community relied more on the Hutterian forms and the crisis spirit of the members than upon its official leaders. Fortunately, the Hutterian forms designated certain formal executive offices such as Servant of the Word and Witness Brother that could be filled by appointment. In the years that followed, the occupants of these offices would come to grow in competence and become fine leaders, although few if any of them would have been able to gain communal confidence at the outset without the crutch of formal office.

The Hutterian forms were undoubtedly of the greatest importance in allowing the Bruderhof to survive this difficult transition period following the death of Arnold. But the trauma of the expulsion from Germany probably helped as well. Festinger and others have discovered that, at times of severe crisis, members who have made a great psychic investment in a group will, rather than become discouraged and give up, more likely redouble their commitment. The Nazi expulsion assured that the Bruderhof would have no debilitating period of despair and apathy. While much of the enthusiasm of the Arnold period was still present, the members of the Bruderhof were forced to choose between quitting and making a total commitment in a foreign land. Most responded by taking up the challenge with renewed enthusiasm.

Very shortly, the Society of Brothers was to face still another upheaval in the form of a new exile. When England declared war on Germany, the British Home Office, although sympathetic to the Bruderhof, felt it necessary to intern those members of the community who were of German descent. Rather than be broken up in this way, the Bruderhof decided to emigrate. But for a group of pacifist 'communists' of mixed nationalities to emigrate during wartime was not an easy matter.

The obvious first choice was Canada, a nation with a long record of hospitality to communitarian groups. Here the Bruderhof could be near their brethren in the Hutterian colonies. But admission was refused by the Canadian immigration authorities.

The next choice was the United States, where there were also some Hutterian colonies, and where the Bruderhof also had a number of influential Quaker friends. One of these friends describes his attempt to get the Shakers to allow the Bruderhof to occupy an abandoned Shaker Village near New Lebanon, New York, which, of course, was ideally suited for communal living. The Shakers at that time had dwindled to a small core of elderly survivors, who had given up any hope of reviving the community:

We consulted Elder Sarah Collins who seemed friendly to our errand until she thought to ask, 'Do they marry?' I realized the import of the question but, of course, answered in the affirmative.

She shook her head firmly. 'It will never do,' she decided, 'true communal living cannot be realized on the basis of the private family.'[46]

In any case, the United States, after hedging for a while, also refused the Bruderhof sanctuary.

It finally turned out that Paraguay, underpopulated and hospitable to conscientious objectors, was the only country willing to admit them. In 1941, about 350 Bruderhof men, women, and children traveled to Paraguay in several groups, during the worst period of submarine warfare. They all got through safely but all the ships on which they traveled were later torpedoed. Three English Brothers remained in England to wind up affairs.

## 4. *Isolated Sect (1941–50)*

The years in Paraguay are seen by the Bruderhof today as an unfortunate interlude necessitated by external circumstances, but the period had an important role in the evolution of the community. Paraguay forged a people out of a loosely connected group of individuals, much as the Biblical 'forty years in the wilderness' forged a nation out of a collection of fugitive slaves. In Paraguay, the Bruderhof decisively broke away from an exclusive identification with Eberhard Arnold and his original circle of German followers. The community became truly international. Englishmen, and later Americans, began to occupy leadership positions. For a while the community (known during the 1940s as the *Sociedad Fraternal Hutteriana*) was trilingual, in German, English, and Spanish. Then, during the period in Paraguay, English gradually emerged as the official Bruderhof language.

But in 1941, as the Bruderhof prepared for its second mass emigration in less than five years, there was only a feeling of being called, once again, to blindly stake everything on faith. An ex-Bruderhof member recounts his memories of the journey as a four-year-old boy:

We little kids didn't understand much of what was going on in England at all. I remember there was a time when we couldn't play with our friends outside of the *hof* anymore because, we were told, our neighbors had started to hate us all of a sudden because we were German.

Then we had to leave. My father told us only that we were going to a far off land. I remember the ship very well. Planes would fly low overhead and we would all have to go below. Once there was a submarine scare and we all had to put on these life jackets.

We docked at Rio and from there to Buenos Aires. I remember the river trip from Buenos Aires up to Paraguay. We went in these funny flat-bottomed boats that were so loaded down and so low in the water that you thought the river was going to come right over them. And there were so many crocodiles, just all lined up like you could walk on them.

A group of Mennonites, who had been settled in Paraguay for many years, gave hospitality and much-needed advice to the first Bruderhof members who arrived from England. Then the community acquired a twenty-thousand-acre *estancia* (ranch) which they named Primavera. There was no one with experience in semitropical living:

We didn't know the first thing about how to survive. I remember they thought, well, it's the tropics, we can build houses without walls. Then the winds and rains came and, whoosh, the houses were gone. The Mennonites taught us a lot. The mosquitoes were hard to get used to, but after a while we didn't even think about them.

Primavera is located in a part of Paraguay whose landscape alternates between forestland and grassland. When the Bruderhof settled in Primavera, it had only one building and no hygienic facilities at all. In the early years there was much disease and death particularly among children.

Meanwhile, back in England, a group of pacifists gathered around the three Brothers who had stayed behind. Some felt they wanted to become members of the Bruderhof, but mass travel to Paraguay was now out of the question because of the war. Letters were exchanged with Primavera and, in 1942, the group bought a neglected farm, which became the Wheathill Bruderhof. One couple was sent from Primavera to Wheathill in an attempt to strengthen the unity between the two groups, but basically each went its own way until after the war. The center of gravity remained most definitely in Primavera.

The Brothers in Paraguay built a sawmill and, with the lumber produced, built houses for the first *hof*, Isla Margarita (Eés la Mar gar eé ta), and then for the second, Loma Jhoby (Lóma Ho boó). In 1942, a house in Asuncion was rented as a business office and display room for Bruderhof-manufactured products and as a house for Bruderhof youth who were receiving training or higher education in Asuncion. In 1946, another *hof* was built, Ibate (Eé ba tay). The Bruderhof had offered to care for sixty European orphans, and Ibate was designed as a children's village. However, there were official difficulties and the plans never materialized, so Ibate became just another *hof*. The three colonies in

Primavera were built within a few miles of one another on the margin between forest and grasslands, 120 miles north of Asuncion, and forty miles east of the Paraguay river.

An ex-member describes the routine of life at Primavera, which was much the same in all three *hofs*:

Dinner at twelve noon and supper at seven pm were eaten at long tables in the big dining room, the center of community life. The kitchen next door supplied the main course, usually meat, some vegetable, and manioca, the Paraguayan substitute for potato. A pudding or something else extra was prepared for mothers nursing children. Old people or those with stomach trouble got specially prepared diet plates. Extra helpings of meat often went to the heavy laborers.

Breakfast at six am and tea at two pm after the noon siesta were family affairs. Some family member would go to the kitchen where boiling water and yerba were ready for making Paraguayan mate, a kind of green tea. He would also bring home two or three slices of whole wheat bread for each one around the family table. It was the same for the two- or three-member groups of single people who generally shared bedrooms and breakfast nook. Sugar for tea, and lard and marmalade for the bread were rationed out by a storekeeper once a week.

Medical care was provided for all three villages in the three-doctor, twenty-one-bed hospital at Loma Jhoby, which also served neighboring Paraguayan patients.

Housing was cramped by American standards, but the rooms had no need of cooking facilities, since the communal kitchen took care of that. A couple would have a bedroom for themselves, sometimes a separate breakfast room, and another room for each two or three children. Dwelling houses, for two or three families, were built long, with many inner doors to allow for adding rooms as families expanded or moved around, a frequent necessity.

Each village had its own school through ninth grade, where the children studied all morning, and either worked or played games under teacher supervision in late afternoon. They were home for siesta and tea, and also for bed at six in the evening. A communal nursery took care of babies during the day, while there was a 'toddler house' for the two's and three's, and a kindergarten-preschool for children four to six years old.

... People were expected to accept whatever work was given them. Men filled such work departments as the cattle ranch, the farm, the sawmill, and the slaughterhouse at Loma Jhoby, or the carpentry and machine workshops in Isla Margarita. Women worked in the sewing room, and in the younger children's departments. The rugged kitchen work was done by a male cook, helped by four women; the laundry had a similar arrangement. Hospital and school were jobs for both men and women.

Each work department had a foreman, who was less boss than co-ordinator; everyone in the department participated in discussions about what to do next, new arrangements, and so on.

Certain menial tasks, or those that interfered with normal life, such as night-watch or washing dishes ... were assigned as 'duties' in rotation by a list posted at the dining room. A woman work-distributor assigned women's tasks, a man those of men.

The essentials of the Bruderhof daily routine fell into place early in the Paraguayan epoch, and have changed only in details up to the present day.

The three *hofs* in Paraguay practiced division of labor to a certain extent. Isla Margarita, the largest *hof*, had woodworking shops, forge, sawmill, brickworks, a fruit-juice factory, and a book bindery for all of Primavera. Loma Jhoby was the site of the Bruderhof hospital. The beef cattle herd and the slaughterhouse were also there. The smallest *hof*, Ibate, housed the bakery, shoemaker's shop, and agricultural farm (including a dairy herd and a poultry flock). Also at Ibate was the Bruderhof central library, in which, in 1950, there were fifteen thousand volumes.[47]

During the years from 1941 to 1950, the population of Primavera increased from 350 to slightly over 600, while the population of Wheathill, in England, rose from three to 181.[48] Almost all of the population increase in Primavera was accounted for by new babies; almost all of the Wheathill, by new converts. During the years in Paraguay, the Bruderhof was more open to anthropological study than it has been since. Therefore statistical information for these years is available and is given in the accompanying table.

By 1950, the Bruderhof had evolved a stable and enduring basis for community in all respects but one – the economic sphere. The years in Paraguay were a time of poverty and a precarious economic existence. The Bruderhof tried a great number of different ways of earning its living but none were really successful. The community was dependent largely on its own agricultural operations for food and there was never quite enough. For instance, the cattle in the milk herd had not been bred for that purpose and so the milk supply was always scanty; virtually all of it had to be reserved for children and pregnant mothers. Also there was never any real market for manufactured goods in Paraguay.

Until the end, Primavera remained dependent upon the generous financial contributions of sympathetic friends – particularly North American Quakers. The Bruderhof justified its continual begging, in large part, by the missionary and social service work it was doing in Paraguay – in particular, at the hospital in Loma Johby. The following is a typical excerpt from one of the frequent informational pamphlets which the Bruderhof sent to its North American mailing list during this period:

As soon as we settled in Paraguay the three doctors began their work. Living conditions in Paraguay are often bad and in the outlying districts there is little knowledge of how to treat illness. Patients began to come in, some of them coming several days' journey to visit the new doctors. Soon a small hospital was built and this work has continued

POPULATION STATISTICS FOR PRIMAVERA[49]

|  | 1941 | 1942 | 1943 | 1944 | 1945 | 1946 | 1947 | 1948 | 1949 | 1950 |
|---|---|---|---|---|---|---|---|---|---|---|
| Inhabitants | 350 | 366 | 370 | 395 | 432 | 466 | 503 | 521 | 590 | 604 |
| Villages | 1 | 2 | 2 | 2 | 2 | 2 | 3 | 3 | 3 | 3 |
| Families | 61 | 62 | 63 | 65 | 66 | 66 | 67 | 73 | 76 | 78 |
| Male (adults) | 100 | 99 | 99 | 100 | 102 | 107 | 109 | 116 | 126 | 142 |
| Female (adults) | 95 | 91 | 89 | 90 | 90 | 97 | 103 | 119 | 119 | 126 |
| Marriages | | 3 | 3 | 1 | 1 | 3 | 1 | 1 | 1 | |
| Births | 21 | 26 | 26 | 24 | 32 | 17 | 34 | 19 | 25 | 24 |
| Deaths | 5 | 5 | 4 | 2 | | 1 | 2 | 2 | 5 | 3 |
| Schools | 1 | 2 | 2 | 2 | 2 | 2 | 3 | 3 | 3 | 3 |
| Pupils | 49 | 58 | 62 | 79 | 92 | 105 | 124 | 139 | 154 | 173 |
| Boys in School | 31 | 36 | 35 | 43 | 50 | 53 | 63 | 70 | 79 | 90 |
| Girls in School | 18 | 22 | 27 | 36 | 42 | 52 | 61 | 69 | 73 | 83 |
| *Hospital Statistics* | | | | | | | | | | |
| Inpatients | 25 | 18 | 28 | 28 | 43 | 88 | 103 | 112 | 350 | 360 |
| Outpatients* | 1100 | 1500 | 1600 | 1300 | 1300 | 2000 | 2660 | 2620 | 3200 | 3600 |

* Approximate figures.

to grow. During the past year it has increased to such an extent that our doctors can scarcely cope with it. Financial and practical help is sorely needed, for the great majority of the patients cannot afford to pay the cost, although treatment is never refused .... Two brothers traveling in the United States during 1949 can be reached at the following address ....

Although the medical work was undoubtedly a success, most members felt that the Paraguayan situation severely limited their opportunities for social action. Transportation difficulties made extensive travel impossible, as a visiting anthropologist describes:

The roads in and between the villages are sand, neither built up nor surfaced, and difficult in rainy weather. Communication is maintained by a few trucks and horse-drawn wagons. The young people frequently use horses.[50]

Moreover, formidable social barriers existed, even between the Bruderhof and the native Paraguayans with whom they did come in contact. Many of the Brothers knew or quickly learned Spanish, but the real language of the country people of Paraguay is Guarani, an Indian language, and this proved difficult to master. The Paraguayans were initially suspicious of the Bruderhof as rich *gringos* while, on their part, the Brothers feared that leprosy and other tropical diseases would result from too close contact with the natives:

It is a custom in Paraguay to take *terrare*, which consists of water sucked up through a metal tube with a filter at the end immersed in a gourd containing yerba tea, which is the national drink. This is passed around and everyone drinks, but for medical reasons we were warned against doing this. The custom, however, is a social one and therefore in refusing we often cut ourselves off socially, though in fact some members always did join in with the local people.[51]

These difficulties were largely surmounted over the years, but the temperament of the Paraguayan people, volatile and independent, remained unsuited for Bruderhof life. The community longed for new members, but only two native Paraguayan families ever joined and neither stayed. Soon after the war ended, the Bruderhof began investigating plans for expansion into more sympathetic environments in Europe and North America.

The isolated sect period, frustrating as it was, strengthened the community in a number of ways. The Bruderhof itself recognized this. In 1948, one of the Servants remarked, 'The years in the wilderness are drawing to a close. We are now a firmly rooted little tree.' Paradoxically, the Bruderhof tree was nourished in Paraguay through a retreat from two of its basic values. The Bruderhof had always been committed to an open-door policy, but, for practical reasons, there was little turnover of membership during the 1940s. In spite of itself, the community was spared the always difficult task of assimilating new members. The Bruderhof has also always been committed to the value of not pressuring its own children to stay. But the isolation and poverty of Paraguay made it possible to build an unusually strong youth cohort, and one that was not very tempted by what it saw of the outside world.

There is another way in which Paraguayan conditions helped the community to grow strong, also involving a kind of suspension of a basic Bruderhof value. All members of the community are supposed to take an active part in decision-making, although in practice the leadership has always taken a major role. In Paraguay, the leadership became quite authoritarian, and this was tolerated largely because of the sheer exhaustion brought about by the life. An ex-member described the situation:

After working for ten hours in the hot sun, you'd want nothing more than to go to sleep, but you'd have to sit it out at the Brotherhood meeting that would last until ten, eleven, twelve o'clock at night, and then be up at five the next morning. And everything that anybody said had to be translated into one or sometimes two other languages. Believe me, you were really grateful if the Servants could bring in a neat little package, and all you'd have to do is say yes or no.

The docility of the community would have been fatally debilitating over the long run. But for a short period of time there was a respite from the need to seek total consensus on every issue.

Contact with the United States increased rapidly during the 1940s. Bruderhof missionary trips to North America brought the community into renewed contact with the Hutterians and made it obvious that the two groups had grown apart. Hutterianism, as we have seen, had served the Bruderhof well, but the community had tended to keep only the basic forms of organization while rejecting specific customs. Smoking, dancing, and playing musical instruments had never really been abolished, but, in Primavera, the community became less covert in these activities. Other customs were accepted for a while, but had started to become an embarrassment to the Bruderhof in its attempt to recruit new members. The Brothers would squirm trying to explain to a bunch of enthusiastic young American families, down for a visit, why the Servant ate special food, why the women wore funny hats, and especially why it was considered good form for a woman, before speaking at a meeting, to begin by saying, 'I know as a mere woman I shouldn't speak, but . . .' The embarrassment was all the more difficult to bear in that it came from defending customs in which the members had never really believed, which went against the grain of their own traditions. Nevertheless, the Bruderhof was anxious, if possible, to stay on good terms with the parent church.

In an effort to smooth over differences with the Hutterians, the Bruderhof sent out two ambassadors in 1949. According to Peters, they had a threefold mission: to allay the fears of the Hutterian congregations about conditions in Paraguay, to invite a delegation to visit, and to ask for material assistance. The embassy was very successful. The Hutterians responded by sending down to Paraguay about forty thousand dollars worth of clothing, tools, and machinery, $22,430 in cash, and two Hutterian ministers to return the visit.[52]

The Hutterian ministers were warmly received by the Bruderhof, but were horrified with what they saw. The smoking of tobacco particularly offended them. This has always been a curious phobia of the Hutterians. The ambassadors also discovered to their dismay that the influx of new young members from the United States had effected a dramatic revival of the long-dormant spirit of the German Youth Movement in Primavera. Work camps, folk dancing, theater, and even movies had become an accepted part of Bruderhof culture.

Neither side was willing to compromise. The Bruderhof felt that modernization was necessary to attract new members, and that their innovations were justified by their missionary success in winning North American converts. The Hutterians felt that the Bruderhof, in its over-concern with expansion, was losing touch with the essence of the Hutterian way of life. When the ambassadors returned to North America and reported to their congregations, the Hutterians formally admonished Primavera and demanded repentance. This was not forthcoming, and the twenty years of unity between the Hutterians and the Bruderhof came to an end.

## 5. *Communitarian Social Movement (1950–58)*

The break with the Hutterites signaled the beginning of a period of liberalization and expansion:

Beards were made optional; most men in Primavera continued to wear them, but the younger generation was clean-shaven . . . . Women's costume became slightly more diverse; slacks were no longer taboo, and were gladly adopted by the girls. The Hutterian confession of faith was dropped as a textbook for baptismal lessons, and replaced by free instruction.[53]

Contact with Europe and North America resumed immediately after the war and, as early as 1947, several Americans had joined the Bruderhof. In 1948, three idealistic Harvard undergraduates dropped out of college to wend their adventurous way down to Primavera, of which they had heard only vague rumors. All three stayed and eventually became members. The United States around 1950 was experiencing a mild revival of communitarian interest, and Bruderhof missionary speakers were much in demand at church groups and college campuses. Europe, and particularly Germany, seemed, by contrast, to be undergoing a time of cynical disillusionment.

By 1953, both the degree of interest and the possibility of financial aid coming from the United States seemed to warrant the foundation of a *hof* in North America. In 1953, six members were sent from Paraguay to the United States for a speaking tour, to make contact with interested friends and wealthy sponsors, and to investigate land for possible purchase. The degree of response was even greater than anticipated. Five members of the small but influential Kingwood Community (all but one member) decided to disband their community and join with the Bruderhof. Half of the members of a larger community, Macedonia, decided to join the Bruderhof, and the other half remained highly sympathetic.

In 1954, an estate of approximately a hundred acres in Rifton, New York, was purchased by the Society of Brothers. Woodcrest, the first North American Bruderhof, was founded on this site in the same year. 1954 was also significant as the year in which half of the members of Macedonia came to Woodcrest. The Macedonia split was important in that it brought into the Bruderhof an entirely new cultural perspective as well as some of its most vigorous and talented members. But it was even more important in bringing the Bruderhof an industry – Community Playthings, a toy-manufacturing business started by two Macedonians in 1947. Community Playthings later became the sole source of income for the Bruderhof, and is responsible for their current prosperity. In 1954, however, it was only a small business, run jointly by the Woodcrest Bruderhof and the remaining members of the Macedonia Community. In this year, the Bruderhof also founded a colony in Uruguay which they named El Arado (Plough).

During 1955, Woodcrest continued to grow. According to a Christmas letter which they sent out, they had by the end of 1955 a population of over 150, including thirty members, fifteen novices, and twenty-five serious guests. During 1955 also, the Forest River Hutterian colony in North Dakota decided to join with the Bruderhof. Land in Germany was also purchased for a colony in the original homeland, to be called Sinntalhof (zíntal hof).

In 1956, expansion and economic growth continued. This was the beginning of the so-called 'nine-hof period', the peak of Bruderhof expansion. With a total population of over eleven hundred, including 418 full members, the Bruderhof had thriving enterprises going in five nations on three continents (see accompanying table). Eberhard Arnold's seesaw had swung again. The Hutterian idea of the community as an isolated sect was in eclipse, and the old Youth Movement idea of the community as an evangelical social movement had returned with the additional elements of internationalism and pragmatic experimentation supplied by the new American members.

The Bruderhof was feeling its oats and thinking of itself as the world's great hope. Community pamphlets of the time proudly catalogued the nationalities represented in the membership: English, German, Swiss, American, Dutch, Swedish, Austrian, Czechoslovakian, French, Italian, Latvian, (Asian) Indian, Spanish, Argentinian, and Paraguayan. Equal pride was taken in

POPULATION OF THE BRUDERHOFS [54]
1956*

| Community | Location | Members | Novices | Guests | Children | Total |
|---|---|---|---|---|---|---|
| Woodcrest | U.S.A. | 46 | 15 | 22 | 84 | 167 |
| Wheathill (2)† | England | 65 | 7 | 26 | 88 | 186 |
| Sinntalhof | Germany | 13 | 4 | 6 | 2 | 25 |
| El Arado | Uruguay | 16 | 0 | 9 | 14 | 39 |
| Forest River | U.S.A. | 34 | 8 | 10 | 64 | 116 |
| Primavera (3) | Paraguay | 244 | 26 | 16 | 352 | 638‡ |
| | Total | 418 | 60 | 89 | 604 | 1171 |

*1956 was the last year in which the Bruderhof allowed the tabulation of statistical material by outside scholars.

†Number of *hofs* in parentheses.

‡Statistical information about the Bruderhof has always been unreliable to say the least. H. Hack, an anthropologist who visited Primavera in 1957–58, reported the population for 1956 as 656, including 83 families and 48 unmarried adults.[55]

the diversity of cultural backgrounds: 'pacifists, anarchists, Moral Rearmers, Communist Party members, vagabonds, Nazis, agnostics, anticlericals, good ordinary establishment churchgoers, and two native Paraguayan families in which the mothers knew no language but the local Indian Guarani.'[56] Bruderhof colonies began to be the scenes of work camps and conferences for young people of diverse backgrounds. Thousands of guests passed through Woodcrest each year, and some of them stayed and became members, increasing the American element, which was rapidly becoming important in the Bruderhof spectrum.

There were signs, however, as early as 1956, that the Bruderhof was overextending itself. Primavera, once the nexus of Bruderhof life, began to feel left behind and bewildered at some of the new attitudes of the post-Hutterian era. An ex-member from Paraguay had this comment:

... a shrewd observer might have pointed out that the Hutterian forms, even though, and perhaps precisely because, they had been accepted as part of a battle for faith, over the objections of modern rationalistic minds, had been devices of integration. The observer might have noticed that people no longer made songbooks for themselves, and that the quality, variety, and enthusiasm of the singing dropped off strongly.

He might have observed that socialism, pacifism, organized church activity and other aspects of worldly life, that once had been nodded toward as ridiculously inadequate patching on a social system that needed to be discarded and replaced, now were more respected, and freely participated in by Bruderhof members. He might have detected the unspoken question: So much we insisted on, so much we made ourselves believe and acquiesce in, was wrong; what else that we think we see now is mere illusion? How many of the things we have given up were right after all?

In North America, the problems resulted from the attempts to do too many things too fast. The ten years' restrained energy of the South American Bruderhofers met the postwar fury of North American pacifism, and there was an explosion. The Bruderhof in the United States felt it could simultaneously stimulate the entire intentional community movement, inspire and convert radical youth, and still serve as a bridge to the progressive elements of the Hutterian Church.

The episode of the Forest River colony provides a case in point. After the break in 1950, the Bruderhof requested of a number of Hutterian colonies permission to send some members to live with them and to act as missionaries in North America. They were turned down by all except Forest River, the only Hutterite colony in North Dakota.

A large faction in Forest River had been extremely receptive to the Bruderhof criticism that the Hutterites had lost their original missionary zeal. This group invited the Bruderhof to send some families despite the fact that a minority faction in Forest River was adamantly opposed to such a move. For a Hutterian colony to make a decision without total unanimity is an extraordinary violation of the community's deepest principles; this has never been satisfactorily explained. It is ironic that the Bruderhof, which, if anything, places even more importance on total unanimity, would agree to come under such circumstances. But they did come, and the opposing faction left in protest, returning to the parent colony in Manitoba.

Despite the warmth and mutual admiration which existed between the remaining members and the Bruderhof people, it was soon evident that this particular merger would not work. The Hutterians could not adjust to Bruderhof internationalism. The enormous long-distance telephone bills, which the Bruderhof ran up monthly as a matter of course, horrified the Hutterians. The Bruderhof members could not get used to the seasonal rhythms of prairie farm life, and were depressed by the isolation of North Dakota, which offered little opportunity for missionary work. In 1957, there was some dissension in the Forest River colony. The Bruderhof members decided to move to the Oak Lake Bruderhof, newly founded near Pittsburgh, Pennsylvania. They took with them several of the Hutterians, including the minister and his family. Most of these Hutterians are still members of the Bruderhof. Along with their children, they add a unique spice to the Bruderhof stew.

Forest River was left with four rather bewildered families and a pile of unpaid bills. Undaunted, they decided to start anew, and are, at the present time, one of the few Hutterian communities that actively seeks, and has actually admitted, convert members. Peters visited Forest River soon after the Bruderhof left and reported no negative feelings toward them:

... the community members at no time used derogatory or disparaging language when they spoke of their newly found and lost brothers. 'They were not farmers,' said young Mrs Waldner pleasantly, 'but they certainly could use their pens, pencils, and paintbrushes.'[57]

After thirty-seven years of poverty, the Bruderhof finally arrived economically in the late 1950s. In 1957, Macedonia was disbanded; all but one of the remaining member families had finally decided to join the Bruderhof. Community Playthings thus became entirely Bruderhof-controlled. The toys became popular with American nursery schools and kindergartens and, by 1959, the greatest economic worry of the North American colonies was where to borrow enough expansion capital.

While all this was happening in North America, Paraguay was the scene, in 1957, of a 'world-conference' to discuss policy matters for the entire nine-*hof* Society of Brothers. At this time, Primavera was still considered the center of the Bruderhof movement, but many of the discussions at this conference concerned means of evacuating more members from Paraguay and building up the colonies in the more populated areas of the world. It was acknowledged at this time that the Bruderhof in Germany was not doing well. Most of the good news came from the United States, and, after the conference, the influence of Primavera declined rapidly and that of Woodcrest rapidly increased.

## 6. *Years of Crisis and Schism (1959–62)*

The years 1959 to 1962 were the period of 'the great crisis'. This was an ugly period in Bruderhof history. Contradictions within the Bruderhof movement, many of which had been acknowledged and wrestled with for years, all seemed to reach the critical point simultaneously. A Bruderhof crisis is a fairly common event, occurring whenever the members of a *hof* are unable to reach consensus on an important matter. But the great crisis involved all of the *hofs*, lasted for more than three years, and radically and permanently changed the basic structure of the community. By 1962, the Bruderhof had undergone a major change in value orientation, and a purge of top leaders; the number of *hofs* had been reduced from nine to four, and half the membership had quit or been sent away.

It is no more possible to delineate neatly the causes of the great crisis than it is the causes of the French Revolution. Some of the underlying conflicts were: the perennial dilemma of Hutterianism as opposed to spontaneity, social outreach as opposed to inner concerns, democratic as opposed to authoritarian decision making, Woodcrest versus Primavera as the nexus of Bruderhof life, a power struggle among the top leaders, national differences in temperament among the Germans, English, and Americans, and earning or begging as a means of livelihood.

The 1950s had been years of rapid change in the Bruderhof. Politically, the crisis can be seen as a reactionary response to the progressive innovations of the preceding ten years; ideologically, the Brothers now speak of it as a return to the original spirit of Eberhard Arnold. The political reaction was brought about by a strange alliance between the very oldest and the very newest elements – the original Germans and the recent American converts. A former Servant of the Word, now in exile, recalls with amazement:

After the world-conference, democracy became a dirty word at the Bruderhof. If you mentioned democracy in connexion with a Brotherhood meeting you really got jumped on. 'We are not a democracy; we're a dictatorship of the holy spirit.' We saw a flowering of the authoritarian spirit in, of all places, America! I will never be able to understand it.

The Germans and the Americans got along from the first in a way that the Germans and the English never did. But although the Germans and Americans experienced an immediate intuitive affinity, a deep-seated bias against Christianity on the part of many of the Americans proved difficult to surmount. Typically, there would be an agonizing struggle with conscience for several months (or in some cases years) and then a sharp sudden breakthrough, a conversion: 'The scales have fallen from my eyes and I have seen the light.'

It has been observed in connexion with many social movements (for example, the Communist Party of America) that the
greater the psychic leap the new member has to make, the more
severely will he then adhere to the tenets of his new belief.[58] The
fanaticism of St Paul can be explained in this way, as a reaction
to his previous state of fanatical anti-Christianity. Precisely
because many of the new American Bruderhof members were still
warring against powerful inner doubts, over which they had only
recently won a great but unconsolidated victory, they felt the
need to be super-zealous. The very liberalization of the Bruderhof
movement that the earliest American converts had done much to
foster became perceived as a threat to the precarious faith of these
and other Americans.

Americans were also responsible for another important, but
unrelated, change. Prior to the success of Community Playthings,
the Bruderhof had always been heavily dependent on outside
contributions as a source of money. The community had always
attracted a circle of admiring liberals who would say, 'What
you're doing is so wonderful and important. I wish I had the
strength of will to join you, but I don't, so here take my money
instead.' And the Bruderhof had always felt that it was right and
proper that it should be so. But this attitude was never unmixed
with a certain hypocrisy. One of the motivations behind the
Hutterian merger was the hope of Hutterian financial aid, and
the Bruderhof would sometimes catch itself giving a rich visitor
a more careful and enthusiastic tour around the *hof* than they
would a poor visitor. The North Americans were used to paying
their own way and came from a society where this was not too
difficult. In the late 1950s Woodcrest began to develop the attitude
that there was something wrong with Primavera's constant
begging for money, and that the South American *hofs* should be
put on a basis of economic self-sufficiency.

After the world-conference, two steps were taken to relieve the
economic pressure in Paraguay. Plans were made for the gradual
reduction of the Primavera population by more than half, and a
carefully researched project was begun to develop two hundred
acres of jungle land for the cultivation of rice. The rice project

absorbed the hopes and the energy of Primavera over the next two years. In January of 1959, the project yielded its first harvest.

Just as Primavera was celebrating this event, a letter arrived from Woodcrest advising the Paraguayan colonies that agriculture had no economic future and that they would be better off getting into some line of manufacture. This prompted a sharp exchange. A Primavera Brother wrote back a sarcastic letter reminding Woodcrest that not many Paraguayans had any money with which to buy manufactured items. Woodcrest quickly replied with a shocked note that suggested that there was 'something radically wrong . . . afoot in the inner life of Primavera, when a Brother's suggestion could be ridiculed.' The fuse had been lit. The bombs would not stop popping for more than three years.

1959 later became known as 'the year the Servants fell.' Almost all of the top leaders got into trouble and were removed from office. The trouble centered around Woodcrest. A leading Servant from the English colonies was caught in a lie while visiting Woodcrest for a conference. He was removed from office, starting a chain of events which, by the end of the year, left the Bruderhofs in England plunged deep in self-doubt and self-examination and totally without leadership. Primavera's crises, although initially less severe, had also left the South American *hofs* tormented and very short on leaders by the end of the year.

Meanwhile, an important religious revival was taking place at Woodcrest. Under the strong spiritual leadership of David, Eberhard's son, Woodcrest was the only *hof* to remain unshaken by the crises of 1959. The Woodcrest Brotherhood had begun to feel that the community had drifted far from the original 'spirit of Sannerz' since the death of Eberhard Arnold. The 'years in the wilderness', had been physically and economically difficult and had not proved conducive to the cultivation of the childlike spirit which had been so characteristic of the years in Germany. Now, with the increased prosperity brought about by Community Playthings, the North American Brothers once again could take time to examine themselves spiritually. Doing so, many of them felt the need for a revolution.

The revolution was signaled by a letter to Primavera in 1959, voicing concern about the existence of a large bloc of unmoved hearts in the Woodcrest household. It referred specifically to guests and prospective members who, though interested in community living, had not responded to the spiritual aspect of the life, and shortly thereafter there was a 'housecleaning' at Woodcrest during which many of these people were sent away. But concern with unmoved hearts soon spread to the Brotherhood itself, leading first to self-examination, then to mutual examination, and in the end to a schism.

'Warmth of heart' very quickly began to take on racial associations. Some of the German members harbored a feeling that the English, and to a lesser extent the Swiss, were cold-hearted, while the Germans and Americans tended to be warm-hearted. It certainly was true that many of the English members had originally joined the Bruderhof more for idealistic and political than for spiritual reasons, and that they tended to react intellectually rather than emotionally to the challenges of community living. But this diversity, which for a quarter of a century had been proclaimed as one of the finest aspects of Bruderhof life, suddenly became, in 1960, an intolerable source of disunity.

Warmth of heart also began to be associated with the policy question of whether the Bruderhof ought to give priority to outreach or to inner purification. In 1958, Woodcrest had created the Woodcrest Service Committee. Closely modeled after the American Friends Service Committee, this was to have opened up the new frontiers of which the Bruderhof had been dreaming ever since the enforced exodus to Paraguay. Instead, two years later, the very term 'social work' had become taboo at Woodcrest and virtually every concern with the world outside the confines of the *hofs* had been dismissed as 'not our task'. Furthermore, those who still were interested in social problems were defined as cold-hearted and a menace to the community. An ex-member explained it in this manner:

Two strands have come to be intertwined in the Bruderhof: one of them is the warm-hearted people who have experienced redemption through Christ and want to build a close, loving community, and the other is those who have come in with ideals and concern to build a community that reaches out to the world with social concern – the cold-hearted. These two strands can no longer go along together. They must be separated.

The shift from outer to inner concerns, as surprising as it seemed, was an inevitable result of the transition from a South American to a North American ecology. In Paraguay, the Bruderhof as an isolated sect could afford to be outreaching with impunity. It took all the missionary zeal that Primavera could muster to convince even a trickle of new converts to break ties with civilization and take a chance on an unknown way of life in an unknown primitive land. Outreach did not challenge the loyalty of veteran Bruderhofers since the surrounding culture was so alien and poverty stricken as to offer little temptation. At the same time, the very alienness of the Paraguayan environment gave the Bruderhof a strong sense of its own relative unity. This tended to breed complacency, and in fact there was little felt need for work on inner problems.

The North American situation was just the opposite. With Woodcrest only two hours' drive from New York City, visitors and prospective members were always pounding down the doors even without any missionary effort on the part of the Bruderhof. Unlike Paraguay, the United States surrounded the Bruderhof with a culture that was both prosperous and sophisticated, and therefore threatening. Boundary maintenance thus became important. On the other hand, the Bruderhof in North America had been ingesting new members very quickly. Most of these new members were only partially assimilated and were still at least unconsciously evaluating the Bruderhof against the many alternative choices of life style available to them. This made it necessary to concentrate on problems of community integration.

During Eberhard Arnold's lifetime, Bruderhof energies flowed simultaneously into outreach and strengthening the inner life. Since his death first one and then the other has been emphasized. If the Bruderhof could have recognized the ecological necessity for different *hofs* to allocate their energy to different problems instead of attempting to set one uniform policy for the entire community, much of the great crisis might have been avoided. Failure to do this had much to do with a long-simmering power struggle among the Bruderhof leaders which found in this policy question a likely battleground.

The principals in the power struggle were Eberhard Arnold's three sons, the husbands of his two daughters, and a few other men. The conflict thus takes on the deep tragic overtones of brother against brother-in-law, with jealousy and hatred finally emerging despite long, heroic battles to repress them. When Eberhard Arnold died, his three sons, David, Peter, and Johann Paul, were too young to take a leadership role. Power was distributed collectively, with Arnold's son-in-law, Hans, more or less the first among equals. By the time the community arrived in Paraguay, in 1941, the brothers felt that they were now old enough to assume command by hereditary right. The community did not accept this and rallied behind Hans to temporarily expel the three boys from the community. They were soon readmitted, but with their power broken, thus securing an era of collective leadership. Many reports have indicated that David in particular deeply resented this treatment, and never forgave the community his expulsion. If this is true, it does much to explain some of the extraordinary events of 1961.

When the Bruderhof began to expand in the early 1950s, the various top leaders chose different theaters of operation. Hans, a true German, gave his heart, against all common sense, to the dream of re-establishing a colony in Germany. Peter and David went to the United States, Johann Paul to Uruguay. Another brother-in-law and a few other leaders kept Paraguay as their sphere of influence. Of course, all these men traveled around quite a bit, so these designations are only approximate. During the years of the great crisis, Woodcrest, under the leadership of Brother David, gained an unprecedented amount of control over all of the other *hofs*. By the late 1950s, while all of the other colonies were floundering, David had not only made Woodcrest an economic success, but had selected from among the new American members a core of loyal, forceful, and competent lieutenants who were to be instrumental in the expansion of his power. By 1959, all of the Bruderhof colonies had come to share the assumption that Woodcrest held the key to the Bruderhof's future.

So when Woodcrest scolded Primavera about its attitude toward the rice project, Primavera took it seriously. One ex-member recalls the events that followed Primavera's chastisement:

A little cloud no bigger than a man's hand grew to a storm of self-criticism, fault-finding, confession, near hysteria, and more confession, as Primavera gave itself a house-cleaning that went on night after night in all three villages for three months. Two women had to be taken to Asuncion for electric shock treatment. Sins, prides, and hostilities emerged that had been covered over as long as fifteen years. At the end, Primavera felt clean, but exhausted. The American Brotherhoods sent members to help with what amounted to setting up community life on a fresh basis.

Why Bruderhof crises develop to frenzied peaks such as this one will become clear only in later chapters. The results of this crisis helped convince Bruderhof members that Woodcrest was right about the need for concern with inner problems rather than with outreach. Throughout the great crisis, the assumption gradually took hold that Woodcrest was the strong and righteous *hof*, while the others were all sorely in need of help.

The great crisis came in waves. Something would happen in one *hof*. This would be settled, and everyone would assume that normal times had returned. Then something else would break down in another *hof*. The Bruderhof began to realize that it had over-extended itself, and it began to think about cutting its losses and consolidating. The first *hof* to be closed was the small Uruguayan colony, El Arado, in 1960. Its leaders were sent to help with crises in England and Germany. In 1961, Wheathill in England and Sinntalhof in Germany had to be disbanded. 1961 was also the year the crisis in Paraguay reached its peak.

In chapter four we shall see how the Bruderhof utilizes energy from the unconscious in the same way as does a mob. Generally this energy is kept under control and used for beneficent ends, but there is always the possibility that it will get out of hand and that the Bruderhof will degenerate into an hysterical mob. This is how some ex-members recall the events in Paraguay in 1961.

Early in the year, Primavera arranged with Woodcrest that David and a small group of other trusted Brothers would come down and try to help set the Paraguayan colonies in order. What happened next is a matter of bitter dispute. Many ex-members report that this group somehow gathered to itself a tremendous amount of authority and, after intensive interviews with each Primavera resident, decided who should be allowed to stay in the Bruderhof and who should be sent into exile. The Bruderhof denies that the delegation ever acted except under the authority of the Primavera Brotherhoods. The debate may be over a moot point. An ex-Servant of the Word from Primavera explains the phenomenon this way:

In the Bruderhof, if you are sincere and someone poses a question, you look inside. You always doubt yourself. But this is the strange thing about it. When the North American Brothers got riding high, they no longer saw evil in themselves and they came on with such self-confidence.

They came on with the word of authority and there was enough wrong with Primavera so that it collapsed by itself. A unique factor was that the young people rose up in support of the North Americans and turned against their own parents because they could see themselves everything that was wrong.

Another ex-Servant adds this comment:

When you send six hundred or so people to searching within themselves for fault, they are incapable of doing anything else. That's how David, with a group of less than ten, was able to take over three *hofs*. If even seven or eight people had stood up to them it would have been entirely different. It might have provoked a split though.

The visitors based their decisions on two criteria. The first was the intuitive impression of the Woodcrest contingent as to whether the individual in question had a warm heart or a cold heart, an awakened heart or an unawakened heart. The second criterion was whether the individual had a positive attitude toward the Arnold family. In connexion with this, each Brother was asked what attitude he had taken, back in 1941, when the Arnold boys had been temporarily expelled from the Bruderhof.

The judging of hearts induced a lasting bitterness in many of those who are now ex-members. Some feel that judgements were made on the basis of nationality, as for instance that Englishmen tended to be more coldhearted than Germans. Such chauvinism may have been expressed by a few— it was, after all, a time of great emotional excess— but was certainly not the basic motivation behind the judging of hearts. More likely, the Bruderhof had suddenly seen how far the community had drifted from the warm – hearted communion days in Sannerz, and realizing that the honeymoon was over, began to panic for the state of the marriage.

The second criterion, a positive attitude toward the Arnolds, tied in with this fear. Rightly or wrongly, the Arnold family had always been associated with the early days of Bruderhof history. Liberals within the community tended to oppose continuing leadership by a single family. Thus it was felt that by determining what stand a Brother or Sister had taken in 1941 on the expulsion of the Arnolds, the liberals could better be identified, and their influence lessened. This was felt to be a prerequisite for the return of the original community spirit. But this criterion also helped to produce the lasting estrangement between members and ex-members which exists today. Many were astonished that the Bruderhof rule against rehashing old crises was being violated. Emotion was high, communication practically non-existent. The darker side of community was expressing itself.

All of Primavera disintegrated under the attacks of the visitors. Over the years almost all of Primavera's competent leadership had taken assignments in the northern hemisphere, so there was no respected leader for the community to rally behind in its own defense. Furthermore, the open hostility of their own children left the Primavera oldsters completely demoralized. The visitors had found in the *sabra* youth (members in their late teens and twenties who had been born in Paraguay or come there as small children) a firmer basis for a new Brotherhood. The repugnance to idealism made suspect those who had joined the Bruderhof 'for reasons' and led to the glorification of those who had a natural affinity for community living because they had never know any other kind. The Primavera Brotherhoods were dissolved and then reconstituted with the *sabras* as a base.

But for Primavera it was too late. The community was dying. Individuals and families were being sent away. Others were quitting in horror or disgust. Those who were left were prodded by the visiting delegation into endless rounds of self-examination and confession. An ex-Servant wrote in a letter to some friends at this time:

. . . things getting worse with David *et al* working the Bruderhof over in Paraguay now. David has been yelling at the circle there telling them they were never Christians. The whole Brotherhood weeping and sobbing and confessing sins. David says we were never a Christian community in all the twenty years in Paraguay.

Eventually, over six hundred people left or were expelled from the Bruderhof (although not all of these were from Primavera). Many left in a daze, not really believing it was happening, totally unprepared for life outside. Years later, some of the exiles with whom I spoke had still not gotten over the shock. A member who survived the great crisis, but left a year later when he realized what had happened, made this comment on the situation:

When I was outside the Brotherhood and I could think honest thoughts and not try to shut them off every minute, it was sort of like *Alice in Wonderland*. We were at the stage where the red queen says, 'Off with their heads. Off with their heads. Off with their heads.' Only here it was, 'Send em away. Send em away. Send em away.' You'd have to be in it to understand.

The mass exodus brought incalculable hardship and misery to hundreds of people, including the very old, the sick, and families with many young children. It was a particularly bad time for such an event to happen. Earlier in Germany or later in the United States, the refugees would have had a much easier time adjusting to a new life. But twenty years in an isolated Paraguayan Bruderhof prepared a person for nothing that he would find in the London, New York, or even the Buenos Aires of the 1960s. To make matters even worse, at this time the Bruderhof did not yet feel financially secure enough to be generous with its outcasts. The Bruderhof convert pledges all of his possessions to the community, never under any circumstances to be entitled to their return. In some cases, the Bruderhof almost enforced this contract to the letter. At least one large family was left stranded in Asuncion with twenty dollars and no knowledge of Spanish, and needed to borrow money from the British Foreign Service to get back to England. This was in 1959.

From the Bruderhof point of view, the separation was a drastic but necessary action. Individuals were sacrificed for the sake of the church, in accordance with the individuals' own membership vows. It is true that were it not for the separation, the Bruderhof today would be a much more eclectic institution than it is. The harshness of treatment could be at least partially justified on the grounds that nobody was (or ever is) really permanently expelled. The Bruderhof awaits only genuine repentance to welcome the outcast back with open arms. Although the community acknowledges the fact that some of the expulsions will turn out to be permanent, it has argued that it would not wish to lengthen the time required for repentance by making it any easier than necessary for the exile.

By 1962, the great crisis was over. The population of the Bruderhof had been reduced from about fifteen hundred to something over eight hundred, the proportion of English members declining drastically. Wheathill, El Arado, and Sinntalhof had been disbanded, and Primavera sold to the Mennonites for $150,000. Only the three North American *hofs* and one in England remained. Of these, Woodcrest was the undisputed center of authority.

Politically, the crisis ended in total victory for Brother David. Hans, his brother-in-law and chief rival, had fallen from office in 1959 under a challenge led by one of David's new American lieutenants, and had subsequently left the Bruderhof. Most of the other leaders were gone or stripped of office. David's two brothers stayed, but were clearly below David in the hierarchy. Various Americans, including members of the visiting delegation, became promoted to the office of Servant of the Word.

Some of the exiles soon returned to the fold, but most wandered disillusioned into the world, where they gradually established themselves. Some still make sporadic attempts to gather together to form a new community. In 1962, a Servant of the Word in exile wrote the following to a sympathetic friend:

You say that we should maintain our brotherhood with the Society of Brothers. The simple fact is that it is they who cut off. I would happily stay in contact with many of them, and with them as a group, but those of us who have become 'unfaithful' are now in the power of evil and so are separated. I knew this when I left and so have no intention of trying to contact them. There is work to be done elsewhere . . . .

## 7. Church-Community (1962–   )

The great crisis brought about an important shift in Bruderhof values. Before the crisis, the Bruderhof thought of itself as an intentional community among intentional communities. It happened to be a religious community – a church – because its members had found that this was the best way, really the only successful way, of sustaining communal life. But being a church did not interfere with the ability to relate to non-religious intentional communities and non-religious seekers of community. For instance the Bruderhof maintained close ties with the kibbutzim.

Since the crisis, the Bruderhof has thought of itself more as a church among churches, one that happens to be an intentional community because this is the best expression that its members have found of the true Christian life. Its outside relationships are now mostly with other churches, monastic groups, and religious denominations rather than with other intentional communities.

The new régime has repudiated its sect and social movement phases. The directions taken during the time between the death of Eberhard Arnold and the great crisis are now thought to have been, in many ways, mistaken. The new church-community is supposedly a return to the true community of Eberhard Arnold. The Brothers believe that 'Arnold's death wounded the community more deeply than was realized at the time, except by a few'.

The repudiation of part of its history is a postrevolutionary excess, perhaps a lingering result of the shock of the great crisis. A saner view would seem to be that only during Arnold's lifetime was the Bruderhof able to be a social movement and a church simultaneously. It is clear from Arnold's writings that he saw the need to combine these functions at all times. Since his death, however, the community has managed only an alternation of the two tasks. Before the crisis, social movement was emphasized to the detriment of church. After the crisis, church was emphasized to the detriment of social movement. Recent reports have hinted that the Bruderhof is beginning to move again in the direction of emphasizing its role as a movement.

The 1960s were mainly years of recovery from the great crisis. 1963 is known as the year of the harvest. About two hundred of the exiles returned to the fold, many of them to the Oak Lake colony in Pennsylvania, which doubled its population (from 120 to 245) between 1963 and 1964. These were years of joy in the Bruderhof. 1965 and 1966 were more mixed; there were periodic crises, although none even approached the severity of the great crisis. In 1966, the Bullstrode community was disbanded and its members were distributed among the three American *hofs*. This left the remaining colonies overcrowded and the Bruderhof began considering plans for a new *hof* to be located somewhere between Woodcrest and Oak Lake. But, as the total population of the Bruderhof has been slowly declining in the last few years, there has been no urgency about these plans.

The Bruderhof in 1966 was a community that had made it. With a relatively stable leadership structure and a booming economy, both for the first time in its history, the dangers which the Bruderhof faced were those of smugness and apathy. As the history of Amana, Harmony, the Shakers, and even some kibbutzim indicates, these are not trivial problems. It is not uncommon for a community to thrive during its period of adversity, only to wax apathetic and disintegrate once it has gained prosperity. The Bruderhof was well aware of this problem from familiarity with accounts of past communitarian experiments, and, in 1966, they took steps to voluntarily cut back on their toy-making business.

The rate at which new converts were joining the Bruderhof also slowed considerably during the late 1960s, raising the question of whether the Bruderhof would eventually follow the path of the Hutterians, devolving into a blood-related ethnic subculture. Certainly more attention than ever was being focused on the Bruderhof children, who seemed to be becoming in some ways the hub of the life. But, in the past, new elements have always entered the Bruderhof in periodic waves. Nothing indicates that this will not occur again in the future.

At some point in the 1960s David Arnold's position of supremacy was made official. He was given the title of *Vorsteher* (bishop), the only Bruderhof member other than Eberhard Arnold to hold that position. But David is no Eberhard Arnold, and the Bruderhof has not regressed to the stage of charismatic community. The form of government in the church-community can best be characterized as democratic centralism. The rank and file in the Brotherhood have a lot of real power; many of the leaders have a lot of real power; but David is definitely at the top, especially when it comes to long-range policy matters.

David's gift, according to men who know him well, is that he 'has the spirit'. You could say that he's got soul. The spirit, in this sense, is soul plus cosmic perspective. He has the ability to evoke emotional catharsis without allowing the experience to degenerate into the mere emotionality of the communion phase. David does not have a bent for leadership in practical affairs; these are left to his many able lieutenants. Nor does he seem to have much of his father's sense of historical evangelical mission. This gift seems to have fallen to his older brother, Peter. But to the over-intellectualized recent American converts, thirsting for a direct experience of God (or even of each other), David's ability to waken cosmic streamings and to discern good and evil spirits is seen as infinitely more valuable than any of these things, and has engendered a fierce loyalty to him in the majority of Bruderhof members.

Whether David will lose or consolidate his position; whether the community will expand, contract, stagnate, or even dissolve; whether it will continue to grow more churchly, reverse itself and become a social movement again, or veer off in a completely new direction, are all very open questions. I would not care to make predictions about the Bruderhof. The community has shown a remarkable evolutionary resilience and receptivity to new influences. An ex-Servant of the Word spent a long while explaining to me how the Bruderhof had really died during the great crisis. But then he recalled the tremendous joy of the 1963–4 period. 'But this is community,' he said. 'This is how it always goes. It's an up-and-down business.'

## 1. *Practical Communism*

One of the first things that the Bruderhof did when its members first got together in 1920 was to pool all wealth and property, according to the example of the first Christians in the Book of Acts: 'Those that believed held all things common . . . .' Community of property has been a cornerstone of Bruderhof life ever since. As one member put it, 'Our life is based so obviously on "From each according to his ability, to each according to his need" that the phrase never has to be mentioned.'

Theoretically, one could live one's whole life at the Bruderhof and, unless he had a job which required contact with the outside world, never see any money. Food, clothing, shelter, all material needs are provided free by the community. The individual must work at whatever community job is assigned him. This is true of all adult Bruderhof residents – members, novices, even short-term guests. But only full members give all of their previously acquired wealth to the community. When a person takes his baptismal vows, he signs over all he owns to the community forever. He is never entitled to get any of it back, even if he leaves, even if he is thrown out. Even the smallest piece of personal property is surrendered, but the Bruderhof never makes an issue out of this in practice. Unlike some monastics, the Bruderhof member is not required to say, '*our* cup', '*our* toothbrush'.

If a Bruderhof member is too old or too sick to work, this of course does not affect his right to material support. In fact, such people may have higher real incomes than the average, for instance, special diets or expensive medical care. The same holds true for families with small children. The goods a family takes are dependent on its needs, not at all on the number of workers in the family. There is no penalty at the Bruderhof for having a large family, and, since birth control is never used, eight to ten children in a family is not uncommon.

Communism in the Bruderhof is more than just an economic arrangement. Members work together, take their meals together, meet together almost every night, raise their children together, and generally spend their entire lives together, within the confines of the *hof*. Bruderhof members are further bound to each other through their dedication to a common cause. They are pledged to die for each other if necessary. Such a commitment would be frightening even within one's family or small circle of intimate friends. But the Bruderhof member pledges himself thus to people whom he hasn't even met yet, to anyone who may happen to join the community in the future. One member wrote:

We do not choose who comes; the door is open to all. But it is a narrow door, and anyone inflated with self-importance or pride cannot fit through. In ordinary life we can choose our friends. Here, those we may have a natural antipathy for are sometimes the very people we are working with all day, eating with and meeting with at night. We come face to face with what it means to love our neighbor – not just our friends but those whom we would ordinarily never choose as friends. Such a life is not everybody's dish. There are many who come and do not stay. They leave as friends – it is just that this price is too high.

As might be expected, in living communistically, the question of fairness frequently arises. This should never be a problem for the ego-free individual, but, human nature being what it is, the Bruderhof tries to do what it can to distribute goods and duties evenly. However, excessive concern with getting one's fair share is frowned on. When an ex-health-food fanatic joined the Bruderhof he noticed that the members who smoked were given a weekly cigarette ration. He asked the storekeeper if he could have carrots, instead of a cigarette ration, to give to his kids. This was refused, and it was very carefully explained to the new Brother that he could never get along in Bruderhof life if he continued to think in terms of equivalences.

The Bruderhof has the advantage, in making practical communism work, that it is a small face-to-face community rather than an impersonal society. This enables the community to be flexible in all of its rules, and to make exceptions where indicated. For instance, Woodcrest waives its no-money principle in one case: that of a woman member whose husband refuses to join the Bruderhof. He lives on the *hof*, commutes to an outside job, and pays the community a certain amount for the support and education of his children. Another Bruderhof rule is that no guest can stay on indefinitely without making a commitment to the life. But this rule is also waived in the case of one semi-invalid old man, who cannot bring himself to join the community, but has no place else to go.

The smallness of the community also simplifies communication. The community can hold frequent meetings for decision making. Announcements to the entire population can be made at either of the two daily common meals. Rules thus take on the flavor of family decisions rather than impersonal directives. For instance, it is announced at supper one day, 'Please don't take leftovers off plates after meals. If there are any leftovers, the kitchen will put them out.'

Despite its advantages in scale, the Bruderhof remains a society in microcosm and must find solutions to all of the universal cultural imperatives; sex, child rearing, education, production and distribution of goods and boundary maintenance within its own communistic framework. Practical communism has been a Bruderhof principle all through its history, but particular applications of this principle – keeping peace in the community kitchen, sex regulation of adolescents, responsibility to the outside world, to name only a few – have evolved slowly and painfully and are still evolving at the present time.

## 2. *Marriage and Family*

The Bruderhof has been called a monastery of families, and in some ways this description is apt. The family is the most important unit in the community life. Unlike the kibbutzim, which have social policies aimed at weakening family structure, the Bruder-hof, following the Hutterian model, does everything possible to strengthen it. Each family lives together in its own apartment. Special times are set aside just for families to be together. Birth control is abhorred: large families are considered natural and wholesome; and each new baby is welcomed by the whole community with joy.

Marriage brings a great rise in status – all the more so once the marriage begins to produce children. The 'mommies and the daddies', as the Bruderhof parents are often collectively called, form a distinct social grouping. An adult who either is not married or has no children is cut off from a great many of the interests and shared activities of the dominant social class of the community. For this reason, and also because extra-marital sexuality is a rarely violated taboo, the incentives to marry in the Bruderhof are very strong.

The man or woman who wishes to marry in the Bruderhof finds that there are certain obstacles in the way, although none are insurmountable. First, his choice of mates is restricted to other Bruderhof single people. For instance, a twenty-year-old Bruder-hof girl, in 1966, would have been limited to a theoretical range of fifty to sixty possible mates. A second obstacle is that, before a marriage can take place, both the partners must have taken their membership vows to the community. A third obstacle, and the most interesting one, is that there is no dating or courtship at the Bruderhof.

The Bruderhof believes that any sort of dating or courtship activity among the young people would lead to the explosion of what one of them called the 'always latent erotic dynamite' inevitably present in a close loving community. Young people in the community do a lot of things together as a group – outings, picnics, work projects. Many of them grow up together. They are all quite well acquainted, relaxed, and comfortable with each other. They are good at communicating their interest with their eyes, although any verbal statement is taboo.

'When a man wants a wife, he goes not to counsel with flesh and blood. He goes and talks with his Brother,' is the Hutterian principle. One talks with the Servant of the Word, not the girl. A girl can tell of her love to a Housemother. According to the Hutterian forms, a man might not even have a particular girl in mind. He can say, 'I want to enter into the state of marriage. Pick me a mate.' However, this is rare at the Bruderhof. Eberhard Arnold wrote:

> If there is a question of an approaching engagement, it is in keeping with our way of life that before the two young people commit themselves by any promise or arrangement, they speak with the Word Leader [i.e., the Servant] so that everything may take place according to God's will.[59]

The Servant most often tells the young man to wait a while and see how he feels about it. If the Servant knows of something that makes this an unsuitable match – if, for example, he happens to know that the girl is interested in someone else – he will tell him to try to forget about it. When time goes by and the young man is still seriously interested, the Servant speaks to the Housemother and the Housemother speaks to the girl and finds out what her feelings are. If the couple are both interested but uncertain, some way may be found for them to spend a little time alone together, perhaps taking walks. Both continue to talk over their feelings with the Servant and the Housemother, and at some point the Witness Brothers discuss the situation. When the couple feels clear that 'we are called to live this life together', and the Servant and Witness Brothers approve, the question is presented to a Brotherhood meeting, which authorizes the engagement.

Engagements can last any amount of time, from a few weeks to several years. The whole community prepares for the wedding, and participates in the celebration.

The Bruderhof marriage ceremony emphasizes the fact that *eros* must be subordinated to *agape*, that the sexual and emotional relationship of the couple must be based on the spiritual brotherhood of the entire group. The couple is asked a series of questions:

> Is the unity of the Church more important to you than anything else? Is the unity of the Holy Spirit more important to you than any-

thing else? Is the highest unity that God's Spirit can have with man's spirit, then, more important to you than anything else? And consequently, is the unity between heart and heart in the whole Church more important to you than the unity between only two? Or, to ask the question in a very practical form: Is unity of faith more important to you than emotional unity, for your marriage?

Is it clear to you, then, that your marriage is not based on a purely human mutual attraction, but rather that unity in your marriage depends on the unity of the whole Church? If so, it will be clear to you that through this unity, of which your marriage is a part, your marriage is truly indissoluble. Or in other words, just *because* the smaller unity between you two is subordinated to the greater unity of Christ's Church, the unity between you is steadfast. This is something very remarkable to the nonbeliever. He would think that the more independently a marriage unity is built upon the natural unity of two the firmer it is. That is an error. Nothing is firm but the eternal. Everything else is uncertain. Only when we make our marriage bond part of the eternal is it a firm bond.

Thus we come to a surprising paradox. We put the question: if one of you were to be unfaithful to the Church, would the other one then remain in the Church and not follow the unfaithful one? It is clear to us that just this radical question constitutes the deepest security of a marriage bond founded in the eternal order. It places each of the marriage partners completely into the unity of the spirit of the Church, and in doing so, into unconditional faithfulness to one another.[60]

If the couple can answer each of these questions affirmatively, then they are allowed to marry. Divorce is not allowed under any circumstances. Even if a person has been divorced before joining the Bruderhof, he never will be allowed to remarry.

Marriage relationships in the Bruderhof seem unusually happy. Couples spend time with each other under a variety of different circumstances, both with and without the children – at meals, work breaks, meetings, outings – not just after work as often happens in ordinary society. Young couples especially, often find excuses to visit each other's place of work. The fact that most evenings are spent working side by side in an absorbing and challenging social movement imparts a youthful vitality even to the marriages of the middle-aged. I saw couples in their forties and fifties coming home from meetings late at night, their faces flushed with enthusiasm, looking like college kids returning from an SDS meeting.

There is of course no opportunity for economic enslavement in Bruderhof marriages since neither partner is dependent on the other for money. In one sense this produces a healthy egalitarianism in marriages – no Bruderhof woman could possibly think of herself as 'just a housewife'. But in the spiritual sense Bruderhof marriages are not egalitarian. Following the writings of Eberhard Arnold, the community recognizes different essential functions for men and for women:

> Man's nature . . . has something of the volcanic which breaks out in decisive moments, pouring out its glowing lava. It is a fighting nature which wields the sword of the Spirit . . . .
>
> In man there is the eruption of solar flames, in woman the flowing, harmoniously spreading light of the sun. These differences are vital and must not be distorted. Although it is a matter of light, these differences are more definite than those between two distinct constellations.
>
> Woman is predestined to a way of love which is not given to man. Man seeks people at the moment when he knows that they need to be shaken and awakened and their hearts changed. Woman is quite different. Her love is steady, faithful, constant. She will give her motherly, sisterly help in a deeper way to those already familiar to her, rather than to the stranger and newcomer, while a man will pour out his energy particularly to the stranger and newcomer.
>
> . . . Man with his great muscular strength or his exceptional gift of a comprehensive outlook is called to especially hard outward struggle . . . . The kinds of work which fall to women do not usually demand great muscular strength of her. Rather, they are in keeping with her loving, loyal, quiet nature. Woman's task is to be loving and motherly, dedicated to preserve, protect, and keep pure the circle of those who are close to her; to train, foster, and to cherish them . . . .
>
> Under no circumstances is man's work of fighting and pioneering, which brings him in conflict with the outside world, to be more highly prized than this cherishing, this inward and creative giving of life and depth to the church-community. There is no difference at all in worth; there is only a difference in calling. If it should be given to us to affirm woman's tasks and not wish for her the work of administration and direction, then our common life will be a happy one . . . .
>
> . . . when the true order of marriage is given among us every woman

will have her true place. She will order, talk over, and agree upon all things with her husband in an inner way. She will have a very strong influence on her husband. She cannot, however, exercise the chief authority or parallel authority.[61]

The position of a single person in the Bruderhof is sometimes difficult. Eberhard Arnold argued that spinsterhood or bachelor-hood was a special grace not given to all, the ability to love everyone and not have a specific attachment to another individual. But an ex-member of the Bruderhof, a woman who had been a single Sister for years, said, 'If you were married and had ten children, you were right in the center of things, but as a single Sister without any family, I always felt that I didn't quite belong' [paraphrased].

A male ex-member maintained that single men are even more alienated than single women. Single men may be not only socially isolated, but personally suspect as well: 'It was felt that if you were a man and you didn't get married there was probably some reason for it: you were a little too queer, or a little too old, or a little too crotchety.' Women are not similarly mistrusted, but more likely pitied and respected.

The one exception to this is the case of older unmarried women, or occasionally, men. If one has lived an exemplary life for many years in the Bruderhof, as an unmarried Brother or Sister, then one's status may rise. It is even possible for such a person to become a leader. But this never happens under the age of forty or so. There is even a certain amount of inequality (by our standards) of work assignments according to marital status. Single girls are assigned to assist mothers with families in the evenings between 5:30 and 6:15. But, of course, the amount of work that each mother does in caring for her family during this time is actually greater than that done by the single helper.

Single people from the age of about thirty have a sort of ambiguous status in the Bruderhof. Below that, they are members of the group called the singles. Although in some ways they are of lower status than married adults, they really occupy a unique unrankable position in the life. Individually, the singles are merely singles. Collectively, they are youth. Youth has a certain mystique even in our own society. In the Bruderhof this is further enhanced through identification of the youth group with the German Youth Movement, the parent movement of the Bruderhof.

Even by Bruderhof standards, the singles form an exceptionally close-knit peer group. This sometimes creates a problem when young people from the outside world join the Bruderhof. Particularly in Paraguay, where the proportion of *sabras* to converts was much higher than in America, it was often easier for a young man to become a Brotherhood member than to achieve acceptance in the youth peer group. Of course, acceptance by this group is made specially necessary by the fact that there are no alternate groups and no individual dating. The singles group forms the closest thing to a subculture in the Bruderhof.

In Paraguay, the age-group between school and marriage was called the youth. In North America there is no such designation. Young people are collegers for the first four years after graduation from high school (regardless of whether or not they go to college). After that they are singles until they marry. Both groups are highly cohesive. They have their own meeting rooms, participate in projects and go on hikes and excursions together, and, in the case of the singles, eat breakfasts and occasional other meals together. Each single or colleger who does not have a family living on the *hof* is given an adopted family. He eats family suppers and Sunday breakfasts with them, helps with the family chores, and participates in the family celebrations.

## 3. *Children and Education*

The birth of a new baby is the signal for an outburst of communal joy. The mother and father spend six weeks in the 'Mother House', alone with the new baby. Someone in the community takes care of the older children, and they come to visit. One evening, the whole community comes to sing songs to welcome the new baby.

When the baby is six weeks old it is cared for in the Baby House from nine to two and three to five-thirty. The mother returns to the common work. The Bruderhof encourages natural childbirth and breast-feeding, and things are arranged to make it easy for the mother to nurse. She can pick up a plate of food at the kitchen and eat it in the Baby House while she gives the infant his noontime feeding. If the baby seems really hungry while she's at work, she'll get a phone call on the job, asking her to come feed it.

The Woodcrest Baby House is well organized and efficient. There is a playroom for each group – the young babies, older babies, ones, twos and threes – as well as a kitchen, a 'getting-well room', and a room where a mother can sit comfortably and nurse her infant. Each playroom opens onto a porch, where the children can play. The Baby House schedule includes activity periods, naps, lunch and supper; breakfast and mid-afternoon snack are provided at home.

There is one woman to care for each four babies, or each eight children, over one year. This job is made easier by all the supporting work done by the rest of the community (the kitchen prepares the food; the laundry washes and folds diapers and clothing). Many of the women assigned to the Baby House are older teenage girls or young single women, bursting with energy and love for children. Thus, work time is for the married woman a chance to get away from children, and for the unmarried women a chance to be with children. The Bruderhof is able in this way to utilize the very strong maternal instincts of young unmarried women, while at the same time giving them experience which will be valuable to them if and when they start raising their own families. Undoubtedly, a latent function of this arrangement is the avoidance of competition and jealousy among mothers. No one can accuse the unmarried girls of showing favoritism to their own children.

One of the impressive things about Bruderhof child-rearing is the way the children are integrated into the life of the *hof*. Every morning when weather permits, each group in the Baby House takes a walk. They may visit the shop were Daddy is working, or the dining room where they see the new decorations on the tables, or the canning shed where the teacher says, 'Have you anything for us to taste?' and each child is given a peach slice. Everyone who walks by the group stops to say hello. I went along on a walk with the twos one Sunday morning. Wherever we went, they kept meeting older brothers and sisters. One big sister came galloping over to pick her little sister up and hug her. Two brothers, one two years old and the other three, met in a very man-to-man fashion: 'We've been looking at the tractor, go and see it.' Among themselves, the twos chatted very comfortably. The whole atmosphere is quite different from that surrounding the morning walk of a two-year-old city or suburban child.

Each September, a group of children makes the important transition from the Baby House to the pre-school building near the main schoolhouse. This occasion is marked with songs and a celebration by the whole community, as are all the rites of passage in a Bruderhof child's life – the move from pre-school to school, the first lunch in the dining room with the adults, the first supper with the adults, and the move to public high school. The children spend two years in the pre-school, and then attend the elementary school, which has eight grades and follows the approved New York State curriculum. All the teachers are Brotherhood members in good standing, with personalities considered suitable for children to take as models. A few have never had formal training as teachers. The school life includes much besides academic knowledge. The children explore their natural surroundings. They tap the maple trees and make syrup. Active games are played at recess. There is much time for arts and crafts. The older children spend some time working in the different work departments. The older schoolchildren and the high schoolers do all the work on the garden, which is an important source of fruit and vegetables, under the supervision of a couple of adults. Any summer morning you can see a group of children bringing a couple of bushels of corn to the kitchen to be cooked for lunch, and on the lawn some six-year-olds may be taking the tips off beans while their teacher reads them a story.

The cohort group, the group of ten or so children born within a year, is an important factor in the life of a Bruderhof child. From the age of six weeks on, he spends at least seven hours a day with the same group of children. They gurgle at each other from their cribs, sit on the potty together while their teacher tells them a story or sings a song, and move up the school together grade by grade.

The change to the public high school in Kingston is a drastic one for Bruderhof children, because it is their first close contact with the outside world. Before this, the children see outsiders only as visitors to the community, or on short supervised trips in the outside world. The Woodcrest children are conspicuous in high school; the community gives them special clothes, much better than those worn on the *hof*, but full gathered skirts, long braids and lack of any kind of cosmetics make the girls especially conspicuous. Academically, they do better than average. Socially, they stick together. Indeed, the fact that they must arrive and go home by bus together makes it difficult to form any close friendships with other children. Often the high school experience reinforces the child's sense of unity with his group and with the community. Sometimes it provokes an identity crisis that leads to a decision either to join the community or to leave it.

The Bruderhof attempts to keep its teenagers 'free from the corrosion of a false social pressure to become "counterfeit adults", and from the forced preoccupation with sex which has spread like a sickness through our American high schools.' This policy often comes in conflict, however, with the open-door policy, as it is difficult for visitors, and especially children of visitors, to make the necessary adjustments. The following story was told by a woman who had been a long-term guest but had finally decided not to become a member:

This Bruderhof woman was going to have a baby and it was due in January. I was talking to one of my children whose birthday's in January and I said, 'Wouldn't it be nice if the baby came on your birthday?' So my little girl thought it would be great and she went to the woman who was pregnant and said, 'Wouldn't it be great if your baby came on my birthday?'

Well, the next thing you know, I was having a talk with the House-mother and a few of the Sisters. They brought up this topic about babies. They explained how they see the coming of the new life in this holy way. They said that the greeting of a new life is something that is given. I said that yes, I agreed, that this was very much how I felt about it. Then they pointed out that by talking about it, emphasizing it, it was taking out the element of wonder and putting in something different.

I questioned this whole attitude of theirs, which brought me into asking them how they explained to girls that they are menstruating, and what they tell a girl before she gets married, and so on. Well, they sort of sidestepped it, and one of them said to me, 'You know, this girl that got married at Woodcrest recently didn't even know how babies came about.' She'd been born in the life, and she'd never been told. I said that I felt something should have been explained to her somewhere along the line. Some of the other Sisters agreed with me. They said to this other Sister, 'Oh, that's kind of an extreme case that you're presenting. It wouldn't happen quite this way again.'

One reason that Bruderhof children are sent to a public high school is to prepare them for the decision they must make between life in the outside world and the life in community. The Bruderhof wants no spiritual deadwood, no people who are in the community merely because they were born there; to stay in the community, a child must feel clear that he is called to this life. Every young person is sent to spend some time living outside the community, so he can choose freely between the community and the outside world. He is helped to obtain further training. Two years studying some practical subject at a state junior college is common. While I was at Woodcrest a number of young people were just about to get their M.A.s in education. (That, of course, was an expensive five-year program. Several students have won scholarships or worked to pay for their education.) A number of women are trained in nursing, physical therapy, child care, and the like. One boy I met was studying auto mechanics part time and working as an apprentice in a garage. All of these young people are living outside the *hof* during their training, usually spending their weekends at the *hof*. If they decide to leave, they will be able to support themselves; if they decide to stay, their training will be an asset to the community. Some never seriously consider leaving the community; some immediately choose to go out; and there are all possible variations in between. Those who decide to stay become the new generation of 'singles', and the cycle of courtship, marriage and family begins anew.

## 4. *Community of Goods*

The absence of money gives a storybook atmosphere to Bruderhof villages. People seem more colorful, more involved in each thing they are doing, because they are doing it for its own sake, not with the thought of some abstract reward. Even the money that does sometimes come into people's lives takes on something of a magical character. A communal treasurer, called the Steward, keeps track of financial affairs and disburses small sums when needed. When two Brothers were chosen to represent the community in an anti-war demonstration in Washington, D.C., I went with them. They spoke to each other of what an adventure it was to be driving a car on their own, with money jingling in their pockets, thinking about what kind of restaurant to choose for supper. Children sell worms to fishermen along the river. The pennies thus earned become a precious secret and a source of prestige in the peer group. But I met one nine-year-old girl at Woodcrest who didn't know what a dime was when I showed her one.

Economic decisions are made by the Brotherhood or by executives with authority delegated by the Brotherhood, as are all other Bruderhof decisions. When the new Woodcrest dining room was built, samples of various shades of paint were put on a wall and a Brotherhood meeting was called. After a long debate, no opinion could be reached. So they decided to paint one wall the color that the majority favored and then re-evaluate the situation. After the dissenters saw how that one wall looked, they decided to go along with the majority. On the other hand, when new curtains were needed for a communal meeting room, the Housemothers and a few women from the Sewing Room chose the cloth.

All goods are bought communally, and some are used communally. Cars, for example, are for communal use, and one Brother is in charge of coordinating cars, drivers, and errands. But *most* goods are used by individuals, and we need to discuss the process of distribution from community to individual.

*Food.* All lunches and most suppers are prepared by the communal kitchen and eaten in the dining room. Lunch is the main meal of the day, usually including meat or fish, a starchy vegetable and a green vegetable, and often fruit for dessert. Supper is light – cold fix-it-yourself sandwiches, or soup and salad, or cottage cheese and salad, often with a 'made' dessert like pudding or pie. Bruderhof food is adequate, although a typical middle-class American would find the portions of meat very small, and a nutrionist might object to the lack of fresh citrus foods and the reliance on tea and bread for energy boosts.

The communal kitchen has been a focus of disagreements and struggles in the Bruderhof, as it has in many other communities. In the early days in Germany, food was very hard to get and some Brothers did not see why they should sacrifice their diet so the children could have more. Others wanted to have more food for everyone, even if of poorer quality. There were disagreements over vegetarianism also, and for a while the kitchen prepared two sorts of food, so the vegetarians could eat according to their own ideals. This did not work out well, and the vegetarians agreed to sacrifice their ideas and eat meat in the interest of unity.

Each family eats breakfast, two suppers a week, and many snacks in its own living quarters. Certain food supplies are available for any member of the community to use as needed: flour, white and brown sugar, margarine, raisins, prunes, cocoa, tea, spices, yeast, homemade pancake mix, and bread. A certain amount of whole milk is available for the children, and skim milk for the adults. There are three eggs a week for each person. On family supper nights, the kitchen puts out food for each family to take and cook – two eggs for each person, or a quarter pound of hamburger, or a couple of frankfurters, as well as some fruit or vegetables, and any interesting leftovers from the week's meals. None of these rules is terribly rigid; no one watches, or minds if you need an extra egg for your baking. The inner attitude must be selflessness and love for one's Brothers, in this as in all other matters.

In addition, there are 'special stores' – certain foodstuffs that are not available on the open shelves but are given out as special treats. These include coffee, tobacco, cold cereal, jam, and wine.

When there is a supply of something unusual, the storekeeper posts a notice. Each mother writes a weekly list, 'I wonder if our family could have . . . ,' and gives it to the storekeeper, who tries to adjust the available supplies to each family's likes and dislikes. On Saturday morning, someone from each family picks up the basket with the stores that they've been given for the week.

*Clothing.* The Bruderhof buys work clothes and other simple clothing in bulk; it also buys and is given used clothing and shoes. New dresses and skirts are made by the Sewing Room. One of the Brothers fixes shoes. He was taught, and is still helped, by a nearby shoemaker who likes the Woodcrest community. Needs and supplies are coordinated by the Housemothers. They sort the used clothing and send garments that need mending to the Sewing Room. Twice a year, each person writes a 'necessity list'. Necessity-list clothing is likely to be second-hand and a bit drab. Someone who happens to need clothing can talk with the Housemothers about it at any time. A little pair of well-worn flannel pajamas may go from the Housemother Room to the Sewing Room, with a note written by a Housemother pinned on: 'Toby M. has outgrown his old pajamas; he could use these if the knee was mended.' One of the women in the Sewing Room puts a patch on the knee and sends the pajamas on to the M. family. Toby's old pajamas are returned to the Housemother Room, to be used by someone else.

Everyone also writes a birthday list of things he would especially like to be given. Usually new clothing is on this list. It is a special occasion when a girl comes to the sewing room for a fitting of her birthday dress. She must keep her eyes closed, so that when she sees the dress for the first time on her birthday it will be a real surprise. If it turns out that she doesn't like the color that the Housemothers have selected, she tries to think of the love of the people who tried to please her, and to remind herself that clothes are not that important anyway.

Bruderhof dress is simple, loose, and casual. There is no costume such as there was in the Hutterian days. However, one observer remarked that an indigenous costume for the women seems to be emerging, consisting of a blouse under a jumper, white knee socks, and black sturdy shoes. There is no sloppiness or drabness about the dress. Young and old tend to dress neatly and attractively, with a love of color, but apparently without the desire to impress.

*Miscellaneous.* In addition to clothing and shoes, the shelves of the Housemother Room are piled with all sorts of goods: toys, books, craft supplies, candy, school supplies and all the sundries that we tend to take for granted, like shampoo and bobby pins. (While we were at Woodcrest my wife observed that she was trying very hard not to lose the bobby pins she'd brought with her; when they were all gone she'd have to go to the Housemother Room and ask for more.)

Most members of the Bruderhof spend a considerable portion of their free time making gifts to give other people. A girl may go to the Housemother Room and ask for gingham and embroidery thread to make a Sunday apron as a birthday present for someone else, who would not ask for them for herself.


## 5. *Community Playthings*

*Community Playthings* is the trademark of the Bruderhof's income-producing industry. It was begun in 1947, in the Macedonia Community in Georgia. Macedonia, at the time, had been hunting around for a communal industry. Two of its members hit on the idea of manufacturing children's furniture out of wood. They also made some unpainted toy block sets. When a large order for blocks came from Hawaii, it was decided that unit blocks were a good item. Today, these blocks are the largest-selling single item of Community Playthings.

At first toy-making was just one of many industries in the various Bruderhof communities. In 1954, sales were only $45,000.[62] The business grew so rapidly, and became so profitable, however, that soon all other cash-producing work departments were abandoned in its favor. By 1956, sales had more than doubled. By 1958, they had increased sevenfold over the 1954 rate, to $314,000. In the early 1960s, the community sold well over one million dollar's worth of its product each year. In 1965, fearful of growing too rich, the community decided to cut back on its sales and to stop dealing through distributors.

The income from Community Playthings supports all three Bruderhof communities. Each *hof* is responsible for the production of some of the items in the inventory. Almost all of the products are sent to Woodcrest, which, in addition to producing its share of the toys, is also responsible for storage, order processing, and shipping. Community Playthings is not incorporated separately from the Society of Brothers. Rather, each *hof* is incorporated in the state in which it is located, and the toy business is provided for in the articles of incorporation of each *hof*. The total income is divided among the *hofs* according to need rather than according to the profits on that *hof*'s products. An effort is made, however, to distribute work responsibilities as evenly as possible among the three colonies.

At Woodcrest in late 1965, there were forty-two men and sixteen women who, under non-communal circumstances, would have had to earn a living. Earning a living for the entire colony, however, required the labor of only thirty men and ten women. These were the Brothers and Sisters directly employed by Community Playthings. It would be incorrect to conclude from these figures that the Bruderhof economy frees almost one third of its labor force for non-remunerative activities. Comparisons are complicated by a variety of factors. Teenagers often work in the shop after school. Men and women from other departments can be enlisted during peak seasons. Many executive functions that Community Playthings would have to perform for itself if it were a private industry, are performed by men not nominally involved in the business. One must also take into account the work-week of the Bruderhof, which is slightly longer than average. Most important, the workers in other departments are performing services which, in the outside world, have to be paid for. Thus they are indirectly earning money for the community by lessening the amount of income the Bruderhof needs to maintain a given standard of living.

Community Playthings is managed from Woodcrest, where

there is a general manager, who is assisted by his wife. Two men also work in his office, plotting shipping routes. As these men are both retired Servants, it seems likely that part of the reason they both work in the office is to make them available for frequent consultation on important community matters. It is such factors as these that complicate precise determination of the labor force.

Twenty-seven men work in the shop, in either the production or the shipping departments. The shop is a cluster of three buildings – a factory and two warehouses – halfway down the hill. There are a production foreman and a shipping foreman. The production department is by far the larger of the two, so that the production foreman has two assistants. There is also a man in charge of shop purchasing.

People in disgrace often seem to be sent to work in the shop, but some of the workers are full Brothers in very high standing. There is neither stigma nor honor attached to being a worker. Only among the teenage girls is being allowed to work in the shop as one's regular chore a highly sought-after treat. (This is rarely allowed except during peak seasons.) Being an ordinary worker is not indicative of a lower level of intelligence or education, although some correlation no doubt exists. But of the three male Bruderhof members of Woodcrest with advanced degrees, two were ordinary shop workers in 1965.

Being an ordinary shop worker is the basic job for Bruderhof men. All male guests are assigned to work in the shop and, until one becomes a Brother, this is the only job accessible. After becoming a Brother, a man remains a shop worker unless or until he is asked by the Brotherhood to fill some other position. There are no particular considerations of seniority in job assignments, so it is entirely possible that one will spend one's entire working life as an ordinary shop worker. The Bruderhof in America has never hired outside labor, although this was done in Paraguay.

Work in the shop is organized in a combination of craft and assembly-line systems. Rough-cut lumber is delivered by truck at one end of the shop several times a week. Packaged finished products are taken away by the shipping crew at the other end of the shop as they become ready. All intermediate steps are performed by Bruderhof workers.

The first three shop operations consist of cutting pieces of wood of the proper length and width, smoothing the sides, and squaring the angles. These are fairly skilled operations performed on the pendulum saw, the rip saw, and the planer respectively. A specific person is always in charge of each of these three machines, although there are substitutes available for each of them. The production foreman keeps in mind the present and future needs for various products, and informs these workers approximately how many pieces of which shapes will be needed.

All the remaining workers are shifted around to various jobs at various times. Some of the more unpleasant jobs, such as paint spraying and checking for flaws, are rotated. Usually, most workers will be occupied with getting a specific job out. This may be the production of two hundred hollow block sets or fifty Vari-play screens. Most of the time, several such jobs will be out on the floor simultaneously. Once a job has been completed, the item will be out of production until the shipping department reports that inventory on it is running low. Some products need only be made once a year. Some must be turned out every month. Unit blocks and hollow blocks are the only products at Woodcrest that were in continuous production in 1965.

Let us suppose that a job lot of one hundred toy gas-station pumps is under production. Each piece requires one flat piece of wood for a base, two pumps (for which block rejects are used), two pieces of red cord, and four metal clips for the ends of the cords. People at early stages of production are responsible for having sufficient numbers of each of these components in stock. The various components are brought to one part of the floor, where several tables are set up. One of the assistant foremen assigns three or four people to the job. Several operations – drilling, screwing, clipping, stamping, etc. – have to be performed. The crew forms itself into the most efficient possible assembly line for this job – one person drills, another screws the parts together, and so forth. Someone will be in charge of putting the finished products into cartons and labeling them. When a hundred have been completed, the load is taken over to the shipping department, where it is stored in the warehouse. Workers fill out time sheets saying how many hours they have spent on each job so that labor 'costs' can be estimated.

The atmosphere in the shop is extremely casual. The only supervision is in the form of guidance, never surveillance. It is not unusual for men to arrive at the shop anywhere from ten to twenty minutes late and this is not questioned unless it becomes habitual. Mass production techniques are used but even there the needs and abilities of the unique individual are generally given primacy over the requirements of the system. Men will consciously adjust their work rates with the aim of maximum harmony rather than maximum output. The following is an account given by a Bruderhof member of such a situation:

We were starting to make a new line of toy trucks. The twenty or thirty wooden parts were cut and semi-finished upstairs, then sent down to us in the basement for drilling, chamfering, some sanding, and finally assembling and lacquer-spraying. Jack, the manager of the plant, was generally at that time too busy upstairs to be able to keep in close touch with the work in the basement. The basement foreman was absent on a journey and his place was taken by one of the five operators, Bill. The methods man, Al, had to design and build the jigs in which the parts were to be held for drilling or assembly operations and then explain each operation to Bill. It was up to Bill to instruct the operator. Al also arranged the general flow of work.

Now Bill was not able to think ahead very far, and as a result he often had one of the men standing idle because the next operation had not been set up for him. In that event Al would willingly do the set-up, and before long he was doing most of this kind of thing for Bill. As the run of vans neared completion, parts for the dump-trucks began coming downstairs. Al had been so busy superintending the van assembly that he was not ready with all the methods for the dump-trucks. Parts for these were stacked about the floor and Bill could not recognize all of them from the production chart. Bill was feeling his slowness and ineptitude, and he resolved to try harder to function as the foreman. Rather than bother Al, he made the decision himself not to drill nail-holes in the hard maple blocks for the cabs. Then, because there were no holes, the nails split many of the cabs. At the end of two weeks the floor was cluttered with parts of three or four different truck models, and nobody seemed quite to know what was happening. Among other difficulties, several trucks were returned to the wheel-assembly bench because their wheels would not turn freely. At this point Al suggested to Bill that the two of them sit down and talk about the whole truck problem. But Bill wanted Jack there, too, because he felt secretly that Jack had been a bit unfair in asking him to take over as foreman just at the time when the new trucks came along . . . .

As I recall the scene, something happened to Jack and Bill and Al when they sat down together. They all saw almost at the outset, that something important had been allowed to slip while they struggled to produce trucks efficiently. I can't explain easily just what that thing was. Al said that he didn't consider himself a good craftsman, and that he really needed help and advice from Jack and also from Bill. He admitted difficulty in waiting for people who were slower to think and to act. It came out that Bill had been alternating between resentment at Al's stepping in, and a readiness to let Al act as foreman rather than try hard enough himself. To deal with this they had to recognize Bill's slowness, and also the fact that he was generally a careful worker, and could correct Al's tendency to be fast and sloppy. As they went back to the job they resolved that each new process should be discussed at Bill's rate of thinking, and that, even if it meant some men were kept standing idle, he should take time to suggest improvements to Al. Bill should consult Al or Jack about such matters as drilling holes rather than risk a guess when he did not know enough about the physical properties of wood.

What happened when they sat down together was of course that they were able to get self-interest out of the way and to see the cause for which they work as the only thing that mattered.[63]

This story illustrates the Bruderhof norm of economic casualness: work hard but don't take yourself too seriously. This norm applies only within the community itself. In relation to the market, to competitors, and to suppliers of business materials and services the Bruderhof acts in an aggressively rational – although ethical – way. Bruderhof business men can take a tough line when they feel that the occasion warrants. Once I was visiting in the home of the director of shipping when he told the following story to his wife:

I got a call today from Acme Trucking Co. The man said, 'Hello T., this is Al here.' I said, 'Hello Al, what can I do for you?' He said, 'Well I'll tell you: we're in a bit of a jam here today, and I was wondering if you could possibly wait till tomorrow on that trucking pick up job that you ordered for this afternoon.' What do you think this means when a trucker tells you that he's in a bit of a jam? It means that he's short of drivers, and some of the jobs are going to go out and others not. I told him, 'Listen Al, every trucking company has a list of its customers in order of importance for just such emergencies, and we like to think that we're right at the top of that list.' He laughed and said that we'd get our truck today.

T. was very amused by this story as he told it. His wife was also amused and rather astonished that he could have said such a thing. T. explained that they both (and especially she) first joined the Bruderhof in good part for idealistic economic reasons. They felt guilty for being a part of capitalist society, and saw in the Bruderhof's complete economic sharing an escape from this. They now realize that this was 'merely idealism', and that they are just as much a part of the economy as ever.

The idea of work as a service, the intensity of commitment to the community, and the extreme degree to which norms are internalized combine to make the Bruderhof a formidable competitor in the field of manufacturing educational toys. This is true despite the fact that the community refuses to patent any of its items. One very successful Bruderhof toy has been copied exactly by another company. There is a feeling that the Bruderhof should not take out patents because they do not believe in owner-ship of property. The community is making use of its land, but if it were not, it would have no right to prevent someone else from using it. The Bruderhof did, however, take out a trademark for the name *Community Playthings*.

Many Bruderhof ideals impede economic efficiency and put the Bruderhof at a disadvantage in a competitive market. Refusal to take out patents is one such ideal. Another is the acceptance of people into membership with no regard to their economic capabilities. The Bruderhof has not hesitated to extend membership to anyone they felt was sincerely called to the life, even if there was reasonable certainty that the applicant would never be a productive worker. But perhaps the most serious economic impedance is the adamant refusal of the Society of Brothers to offer any incentive (even praise) for good work.[64]

These disadvantages are more than compensated for by the low labor costs of Community Playthings. Of course, there are no direct labor costs in terms of wages at the Bruderhof. But, due to the voluntary simplicity of Bruderhof life, the real income of the Bruderhof worker, measured by his standard of living, is below that of labor in the free market. Furthermore, since the Bruderhof purchases consumer goods in quantity, this same standard of living costs less than if it had been purchased by an individual worker's family.

The economic position of the Bruderhof is further improved by certain advantages intrinsic in the communal life. The main such advantage is the extraordinary high degree of commitment on the part of the workers. This is especially an advantage in a craft industry producing a product for rugged use and long durability. An indication of this spirit of commitment is the fact that in all the work departments the tempo will pick up rather than slack off toward the end of the day as happens in most factories. Also, every worker is always on the lookout for better manufacturing methods. In a sense, every worker in the Bruderhof shop is his own time-and-motion expert.

Another factor giving the Bruderhof an advantage in productivity is its ability to mobilize labor for particular emergencies. Everyone can be asked to work late during particular rush times such as Christmas. Teenagers can be called in for emergencies to work Saturdays or after school. Furthermore, people from other work departments can be called in to the shop (or to the kitchen) to meet a sudden emergency, letting the sewing, or the laundry, or the housecleaning wait.

Sometimes the entire community participates in a work evening in order to do a particularly tedious job. One day while we were at Woodcrest it was announced at lunch that there would be a catalogue project that night and that all who could do so should attend. Approximately 120 people, including children, did attend. We addressed and bundled 10,412 catalogues during that evening. This way, the Bruderhof's 150,000 annual catalogues can be sent out fairly quickly. A work evening is a festive occasion with refreshments and often music. It is considered more of an entertaining event than a chore, a novelty in a generally rather predictable life.

Bruderhof toys are well made and very expensive. Few are sold to private individuals. Most are bought by schools and other institutions which require sturdy equipment that can stand a lot of rough handling. One of the reasons for the phenomenal rise in the fortunes of the business is the amount of federal money that has recently been pumped into education. Operation Head Start has been one source of particularly lucrative contracts for Community Playthings.

## 6. *Other Work Departments*

Community Playthings earns all the money that the Bruderhof needs, but of course many other sorts of work are necessary for communal functioning. The community decides where each person should work. Major decisions, such as who should teach in the school this year, are reached in the Brotherhood. Day-to-day work assignments are made by Brotherhood-appointed executives known as work distributors.

There are separate work distributors for men and women, but that for the women is kept much busier since most men stay at the same job for months, or even years, at a time. At lunchtime, the women's work distributor almost always speaks to several women, telling each what she is assigned to do that afternoon. Women are often shifted from one job to another, in a complex pattern resulting from changes in physical state, changes in spiritual state, and the demands of the work. A woman who has just had a baby doesn't return to work for about six weeks, so someone must cover for her. After she does return, she must be given work that can be easily interrupted whenever she has to go to nurse or attend her child. A woman experiencing serious spiritual diffi-culties is shifted out of work in the Baby House or school. Whenever there is a love meal or other celebration, several women are assigned to help decorate the dining room. It can be said without exaggeration that, in the woman's sphere, almost every day presents a unique set of demands.

In both the men's and the women's spheres, work is not assigned solely according to the criterion of efficiency. One sometimes finds a doctor or a lawyer sanding toy blocks in the shop, or an intelligent and charismatic woman peeling potatoes in the kitchen. Sometimes this is punishment, but much of the time it merely reflects the peculiar Bruderhof mystique surrounding 'the practical work'. This mystique is not nearly as strong as it is in the kibbutzim, which at times have insisted that everyone take equal turns at mental and physical labor. However it is definitely present as a feeling that certain tangible benefits accrue from immersion in the substructure, as opposed to the superstructure, of the community.

The distinction between practical and nonpractical work dates back to the earliest years of the Bruderhof, when most of the members were involved in religious publishing. In those days, farming was the practical work while writing and publishing were the nonpractical work. Although the Bruderhof no longer does much farming, publishing has re-emerged in recent years as the most important manifestation of the community's non-practical work.

The Plough Publishing Company is organized as a nonprofit corporation within the Bruderhof. The sales department of Plough is located at Woodcrest. Typesetting (which is done by hand, by skilled Bruderhof craftsmen) and printing are done at Oak Lake. The community publishes two or three books a year, mostly of a religious nature. Among its publications are the works of Eberhard Arnold and Christoph Blumhardt, various Christmas story books, and children's books written by Bruderhof members.[65]

Aside from Community Playthings and Plough Publishing Company, there are ten work departments at Woodcrest. Six of them are exclusively for women: Housemother Room, kitchen, laundry, Sewing Room, cleaning crew, and Baby House. Three departments employ both men and women: the office, the school, and the archives. And one, the maintenance department, is made up exclusively of men. The following list shows an approximate work distribution for women, at any one time:

| | |
|---|---|
| Housemother | 5 |
| Kitchen | 7 |
| Laundry | 6 |
| Sewing Room | 4 |
| Cleaning Crew | 5 |
| Baby House | 6 |
| School | 8 |
| The Archives | 2 |
| Office work | 10 |

When I was at Woodcrest there were five Housemothers, mature women who supervised the women's work and the general welfare of the community as a household. They are the female leadership of the Bruderhof. A woman with an emotional or spiritual problem often takes it to one of the Housemothers instead of to a Servant. One Housemother is the women's work distributor. All the Housemothers are supposed to bear in mind all the hundreds of things that need doing; they make the hundreds of executive decisions involved in running the household. When guests are coming, they see that the guest rooms are prepared. When anyone in the community has a birthday, the Housemothers prepare a birthday box for him. They decide who gets what clothing. Anyone can request something from the Housemother Room, clothes or craft goods or drugstore supplies, and the Housemothers decide if it would be good for him to have it. In addition to this, Housemothers counsel the Bruderhof women with their problems. In personnel matters, although not in matters of policy, the Housemother functions as a female Servant of the Word. Most Bruderhof women look happy and relaxed, far younger than their years; the Housemothers (and the mothers with ten children) are the only ones who often seem rushed and harried.

The kitchen prepares lunch, snacks, and most suppers for the whole community. Six or eight women do all the cooking for three hundred community residents.

Two men serve food at each meal, and two others wash the dishes; these chores are rotated. Special diets are prepared for those members whose health require it, and a tray is taken to anyone who is sick in bed. The kitchen is cheerful and well-equipped, with homemade drawings and signs on the cupboard doors. A guest told me how impressed she had been, while working in the kitchen; not used to standing on her feet so much, she had sighed with tiredness. The girl working next to her noticed it and asked her if she'd like a stool to sit on. 'I was so amazed that she noticed how I was feeling; it was so kind,' she said. The atmosphere in the kitchen is remarkably peaceful. Even during the hurried last minutes before a meal, no one ever loses her temper.

The communal laundry has two enormous professional washing machines, named Pooh and Piglet, and a small one named Eeyore as well as a large dryer. Each family puts its laundry into a net nylon laundry bag with the family name sewed on, and the clothes are washed and dried in the bag, thus easing the sorting problem; also name tapes are sewed onto most things. One day is set aside for diapers, which are washed by professional diaper service methods. Diapers and sheets are communal property; no one necessarily gets back the same sheet that he put in. Family laundry is dried, sorted, and folded. The laundry also does some ironing for women who have large families and need the help.

The Sewing Room makes new skirts and dresses, and does a great deal of mending, lengthening and shortening. About four women work there. The eighth-grade girls come in one afternoon a week for a sewing class. There are cupboards to hold the boxes of thread, bias tape and buttons, the new cloth for dresses and scraps of old cloth for patches. Seven sewing machines sit side by side. There are two ironing boards. The late afternoon sun streams through the windows. Often Emmy Arnold comes in to spend some time here with her knitting.

Personal apartments are cleaned by the people who live in them, but communal areas are cleaned by the cleaning crew – five or

seven women at any one time. They make sure there are enough
cleaning supplies in all the houses, clean the meeting rooms, the
dining room, the hallways and bathrooms in the living quarters,
wash the school windows, whatever area is suggested by the work
distributor or scheduled for cleanup. There are dust pans and
professional-looking brooms on each floor of the houses, and
plenty of cleaning equipment.

The Archives is a small work department, mostly involved with
the preservation of old Bruderhof documents and the translation
of Eberhard Arnold's writings into English for eventual publication by Plough. An inner room in the Archives contains a small
library in which may be found many rare Hutterian manuscripts,
manuscripts of Eberhard Arnold's works, volumes on church
history, and a priceless old Anabaptist Bible in German. The
maintenance department is nominally composed of handymen
but, as it provides a comprehensive view of how the entire *hof*
functions, it often serves as a training ground for young Bruderhof executives or those being groomed for executive positions.

The Office is the most difficult of the Bruderhof departments to
define. In one sense, it is composed merely of the second floor of
the Carriage House, above the communal dining room. This floor
is divided into a number of small offices, of which some are part
of Community Playthings, others are headquarters for Brotherhood executives, and still others are devoted to clerical work for
the community such as bookkeeping and the handling of incoming and outgoing mail and telephone calls.

Men's jobs can also be shifted to meet needs. All of the eleven
adult men not employed in Community Playthings in late 1965
were familiar with shop procedures, and could fill in there in
emergencies. Four were employed full time in the community's
executive hierarchy. One was the community physician and also
served in the hierarchy. One was principal and another a teacher
in the communal school. One was the community storekeeper.
Three were maintenance men.

Community Playthings and the other work departments often
appear to be operating almost effortlessly, with no frictions, no
resentments, and no failures of communication or coordination.

Indeed, the working life of the Bruderhof does flow on smoothly most of the time, in a happy union of Germanic industriousness and sober responsibility with American enthusiasm, self-reliance, and inventiveness. But the thought of a self-supporting economy of almost eight hundred people running without friction is a utopian dream, and the Bruderhof is no utopia. When disputes do arise, they are handled by the Bruderhof social control mechanisms to be described in later chapters. The following example provides a general picture:

I was folding sheets with her. I could tell by the way she tugged the sheets that she – well, this is going to sound a little silly, but I became conscious of this as I worked with her – at some point, one of you has got to decide whether to turn the sheet inward or outward to get to the center fold. Well she would sort of tug it, so I would go her way. But sometimes I would tug it, but she wouldn't go my way. She still wanted me to do it her way. So I did it, but I told her that I was aware of what she was doing. I said, 'If you want me to always do it the same way, just say so, but please stop playing these cosy little games with me.' Well, she just threw the sheet at me and walked out of the laundry.

Then the Servant of the Word called me in and said, 'D. can't work in that laundry when you are there.' I thought he was kidding. But he said that it was a very serious situation when a Sister says that she can't work in the laundry because somehow or other I was polluting the atmosphere. So I said to the Servant, 'Well, what's wrong with her?' Then he got really angry and said, 'Did you ever think of asking what's wrong with you?' I said, 'It's true. Maybe both of us better sit down and say what's the matter with both of us.' He shouted, 'I told you, you've got to say, what's the matter with you!'

## 7. *Maintaining Community Boundaries*

In facing the outside world, the Bruderhof attempts to steer a middle course between two dangers. One is that of excessive pride, manifested in smugness and in contempt towards all those who are not following 'the one true path'. The other is despair, manifested in the feeling that communitarianism is irrelevant to the problems facing the modern world, and that Bruderhof

Christianity is merely a rationale for escaping from the complexities of life. Ideally, the Bruderhofer seeks to believe that he is a member of the most important of social movements, but that this is not particularly to his credit. He is merely surrendering to God's will, and anybody who wants to can do the same.

Actually, most Bruderhof members have probably fallen victim to each of these traps at various times. The danger of pride is particularly virulent because the Bruderhof ideology calls for the renunciation of the individual ego. How tempting to take on a collective ego in its place. If the Bruderhof is so special, it is only natural to feel special oneself by association. Enthusiastic guests enhance this tendency. When individuals become ensnared by pride in the collective ego, it is a fairly easy matter for the community to correct them. When the entire community becomes thus ensnared, there is trouble. This has happened several times in the community's history. Each time, has the letdown come in the form of a crisis.

The other danger, that of despair, threatens the community during times of trouble in the outside world, such as war, depression, fascism. At such times, the member's old friends and relatives may bitterly accuse him of escapism (How can you go on calmly living in your little community, making toys, and singing songs, when there's a . . . ?). One Bruderhof member wrote an essay, in response to this kind of doubt, to show that communitarian living is the very opposite of escapism:

They tell us we are withdrawing from the world and its history. They say we are spending our lives only with those who think as we do, that we are thus depriving ourselves of all chance to act effectively on behalf of our convictions 'in history', 'in the world', in the place 'where we have been put'.

What can we answer to this?

. . . I cannot believe that merely being in the maelstrom of history automatically means living in this history. You may be in the whirl of the big city, take part in its outward life and be exposed to all the consequences of historical happenings, but to have a true relationship to history is much more than that. World history is events, human events, and a man shares in it only if he does not simply let it happen to him and around him, but does his part to determine its course. This sharing in the formation of history is what I should call working in the world. That is really living with history . . . .

. . . we must not admit limitation of our actions through circumstances; circumstances are nothing other than the consequences of our own human actions down through the centuries. We must not adapt ourselves to history. We must be willing to direct history. Is that utopian, megalomaniac? We do not believe it is . . . .

. . . We know we stand with the world from the moment that we declare common cause with it, to the extent that we cannot separate its distress from our own, so that, in fact, its distress becomes our own and we make our redemption dependent on its redemption.

. . . this endeavor is so far above us it can never be carried out by partial means. As long as we do nothing but undertake minor, partial repairs here and there we cannot hope for anything to come out of it. If we want everything, we have to give everything. It is impossible to win the new and at the same time cherish something of the old, once we have seen the untruth of the old . . . .

In the place 'where we have been put' our real life-responsibility was hemmed in by conditions which we rejected and felt to be wrong. Should we have stayed in that place when we were shown and given the possibility of a new way of life? Is it not rather the person who stays where he is to seek his own personal salvation who is separating himself from the world, even if he lives in a city with ten million other people? . . .

All of us hope for a future of peace, love, and brotherliness. The fulfilment of this wish is not bound to any place. It depends if people make a reality of it. And so we want to make use of our lives to show and shape – now in the present time – the image of the future. We have turned toward the future, changed our direction in the present. And since our existence spans the arch between present and future, we believe that it is history we are living.[66]

There exists a formidable strain, both within the Bruderhof and between the Bruderhof and its exiles, over the opposing needs for outreach and concern with internal matters. The question is by no means settled in anybody's mind. Every Bruderhof member speaks of the intense longing for outreach burning in each Brother's heart. The only time people ever became overtly angry with me during my stay in the Bruderhof was when I suggested that I did not see any evidence for this longing. Emmy Arnold explained to me: 'We are turned a bit inward now. This is sometimes necessary. But we desire to be turned outward toward the world.' The Bruderhof explains its deemphasis of outreach in terms of a lack of inner strength. The idea is that, when inner purification has been attained, the community will then be 'given' the strength for missionary activities.

Ex-members are more cynical. They believe that the Bruderhof's leading Servant of the Word is not really interested in outreach but would like to model the community after the pattern of the Hutterians. One former Servant of the Word told me:

> As long as [the *Vorsteher*] can keep his cool, there'll be no changes in the Bruderhof. There'll be more and more inward gazing. There'll be no outreach until perfect unity has been achieved – that means never.

The truth probably lies between these two points of view. The Bruderhof does not need outreach to fulfil its purpose as a movement. It can do this merely by existing as a community in brotherhood and peace – a goal which can reasonably by given first priority since there would be no purpose in reaching out if there were nothing to show people once they were gathered in. But it is probably also the case that, as the community grows older, it is tending to get lazier and more set in its ways, and to welcome excuses for avoiding disruption and risk. It is certainly possible that one of the reasons Brother David came out the victor in the great crisis is that he represented the security of strong boundaries against the uncertainties of the outside world.

The relationship between Woodcrest and the surrounding community has been good, although rather distant and formal. Once a year, the community holds an open house, at which a short talk on a spiritual subject may be given. In 1965, the open house featured the Woodcrest choir singing Haydn's *Creation*. Guests are served refreshments and given a tour of the *hof*. One or two hundred people come to these open houses, some from as far away as Poughkeepsie. But during the rest of the year, friendships with members of the outside community are strongly discouraged. According to the Brothers themselves (and a very few outside informants, insufficient for a true sample of opinion), the Bruderhof is rather liked by its neighbors. There is no Communist smear against them, although sometimes they are referred to fondly as 'the only true communists', in contrast to the Russians.

The Bruderhof takes no stand in politics, either local, state, or national. The members are pacifists and are strongly in favor of the nonviolent civil rights movement. Only once, during the Johnson–Goldwater campaign, were they tempted to vote. This was discussed in meetings for a long while, but it was finally decided not to vote, even against Goldwater. 'We decided that politics was just not our way.' Bruderhof political activity is limited to a very reticent participation in nonviolent anti-war and civil rights demonstrations. Even in this activity they tend to stand on the periphery, and withdraw if any sign of non-loving confrontation with the authorities seems about to take place.

In its early days, the Bruderhof was part of the German Christian Youth Movement, and many who remember these days are nostalgic for them. Part of the great interest in the civil rights movement stems from the desire, especially of many old-time Bruderhof members, to 'hook on ' to a larger movement. A great amount of energy and time goes into making and keeping up contacts with other communities and Protestant monastic groups. During the summer of 1965, the *Vorsteher* and his family went on a trip through Europe, making contacts with various groups in Germany and France. Relationships with American communities, especially nonsectarian ones, are rather cool, however. Some efforts in recent years have been made to re-establish good relations with the Hutterians.

As Bruderhof outreach has declined in the past eight years, so has inflow. Both the number of new members and the number of visitors and guests have fallen drastically. Only a few new families have joined the Bruderhof in the last few years. During the four months of our stay at Woodcrest, we were the only long-term guests in the community. Every weekend brought a handful of visitors, but these were mostly curiosity-seeking tourists.

The guest warden is an officer of the community with the specific job of giving tours and talking to casual guests. He is called away from his regular job whenever a guest appears. Such a guest is not given freedom to wander around the *hof*; his tour is carefully supervised by the guest warden. If he is staying for more than one day, the guest will generally be asked to work in one of the community work departments.

The Bruderhof does not like guests who will not accommodate themselves to the communal routine or who gawk at the community members as if they were animals in a zoo. To all others, the community gives a very warm and generous reception. This is true for any guest, but especially for those that have expressed a serious interest in the community. One woman described a time when she had been a guest of the community for a weekend. A short while later she came for a longer visit. When she arrived, there was a big 'welcome home' sign for her. At that moment, this woman felt so overwhelmed by the love of the community that she decided to join.

However, even a very serious guest will be excluded from all of the business meetings of the community. The information that he is given will often be the official line, rather than the strict truth. In fact, it can be said that there are three levels of exposure to Bruderhof life. Immediately, the guest is exposed to the level of appearances. As he stays on and becomes more serious in his intentions, and even more so if he decides to take the novitiate, he gradually becomes exposed to the level of meanings. We have been discussing these two levels so far. But until he is baptized into the Brotherhood, he does not become aware of the deepest level, the infra-structure that binds the community together. It is to a discussion of this level that we now turn.

## Chapter Four □ THE POWER OF THE UNITED BROTHERHOOD

What holds the Bruderhof together? Most distinctive social orders are based on some combination of tradition (We live this way because people have always lived this way.), sovereignty (We live this way because if we didn't they'd call the cops.), and charisma (We live this way because our great leader has shown us that this is the best way to live.). The Bruderhof began as a charismatic community, but Eberhard Arnold died over thirty years ago and no one comparable has ever taken his place. The community exercises a certain amount of sovereignty in its legal control over the individual's material assets, but this is quite limited and has not been enough to deter the hundreds of Bruderhof ex-members. Over the years, traditions have grown up, and these undoubtedly have an effect, but, as we have seen, an intentional community is interesting precisely because it is not and never can be a traditional community. Clearly we must look elsewhere for the glue that holds together this particular communitarian collage.

The secret of the Bruderhof has to do with its utilization of a particular mode of human interaction which is known to sociologists as collective behavior. This mode of interaction liberates great quantities of energy which, under ordinary circumstances, are repressed. Instances of collective behavior in ordinary society are found in such diverse phenomena as lynchings, football rallies, and encounter groups. It is perceived by participants as a merging experience. Loss of individual autonomy is felt in many ways, including loss of physical boundaries, loss of responsibility, loss of will, and loss of one's traditional set of values. But this loss of autonomy, which for convenience may be called ego-loss, does not result in a sense of disintegration, but rather in the awareness of the emergence of a new entity, the group. This group is seen as a united *gestalt*, existing above and beyond the sum of the existence of its members.

Collective behavior and associative (or normal) behavior are two basic forms of human interaction. In the former, ego boundaries are broken down and people's identities seem to merge. In the latter, people react to one another as unique individuals. Herbert Blumer writes:

> One gets a clue to the nature of elementary collective behavior by recognizing the form of social interaction that has been called *circular reaction*. This refers to a type of interstimulation wherein the response of one individual reproduces the stimulation that has come from another individual and in being reflected back to this individual reinforces the stimulation. Thus the interstimulation assumes a circular form in which individuals reflect one another's states of feeling and in so doing intensify this feeling. It is well evidenced in the transmission of feelings and moods among people who are in a state of excitement. One sees the process clearly amidst cattle in a state of alarm . . . .
>
> The nature of circular reaction can be further helpfully understood by contrasting it with interpretive interaction, which is the form chiefly to be found among human beings who are in association. Ordinarily, human beings respond to one another, as in carrying on a conversation, by interpreting one another's actions or remarks and then reacting on the basis of the interpretation. Responses, consequently, are not made directly to the stimulation, but follow, rather, upon interpretation; further, they are likely to be different in nature from the stimulating acts, being essentially adjustments to these acts. Thus interpretative interaction . . . tends . . . to make people different; circular reaction tends to make people alike.[67]

It has long been known that collective behavior experiences are capable of bringing forth tremendous quantities of energy not ordinarily available. But like the nuclear energy of the uranium atom, this energy has not been thought to be available in any kind of controllable or useful form. The argument of this chapter is that the Bruderhof has evolved an institutional structure whose precise function is the controlled utilization of collective behavior energy.

Ralph Turner has discussed the regenerative functions of collective behavior:

> Collective behavior contributes to solidarity by countering the distance-provoking effects of formality in society. One of the endemic sources of strain in society is the antithesis between regulated order and interpersonal intimacy. One of the costs of orderliness and predictability, achieved through adherence to rules of interaction and attention to statuses, is the augmentation of reserve and segmentation in the relationships between people.
>
> ... by breaking the daily routine and bringing people together in a situation in which customary reserve can be suspended, some social revitalization can be achieved.[68]

Collective behavior emerges when normal or institutional group behavior breaks down. Institutional group behavior is marked by the presence of rules, roles, rituals, symbols, norms, and goals. In short, it is game behavior. It achieves order at the cost of spontaneity and intimacy. We are very familiar with the literature of negative manifestations of collective behavior, such as panics, riots, and lynch mobs. But Turner and others increasingly emphasize the positive contributions of such behavior in releasing energy, creating enthusiasm, and achieving social revitalization. I contend that even such positive manifestations of collective behavior as have generally been recorded use only a small fraction of the total available energy, and that the Bruderhof is structured in a way that allows much more use of this energy.

To use the terminology of the Bruderhof, the community is a vessel in which to catch and hold the spirit. The spirit is ephemeral and yet the source of all renewal and all creativity in society. Although rational structure necessarily stands in antithesis to the spiritual experience, it is possible to use structure to maximize accessibility to such experience when it comes. Ideally, this is what the structure of marriage does for the spiritual condition of being in love. The purposes of the Bruderhof structure may be seen as the following: maintaining openness to the coming of the spirit, holding on to it and partly taming it once it does come, and helping the community muddle through those intervals during which the spirit has fled. These tasks are accomplished through the major institution of Bruderhof life – the Brotherhood.

## 1. *The Brotherhood*

When a Bruderhof member speaks of the Brotherhood, he is speaking of an institution which has extension into both his inner and his outer worlds. In German, there are two distinct words for these two dimensions: *gemeinde* and *bruderschaft*. The *gemeinde* is the congregation when it is filled with the Holy Spirit. The *bruderschaft* is the physical assembly of the members of the community. In English, both of these concepts merge into the word 'brotherhood'.

The *bruderschaft* is permanent but the *gemeinde* is ephemeral. Eberhard Arnold always used to rebuke the community when it confused the two: 'We are not the *gemeinde*. The *gemeinde* sometimes comes to us.' During times of severe crisis at the Bruderhof, it will sometimes be said that the Brotherhood has ceased to exist. By this it is not meant that the physical Brotherhood is no longer meeting. If anything, during such crises, Brotherhood meetings are more frequent than usual. But when the unseen spirit that gives the Brotherhood its special power has departed, the Bruderhof member is bereft because, in his inner world, the Brotherhood no longer exists.

The Brotherhood is composed of all of the baptized men and women of the Bruderhof who are not currently in exclusion. At Woodcrest in early 1966, there were approximately seventy-five Brotherhood members. Since it is rare, although not unknown, for a person under the age of eighteen to be a Brotherhood member, and since at that time there were 129 persons over eighteen who were living at Woodcrest, about 58 per cent of those eligible by age were Brotherhood members. The other 42 per cent were completely excluded from the decision-making process while remaining completely under its authority. These included novice members, guests, Brothers being punished by temporary exclusion, and permanent residents who had decided not to become members or who were still making up their minds.

It is difficult for members of a highly decentralized and pluralistic society to appreciate how totally the Brotherhood dominates the Bruderhof – both in its communal existence and in the individual lives of its members. All statuses in the community are held vis-a-vis the Brotherhood. All decisions, except the most trivial, are made through the Brotherhood. All self-examination as to the state of the community's life and work is made in terms of the state of the Brotherhood. Most important, the Brotherhood is at once the vessel that receives the energy-laden spirit and the machinery through which the raw spiritual (or collective behavior) experience is refined into useful energy.

There are two different forms of Brotherhood assembly. One is called the Brotherhood meeting and the other is called the *Gemeindestunde*. The Brotherhood meeting is the decision-making meeting and is closed to all except members. (I never saw one.) It is held several times a week in the evening, usually for two to three hours, depending on the volume of business. The *Gemeindestunde* is the meeting for prayer, and is open to a wider circle than the Brotherhood meeting, including novices and sometimes guests. The *Gemeindestunde* is held once or sometimes twice a week, also in the evening.

The typical *Gemeindestunde* begins with a reading or a talk by the Servant of the Word or some other Brother on a theme drawing attention to the reality of the inner life of the Bruderhof. Readings are often from the works of Eberhard Arnold or Christoph Blumhardt. Other religious authors, such as Leonhard Ragat, Dietrich Bonhoeffer, Alfred Delp, John Woolman, or any of the old Hutterians, are also occasionally selected. This is followed by a period of silence resembling a Quaker meeting. The silence is broken only by those who feel 'a leading of the Holy Spirit' to speak out. Finally, there is the common prayer, spoken by the Servant, whose job it is to find and articulate the unconscious prayer that is moving in the hearts of the entire united Brotherhood. The Servant takes this task very seriously and will never begin a prayer if he does not discern complete unity in the circle. Thus, a *Gemeindestunde* sometimes ends without coming to prayer. When there is prayer, the entire Brotherhood kneels in a circle with hands outstretched, palm upward, signifying childlike expectation that God the Father knows what the community needs and will provide it.

So seriously does the Brotherhood take the requirement that there be absolute unity in the *Gemeindestunde* that a Brother or Sister who has a grudge against someone or a bad feeling toward the community will not come to the meeting. If he does come, he will make every effort to solve the problem, either by talking with the person with whom he is quarrelling before the meeting, or making a confession at the meeting itself. If he still has not succeeded in establishing unity, he will leave before the circle comes to prayer. An ex-member commented:

> During *Gemeindestunde*, if someone had a feeling against a Brother, he'd just get up and go out. He might ask another Brother to go with him and talk it over. If this was a couple of more important Brothers and the *Gemeindestunde* was drawing near to a close, they would postpone the final prayers until they came back, or just weren't going to come back. [Question: What do you mean, 'more important Brothers?'] I don't know for sure – Witness Brothers maybe. They would never have used those words, 'more important Brothers'.

At the *Gemeindestunde*, attention is drawn to the nature of the Brotherhood as *gemeinde*, a sacred domain in which, at times, the members lose their separate identities and become the Church or Body of Christ. This in itself serves as a source of strength for the community. The petty problems of everyday living are placed in cosmic perspective; they are pictured as battles by an outpost of God's Army against the forces of evil and disunity. Members leave the meeting recharged with dedication to the great task and to their individual jobs.

Emphasis on the Brotherhood as *gemeinde* is not restricted to the *Gemeindestunde*; it pervades the entire life. It is just that the *Gemeindestunde* is a time when this aspect is exclusively emphasized. For instance, unity is always stressed as the highest value within the Brotherhood, but it is understood that at decision-making meetings controversies will inevitably arise and that unity must be thought of more as a goal than as a constant fact. But at the *Gemeindestunde*, it is not possible to pray disunitedly for unity. Unity is a precondition for prayer. If there is no unity, there is no *gemeinde*, and, therefore, nothing which can pray.

The basic theory of Bruderhof decision making, as practiced in the Brotherhood meetings, is far different from that underlying democratic legislative decision making. Democratic decision making is based on competing interest groups and a range of issues. The legislature is a forum in which these groups negotiate so that the final decisions reflect the numerical power of the various interest groups and the intensity of their positions. For example, a persecuted minority group, such as the Negroes in America, may be able to elect a small body of legislators. By trading their support on all other issues for support on civil rights legislation, they can greatly increase their ability to pass it.

The theory of Bruderhof decision making is quite different. It is based on the assumption that the right decision exists. The task of the Brotherhood is to find it. There is no such thing as an interest group. The right decision is right for the entire group and for each member, equally. But no person acting alone can ever find this right decision. For this reason, everyone in the Bruderhof has a duty to become involved in every decision and to speak his mind if any relevant thought occurs to him, even if it contradicts the entire rest of the Brotherhood:

> In line with the theory of the pre-existent decision, defined as God's will, one had to *listen* and *look* to find the decision. But to do this properly, one had to be empty of self – otherwise you were deaf and blind. Otherwise, you were not *transparent*, you were not 'hollow' so that the spirit of God could flow through you . . . . [69]

When the decision is fairly clear, someone who disagrees in an angry or resentful way is often said to 'bring in a disturbance'. In order to differentiate this from performing one's proper duty of speaking out, the attitude, not the objective content, is the focus of attention. The proper way to dissent is never to say, 'I object,' but rather, in a tentative voice, 'I have a question.'

A hostility to cliques in which issues get discussed follows naturally from the theory of the pre-existent decision. Such cliques are called, derisively, kitchen brotherhoods. They are broken up whenever possible. At one time, some of the younger schoolteachers tried to introduce reform of the school. They were severely rebuked for factionalism, even though their faction grew out of a common task and common expertise. The Brothers see kitchen brotherhood meetings as opportunities for viewpoints to become hardened before there is opportunity for full discussion.

Not all Brothers have an equal contribution to make in finding the correct decision. Some never or very rarely find anything to say. Others may acquire a reputation for generally having a clear leading, and these will be listened to with greater attention than others. The Servant of the Word always falls in this category. In trivial matters, which make up the great bulk of Brotherhood business, those that have full-time jobs preparing the decisions for consideration are usually heeded.

An image that the Bruderhof uses in discussing its search for the right means of conduct is that of a dark room full of people holding candles. Each candle makes a contribution to the illumination of the room, but it is still necessary for someone to use the combined light to make a clear statement as to the nature of that which is seen. This is the proper task of the Servant of the Word. His role is not to lead, but to integrate and give form to the many contributions of the individual Brothers. Eberhard Arnold outlined the proper function of the Servant as follows, in a guideline still accepted and followed by the Bruderhof:

It is important to grasp in a new way the meaning of leadership in the church-community. Leading usually takes place through suggestion or transference of the will of one to the others. This can never be so with the church-community.

... we are united in deepest openness and obedience to the Holy Spirit. When we are united, when this is revealed to all, *there must be someone to put into words and action that which is felt by all* ....

The Word leader [Servant] is the spokesman for that which lives in the others. The Word leader cannot speak or act out of himself. He says or does that which moves in the others and wants to be expressed in word or deed. Never should there prevail a human leading. Everybody can be the spokesman for the life of the whole community. We have no principle of leadership and no majority system. We do not want one human opinion to rule over the others. We believe that *the Spirit of truth manifests himself to all and never contradicts himself.* We believe in the revelation of truth in the living community.

. . . He who has this task [of Servant of the Word] must first grasp the inward and outward situation of the whole group and bring it to clear expression in word and action. He must bring to expression that which is holy, which moves and fills the hearts of all, *even if it is unspoken and undone.*[70]

The leadership function of the Servant will be discussed in great detail in the following chapter. Here it is only important to note his special role in the decision-making process. It is certainly not the case, by any means, that the Servant's suggestions are always followed by the Brotherhood. Nevertheless, there is a constant strong pressure on the rank-and-file Brothers to conform to the will of the Servants and others who speak with a certain amount of authority.

This pressure to conform stems from the very nature of the Bruderhof decision-making system. The idea of the pre-existent decision makes it a serious matter to be caught on the wrong side of an issue. One is not merely expressing a minority opinion, but possibly showing that he is out of touch with the Holy Spirit. Furthermore, the need for absolute unanimity, far from giving power to the individual dissenter, places a great burden upon him not to dissent unless he is pretty sure that he's right. It is an interesting paradox that, at least in a highly cohesive group, making the power of dissent equivalent to the power of veto is a means of weakening rather than strengthening dissent.

In 1950, when the Paraguayan Bruderhofs broke with the Hutterians, G. was Servant of the Word at Wheathill Bruderhof in England. G. was one of the early founders of the Bruderhof in Germany and had been a close friend and associate of Eberhard Arnold. The ascribed charisma which this status gave him was considerably enhanced by a great deal of personal charisma. One member said of him, 'He has an ability to call attention to the cosmic significance of everyday events more than any other member of the Bruderhof.' G. objected very strongly and intemperately to the decision of the Paraguayan Brotherhoods to break with the Hutterians. After some discussion, the Wheathill Brotherhood sent to Paraguay a unanimously endorsed, strongly worded letter of accusation. G. was invited to come to Paraguay.

When G. arrived in Paraguay he found that the situation was quite different than he had thought. He was convinced that the Paraguayan Brotherhoods had been right and that his own suspicion and anger had come from the fact that he had 'cherished a resentment' against one of the Servants in Paraguay. G. was placed in exclusion with his own consent. When the Wheathill Brothers heard what had happened, they, one by one, began to confess that they too had had doubts as to the validity of G.'s original opinion but, troubled with self-doubt and problems on their own, they had not paid sufficient attention or had enough confidence to be able to offer dissent. Each had assumed that, since nobody else was objecting, his own doubts must be due to some personal problems. The ex-member who told me this story said that this phenomenon was quite common in the Bruderhof. He referred to it as the Phenomenon of the Emperor's New Clothes.

Although the Brotherhood is made up of an assembly of persons, every person is an isolate vis-a-vis the Brotherhood. The entire socialization process of the Bruderhof is geared to produce in the individual feelings of his own selfishness, worthlessness, and inadequacy. The collective self is an absolute good. The individual self is an absolute evil. Obviously, such a presentation is viable only if the community actually can provide each individual with a sense of collective self that is more satisfying than his individual self.

## 2. *Joy*

The big payoff is an experience which the Bruderhof calls joy. This joy is a twofold reward: it provides direct emotional gratification to the individual, and it is his primary evidence that he and the community are in a state of grace. As we shall see, joy is a product of the collective behavior experience. As such, it is an experience whose presence or absence is highly contagious. But joy, like any other emotion, can only be felt by an individual, not by a group. Thus we find that joy in the Bruderhof, although perhaps triggered by a collective experience, is not one phenomenon but many. Each person, according to his nature, perceives it differently.

A Servant of the Word at Woodcrest was surprised when I asked him to explain the Bruderhof experience of joy. To him, joy is the natural state of man when connected to the Holy Spirit. It is life without joy that is unnatural and needs explaining. On the other hand, two ex-members described the experience with horror as mass psychosis. While this harsh judgment undoubtedly had something to do with their resentment at having been asked to leave the Bruderhof, they had always felt that the euphoria was in some way eerie and unnatural and had to be accepted on faith. In such cases – a small minority – joy is not the payoff and other reasons for maintaining commitment must be found. In the case of these informants, motivation was provided by strength of will and ideological conviction.

Some members have described Bruderhof joy primarily in terms of participation in a glorious historical movement – of oneness with the apostles and great saints of history. Others have stressed the factor of escape from the wretchedness of lonely individual existence. Still others have been most aware of the self-unifying aspect of joy – tying together the various strands of their lives. Many have emphasized the importance of joy in giving meaning to life.

There is no exact word to describe the phenomenon that I am here, for convenience, calling joy or euphoria. In some of its forms, perhaps, exaltation would be a more accurate term. This emotion is rarely light-headed or light-hearted, and often not even exuberant. As one member put it: '. . . the joy can be solemn. It's definitely not just happiness. You could feel it inside, the welling of the greatness of things.' In other forms the word 'peace' might most accurately describe it. An ex-member said:

The real euphoria of community living comes from the continual fulfilment you feel, that you're at peace with yourself and you're at peace with your neighbors, and you're doing what you really think you should be doing, you're doing it sincerely, you're doing it enthusiastically. And that carries itself over into the work, especially the concrete work.

Bruderhof members speak of patterns of joy. They recognize a certain indissoluble relationship between joy and struggle:

The euphoria has to be regained again and again. The Holy Spirit is always a visitor, never a possession. God doesn't need us, but if we are worthy, His Spirit comes to us [paraphrased].

Periods of intense joy tend to follow periods of crisis. One ex-member went so far as to distinguish two distinct types of joy. He said that, for him, post-crisis joy was so great as to be an entirely different experience from the ordinary, everyday joy. Another person spoke of a particular ceremony, 'the laying on of hands' to receive back into the Brotherhood members who have been in exclusion, as euphoria at its absolute peak.

However the joy may be interpreted, there is no doubt that it is central to the Bruderhof experience. This can be seen in the way that the members, and especially the ex-members, talk about it. A number of apostates confessed that they were afraid to go back to the Bruderhof, even for a short visit. They were afraid that a whiff of the joy would draw them back into the fold again, despite their firm resolutions to the contrary. A majority of the others with whom I had contact exhibited manifestations of what has come to be known among them as 'exile syndrome', a dispirited, purposeless drifting, viewing any possible life outside the Bruderhof as dull, pale, and meaningless. Exile syndrome generally wears off after a year or so, but in some it has persisted more than five years. It might almost be said that Bruderhof joy is habit-forming.

The reader's evaluation of this phenomenon of joy will be crucial to his evaluation of the Bruderhof as a whole. If he feels, as I do, that it is genuine and, moreover, touches the very core of what it means to be human, then it will be important for him to understand the Bruderhof and to relate it to the future of his own world. Reading about the great crisis and about the socialization system to be described in chapter six will bewilder him, but not deter him from this effort to understand. But if the reader thinks of Bruderhof joy as an opiate or delusion, a rationale for withdrawal and conformity, he may still have a sociological interest in the community as a deviant phenomenon, but will not be impressed with it as a relevant social movement or social experiment.

Since joy is an emotion, we naturally turn to psychoanalysis in search of criteria by which to test its reality. We find, however, that psychoanalysts themselves tend to treat such emotions as primitive terms requiring no further elucidation. Bertram Lewin writes:

> Particularly in the field of emotions, we tend to assume that we know elements, mental states which need no further dissection because they are irreducible. Rage, fear, joy, sadness, impress us as self-evident and atomic, for they are the clear points in what T. S. Eliot calls 'the general mess of imprecision of feeling'....[71]

Because joy is rarely if ever a cause for psychiatric complaint, there has been even less of an effort, than with more destructive emotions, to delve into its causes, Lewin goes on to say:

> ... we [psychoanalysts] were slow to view through the glass of analysis one member of the class of affects. I refer to the feeling of elation, variously known as joy, bliss, euphoria .... Can elation too be a defense, or a resistance, ... that needs reduction? A human enough prejudice opposes this idea .... There are, to be sure, 'out-and-out manics,' but ... elation as such ... is not in its mild forms apt to bring persons into analysis, or once they are there to provoke much desire for change or therapeutic effort.[72]

A further obstacle in the way of our evaluation of joy is a linguistic one. We tend, more than with any other psychological state, to take a person's own word for the validity of his emotions. We recognize that emotions may be consciously fabricated, as by movie actors and hypocrites, but, once we judge a person to be sincere, there is not any convenient way in the English language to express doubt as to the validity of his emotions. To quote Lewin again:

> Psychiatry lacks a convenient term for a false emotion, one which would be the analogue of the term delusion (a false idea), or hallucination (a false perception). We have no word like the Hippocratic *paracrousis*, which, borrowed from music, meant a 'false note or discord', a 'striking falsely', and which might have served, if it had not become obsolete, to denote a discrepancy between the ego's inner emotional perception and the objective situation – not a minor discrepancy comparable to an intellectual error or to a simple sensory deception, but a marked, serious incongruity.[73]

Bearing in mind these difficulties, we can begin to attempt an evaluation of Bruderhof joy. A logical starting point is to ask what Bruderhof members themselves think of it. Most, of course, would not even entertain the notion that their joy might be anything but an authentic spiritual visitation. A few are more cynical, as illustrated by the following story told to me by an ex-member:

> Maybe the codification and prescription of feelings is typically German. We had a member named W., a German theology Ph.D. He used to recall with amused scorn, a probably apocryphal anecdote about what used to happen on the *Kraft durch Freude* tours (Joy through Strength: a Nazi excursion-system for the working class). They would be taking a ship out to the Azores. Around sunset time, the tour-leader would bark: '*Antreten! Natur bewunder!*' (More or less: 'Up to the rail! Admire the nature!'). This I used to feel (and I shared his sentiments) was W.'s way of obliquely satirizing a tendency we had to go around self-consciously prescribing that we all had to be joyful [paraphrased].

It is probably the case that W. had put his finger on an endemic Bruderhof conceit – a pretense that there is joy during times when there is no joy. Nevertheless, neither W. nor the man who told me this story would deny, judging from other comments, that the joy often was real and was crucial to the entire Bruderhof experience. In fact, I never met a person who had been connected with the Bruderhof in any capacity (and I met some who really hated the community) who denied the reality and the power of the euphoric experience, even though there were a few for whom it was strongly negative rather than strongly positive. Another bit of evidence for the reality of the experience is that for many visitors (myself included) the joy is the first thing to be noticed upon entering the *hof*, even before exposure to the ideology, the economics, the singing, or the style of life. This would seem to weaken the counter-hypothesis, that the joy is a delusional epiphenomenon of the Bruderhof's pressure for conformity. In my case, at least, the joy struck a clear chord, not the false note of *paracrousis*.

Even if we admit that the Bruderhof experience of joy is real, it remains to determine its causes and its role in the liberation of energy. A clue to both of these problems is provided by Sigmund Freud's analysis of mania in the manic-depressive, as discussed by Bertram Lewin:

> The energy previously tied up or employed in the struggle between the two agencies of the personality (i.e., between the ego and the superego) was now freed and placed at the ego's disposal, which put the patient in a psychic economic position to indulge in a triumph or celebration. Freud's comparison was to a poor devil, suddenly relieved of drudgery by a legacy, finding the time and energy for a celebration. Freud's other explanatory suggestion about mania was that it corresponded to a possibly biologically determined intermittent necessity for the differentiated parts (agencies) of the total personality to coalesce periodically, so that the part that arises later in development disappears in its part of origin. Thus in mania the super-ego regressively rejoins the ego, as the ego rejoins the id in sound sleep. Freud saw a social recognition of the recurrent need for such structural regressions in the various carnivals, Saturnalia, and other socially institutionalized holiday letdowns in instinct restriction. *The explanatory concept, familiar enough to a neurophysiologist, is that of regression to a simpler structural state, permitting a release of energy* [emphasis added].[74]

As Freud shows, in *Mass Psychology and the Analysis of the Ego*, it is precisely this structural regression, of the super-ego into the (collective) ego, which takes place during the typical collective behavior experience. Not all joy is triggered by a collective experience, of course, nor does every instance of collective behavior result in joy. But in the case of the Bruderhof it is clear that the two must be examined together.

An ex-member of the Bruderhof who is familiar with encounter groups remarked that the experience of joy in both was very similar. For him it was, in each case, a reawakening of hope for nurturance that would finally be satisfying at the breast of the Good Mother (the community or the group). In this respect, it is interesting to note that encounter groups have been observed to go through phases similar to those of the Bruderhof's crisis-euphoria cycle. William Bion has described a four-stage encounter group cycle. The first stage is a shared mood of expectancy when the members discover that they are allowed to be spontaneous. This may trigger an outburst of euphoria, as the individual members give themselves permission to regress to a state of undifferentiated collective ego. Usually this cannot be sustained, and a third stage of disillusionment follows, in which the various members begin to doubt that there are enough goodies to go around and thus compete with each other for attention. When the group has had its fill of this, a fourth stage of reconstitution sets in. The members realize that they are all wretched together and they might as well make the best of it. This triggers another period of expectancy and the cycle begins anew.

In the Bruderhof these four phases would be called expectation or waiting, joy, crisis, and clearance, but the process is very much the same. In encounter groups, the timing of these four stages is a hit-or-miss phenomenon. It is still more so in mobs, rallies, and other manifestations of collective behavior. The Bruderhof adds an element of regularity through the controlled utilization of the collective behavior experience.


## 3. Harnessing Joy

The problem of taming the collective behavior experience is really two problems. First, the experience must be made to happen with a consistently high degree of regularity and intensity. Second, the experience must be transformed into a useful form of energy. Each of these problems contains a number of sub-problems. Let us consider the two major problems separately.

The literature on collective behavior records many instances of extraordinarily high intensity – sufficient sometimes to change a person's entire future life or to move him to feats of courage or love or ability rarely perceived in ordinary life. Yet most collective behavior experiences are not this intense. Why not?

Three major forces can be identified which dampen the intensity of the collective behavior experience. These are: disunity of the group as to values, norms, and goals; lack of full participation in (or surrender to) the experience; failure to understand and/or give a positive interpretation to the experience. Of course, these forces are not mutually independent. But they do pose three distinct obstacles to the creation of a structure conducive to intense collective behavior experiences.

Disunity within the group and inability to participate fully in the ego-merging experience are both counterforces to intensification of the experience. We know from experiments in social psychology performed by Asch and others that suggestibility (which is obviously highly related to potentiality for ego-loss) is correlated with strength of character – perhaps with the degree that one's personality is inner-directed. Inner- directed people are unlikely to take part in lynch mobs or revival meetings, and a preponderance of such people in a group makes it more difficult for the group to have an intense collective behavior experience.

However, ego-loss by itself is not sufficient for such a collective experience. There must be some communality – whether of interests, life styles, values, or goals around which the group ego or the group mind may emerge. Hence the importance of a pre-existing unity within the group.

Even if the two above prerequisites are met in a group, the experience itself can be terrifying, and this is so to the very extent that its potentiality is perceived as intense. Men characteristically form themselves into institutional or game-based groups not only because of the greater efficiency that such a mode affords but also because of the greater safety to the individual. Even the non-task-oriented recreation of civilized man usually takes place in a game setting, and, where it does not, he must resort to artificial means, such as getting high, to break out of the game world. It follows from this that, in addition to unity and readiness to participate, the group needs some way of overcoming the fear of the collective behavior experience. Otherwise the members of the group will act so as to avoid such experiences and to cut them short when they do occur.

Unity provides a basis for mutual trust, and is a great asset in overcoming fear. But, even among trusted friends, fear of the unknown remains, and there is a fear inherent in the loss of individual standards for evaluating behavior unless new collective standards appear which each individual is convinced are good and in his interest. An interpretive framework, then, is the third functional need – one that explains to the individual what is happening, why it is happening, and why it should be happening.

It is interesting to note that primitive men often seem to possess qualities resembling the three that we have been discussing. As Emile Durkheim has pointed out, in societies without much division of labor, people are bound to each other much more by their feeling of being identical than by the more modern feeling of mutual need based on differences.[75] This corresponds to Bruderhof unity. The tribe and kinship group are so vital to the primitive man's survival, that he can have little sense of a discrete autonomous self. This corresponds to a high propensity for ego-loss. Finally, primitive religions tend to give greater emphasis to shared emotional experience, whereas 'higher' religions often emphasize ethics and theology. Thus primitive religions can be looked upon as providing more of an interpretive framework for the collective behavior experience than do the more cerebral religions. From this point of view, the Bruderhof mechanisms for intensifying collective behavior are really mechanisms for simulating tribalization among people who are products of a very untribal civilization.

The next major problem in harnessing the collective behavior experience is that of transforming it into enthusiasm for and commitment to the group. In order to do this, the members must come to think of the experience as something positive, unfrightening, and reliable. The interpretive framework bears most of the burden of showing the experience as positive. A good interpretive framework must make the collective behavior experience understandable and highly enjoyable. Naturally it helps if the experience can be interpreted as something possible only within the group.

The latter problem, that of making the experience reliable, is much more difficult. Again we can think in terms of three major sub-problems, all of which seem to be intrinsic to the experience itself. One is that collective behavior is always ephemeral in nature. The second is that its occurrence in a collectivity is always sporadic and unpredictable. The third is that it tends to create emotional waves of extraordinary intensity among the participants, ranging from passionate attraction to equally passionate repulsion.

Why collective behavior phenomena exhibit these qualities is an unsolved but very interesting problem. It is these apparently ineradicable attributes of collective behavior that make it impractical for a complex society or social group to seek its major source of group commitment in collective behavior, even when such behavior is typically intense. The Bruderhof, however, has evolved a social structure which does not eliminate these unfortunate attributes, but rather accommodates for them and eliminates their ill effects.

The problem of ephemerality lies in the fact that the feeling states and attitudes of a collective behavior experience generally endure in individuals only briefly if at all after the experience is over. Religious leaders have always decried the short-lived effects of the great religious fervor generated by revival meetings. The lynch-mob town returns to business as usual the next day. In task groups this problem is manifested in the tremendous enthusiasm generated for new projects, which rarely carries through to the end of the project. One important question is how the Bruderhof retards this rapid evaporation of the Spirit.

The sporadic nature of collective behavior really poses two problems. The first is that one can never predict when such an experience will occur or plan for it. The second problem is that there will necessarily be periods of time, of uncertain duration, in which there will be no intense positive collective behavior experiences to generate commitment. How does the Bruderhof muddle through such 'dry periods'?

In addition to being sporadic (or discontinuous), collective behavior in a group seems to have a sort of wave nature to its intensity. It's important to realize that too great an intensity is just as much a threat to a function group as too low an intensity. Specifically, every group has norms against spontaneous conduct that it does not want broken even in the collective behavior state. Important among these for the Bruderhof are sexual norms. Furthermore, it is important that the collective behavior induce commitment to the group life as a whole, not solely to the collective behavior state. The latter becomes a danger in really intense experiences. The problems of too low an intensity are the same as those of overcoming 'dry periods' except that at times it seems as if collective behavior can exhibit negative intensities which generate actual repulsion. The Bruderhof's great crisis is a chilling example. Finally, the Bruderhof structure must be capable not only of existing on all of these levels of intensity, but must also be capable of moving freely among them at any time, again due to the sporadic nature of the experience.

In summary, these are the major problems involved in transforming collective behavior experience into commitment:

A. Triggering the experience

B. Making it intense and positive
   (1) fostering unity and isolating disunity
   (2) creating ability to participate fully in ego-loss and ego-merging
   (3) surrounding the experience with a positive interpretative framework

C. Making it reliable and usable
   (1) mitigating its ephemeral nature
   (2) mitigating its sporadic nature
   (3) dealing with constant variations in its intensity
      a. too high a positive intensity
      b. too high a negative intensity

## 4. *Unity*

Unity is the highest value in Bruderhof life. The chief theological justification for this comes from the description of the Last Supper in the Gospel of John. In this view, sin is seen in its original etymological meaning of 'separation'. Anything which separates one from the original unity of God is sin. I have already mentioned the strongly enforced norm in the *Gemeindestunde* that the Brotherhood cannot pray until it has come to unity.

It is obvious that unity is an extremely functional primary value for an intentional community. Not only does it serve the purpose of intensifying the collective behavior experience, but it also provides a value upon which to base consensus-maintaining procedures and norms – thus serving the system of social control. In any strongly value-oriented collectivity, it is important to ensure that adherence to the values does not conflict too much with the actions necessary to survival. This has been the bane of many social movements. Early Christianity provides an example of what happens to the value of love when it conflicts with the reality principle. Studies of the kibbutz have chronicled the downfall of the value of equality under the pressure of mundane system requirements. But it is hard to imagine, at least in a small intentional community, how the value of unity could come into conflict with the reality needs of the community.

After unity, the Bruderhof states its three major values ('what we live for') to be love, peace, and purity. All of these are interpreted, however, in a special way, in the light of the value of unity. Bruderhof love, as we have seen, is not *eros* but *agape*. That is, it is love based not on attraction to personal attributes of another person, but on a shared feeling of partaking in God's all-encompassing love. 'Likes and dislikes of people are no part of this life. They can be no part of it,' said the wife of the Servant of the Word at Woodcrest.

When asked if special friendships ever naturally occurred, Emmy Arnold, the widow of the founder of the community, explained, 'Special liking of one person is reserved for marriage.

We are monogamous – not like the Oneida Community.' This curious response is very revealing. It indicates the acute awareness that the Brothers have of the constant danger, in a close community, of strong latent sexual feelings becoming manifest. Special love must be discouraged not only because of natural antipathies, but also because of natural attractions.

The Oneida Community was one of the more famous and successful of the nineteenth-century American intentional communities. John Humphrey Noyes, the community's founder and charismatic leader is the only person in the history of American communitarianism of comparable stature to Eberhard Arnold. Unlike Arnold, however, Noyes did not make provision for the continuance of the experiment after his death. Oneida never passed beyond the stage of charismatic community. It dissolved soon after Noyes died, although many of the members' descendants still live in the town and operate the communal business.

Although Oneida was a Christian community, similar in essence to the Bruderhof, they practiced a unique institution known as 'complex marriage', wherein all husbands and wives were shared in common. Complex marriage was seen as an opportunity to practice *agapic* love on the physical plane. Members were not supposed to be unduly influenced by physical and emotional considerations in the choice of sex partners. Furthermore, any strong attachment between two people, whether emotional or spiritual, was seen as a threat to the community and actively discouraged. Maren Lockwood Carden writes:

> By the community standards the most serious disadvantage of complex marriage was that couples frequently fell in love with each other. Community reports include frequent criticisms of men and women who failed to suppress one of these 'exclusive' or 'special' attachments. The rule of ascending fellowship was invoked to prevent young men and women from having sexual relations, in part because they were so likely to fall in love. If it was suspected that a woman refused a man's attentions because of greater love for another, she was severely criticized for lack of the appropriate 'public spirit'.[76]

Bruderhof love is not an independent value, but merely the emotional aspect of unity. Within the united Brotherhood, love is the natural condition. Experiencing love from one's Brothers is absolutely conditional on remaining a member of the community. One apostate couple, in which the husband had been a member of the Bruderhof for twenty years and the wife for ten years, spoke of the shock and bitterness at the reaction of the community to their exclusion:

We were sent to live in a cabin nearby. The two men who were taking us to our new house walked several feet in front of us, and didn't talk to us during the entire walk. Later, when we happened to meet a Brother on the street, he would never talk to us. Sometimes they would even turn their heads away . . . . One of the doors of our cabin faced toward the store (an outlet where the Bruderhof sold things that they made). One day a Brother put a bench in front of that door so that we couldn't use it but would have to use the side door (which was less visible to the store). I tell you it was just crazy! But who was crazy I wonder? Because we ourselves had acted the same way many times when a Brother had been excluded, and we had never thought about it at all [paraphrased].

Peace is another value held by the Bruderhof that is interpreted in terms of the value of unity. Of course, as I have mentioned, the Brothers are absolute pacifists who would not use violence under any circumstances:

We hold the desire not to ever fight back under any circumstances. If you do fight back you keep your life, you can still eat, but you lose all that you've been living for, if this is the principles of love and brotherhood.

And yet there is a suspicion that mere nonviolence is not enough. This is understandable in terms of the general Bruderhof emphasis on attitudes rather than behavior. The Bruderhof admires Gandhi and Martin Luther King, but with strong reservations.

Their way is much better than killing, that goes without question. But it's still force just as much as any other form of political action. True change must come spontaneously from the heart.

It might be said that love, for the Bruderhof, is the emotional aspect of unity and peace is the sociological manifestation of unity. In this sense, purity, the fourth Bruderhof value, can be understood as the moral touchstone of unity. It is in terms of the purity of actions and relationships that unity or disunity is discerned and controlled. Bruderhof members really worry about purity. They believe that one rotten apple spoils the barrel. Much of the system of social control, to be described in chapter five, is directed to keeping dissonance on any level out of the Bruderhof life. On the level of the individual, the value of purity requires purity of purpose (singlemindedness) and purity of conscience. There is no such thing, in the Bruderhof, as being a little bit sinful. Any deviance is as great as total deviance (although, of course, the remedy for the one need not be nearly as drastic as the remedy for the other).

On the group level, purity demands that there be complete unity in the Brotherhood. Even a single deviant cannot be tolerated. On both the individual and the group levels, purity is maintained through separation of the good from the bad. The idea is to isolate the sin; sometimes this has to include isolating the sinner.

On the inter-*hof* level, purity is also guarded carefully. Frequent exchange of members, especially leaders, and very frequent cross-visitation helps to augment inter-*hof* cooperation and destroy 'local patriotism'. There is even a provision of the exclusion system for excluding an entire *hof*. This is an extreme measure only rarely used. But if a *hof* considers itself in trouble it may ask for leaders of the other *hofs* to come and set things right.

During my stay at the Woodcrest Bruderhof, I was puzzled by an apparent contradiction between the great emphasis on isolating Brothers and children from any outside 'impure' influences on one hand, and the tremendous freedom given to high school and college students on the other hand. Great care is taken to see to it that the children never hear visitors, delivery men, or other outsiders say a dirty word. Play with neighborhood children is discouraged. The adult members very seldom retain membership in any outside organization, and at one time even their mail was censored and their newspapers and magazines were checked for objectionable material which was clipped out.

The high schoolers and the collegers, however, are treated completely differently. They are encouraged, and sometimes even prodded, to get into contact with the outside world. After college, unless they are absolutely certain that the Bruderhof is the life for them, they are urged to spend some time 'out on their own' in order to learn first-hand how people live in the outside world. 'Out on their own' does not mean fully abandoned though. The Bruderhof does remain in communication with these young people, helps them get jobs, and sees to it that they are boarded with wholesome Christian families.

There is really no contradiction between these two approaches. Both are products of the rotten-apple theory of purity. Adults and children are 'members' of the community – adults because they have chosen this way of life, and children because they have not yet reached the age of choice. As such, they themselves must be kept pure because they are the community and the community must be kept pure. But teenagers are not 'members' of the community in the same sense. They are in a transition period during which they need to make up their minds. Theoretically they should consider themselves – and be treated – no differently than any stranger who visits the community to consider joining. Naturally, the Bruderhof cannot help, in practice, treating them quite differently. But there is a concern that Bruderhof children not simply drift into the community because it is the path of least resistance. If it is hard for them to join the community and easy to go into the outside world, impure elements will be discouraged from joining. In this way, they hope that unity through the generations will be preserved.

If unity is important within the larger household, it is absolutely crucial within that select circle of the community – the Brotherhood. This is tricky because the Brotherhood is, after all, a decision-making body. Nor are the Brothers hypocritical about their desire that unity not degenerate into conformity. Perhaps no problem has so constantly plagued the Bruderhof as this one. A former Servant of the Word, who is now an apostate, commented:

There are a few moments where I can say there was real unity on the

Bruderhof. Very precious moments. And I wouldn't like to miss those. And they were genuine . . . . But the question of unity has become, in my opinion, a kind of dogma. I have seen on the Bruderhof, through all the years, this so-called unity work to the disadvantage of the group. (Q: All through the years from the very beginning?) I think so, because this asserted such a strong group pressure on the individual conscience, that the individual conscience couldn't function any more, and people got intimidated. And many times where it was a so-called united decision, it turned out afterwards, when it was a crisis, that people had been feeling differently. This became a pattern. So is it real unity? In my opinion, no. And yet, if a group makes a decision as a unity, and this unity is manifested and declared as the voice of God, who are you as an individual to stand against the voice of God? You must be a very presumptuous individual to do that.

The problem is that, in a total institution such as the Bruderhof, approval of the group assumes overwhelming importance. Only a very courageous man can resist. An ex-member reported:

You get the feeling, 'everyone is against me'. This is not always an illusion. The bandwagon effect is really there . . . [and the people who] participate in it are often subjectively sincere. Once it's pointed out to me, I really do feel this way [hostile] about this person. You do get a kind of amplification effect sitting around in a circle like that in the Brotherhood meeting.

This is the negative side of joy. In unity, the individual loses his autonomy and along with it often his sense of responsibility. 'I never thought less during any time in my life,' said a woman speaking about her ten years as a Bruderhof member. The unity of the *gemeinde* is structurally similar to the unity of the mob. The danger is always present that the collective emotions which the feeling of unity gives license to will be mob emotions rather than exalted feelings of rapport with the Kingdom of God. One ex-Brother described a shattering experience that he had before the Brotherhood:

[Q: Were you at the Brotherhood meeting that made the decision to send you away?] Oh, I was at it! [grim laughter] I'll never forget that. If you sit and have some thirty or more Brothers all in a circle, and you're one of them, and they all point the accusing finger at you, and you feel it go through the whole Brotherhood, you can't forget it too quickly. [Question from respondent's eight-year-old son: Was mother even against you then?] Well, she wasn't against me, we won't say. But she was for . . . she felt the Brotherhood must be right. [Q: Did anybody speak up in your defense?] Not as such, no. [Q: Did anyone even question?] Yes, there were some questions. But the ones who I felt were most understanding were just quiet. One of the teachers said: 'Well, I remember the day before yesterday, the children were out ice-skating, and I could see how mean B. [another son of the respondent] was. I saw him just stick out his foot and trip one of the girls and she fell flat on her face.' And then a murmur would go through the whole crowd, of agreement, how mean he must have been. Then another said, 'We think B. is your favorite child . . . '

If a person turns out to have been wrong about a decision, he must stand up before the Brotherhood and make a public confession – even if many others were also wrong. The mood of mass confession is completely different from the mood of individual confession. The former is solemn and serious but not always in an unpleasant way. Especially if the Brothers see the light beyond the present crisis, there is an exciting feeling of shared expectation in the air. Such 'clearances', as the Bruderhof calls these mass confessions, are often followed by intense euphoric experiences. An individual confession, on the other hand, is merely an irksome duty, and generally is a bore to the Brotherhood. Brothers cannot help but be aware of this fact. One apostate, explaining why he did not speak his mind on occasions when he strongly dissented from a Brotherhood decision, said, 'It was safer to go the wrong way with the majority and confess later when all the others did, than to go it alone and risk being knocked down alone.'

'Consenting with a heavy heart' is a partial means of escape from this dilemma. This is a behavior pattern borrowed from the Hutterians, whose complex business organization often necessitates rapid decision-making. If a Brother cannot consent to a decision but action cannot be postponed, he may consent 'with a heavy heart' indicating thus that he does so only for the sake of expediency. In the Bruderhof too, this form of consent, at one time in the past, was used in decisions relating to the business enterprise. Expansion of the pattern would be of great aid to the Bruderhof in preventing dangerous situations of pseudo-unity.

The enforcement of unity as an ultimate value is important in making unity a structural condition of Bruderhof life. It is not sufficient. The structural situation itself is an important determinant of the degree of unity to be found in the life. In *Conflict and the Web of Group Affiliations*, Georg Simmel states:

> ... to belong to any one ... group leaves the individual considerable leeway. But the larger the number of groups to which an individual belongs, the more improbable is it that other persons will exhibit the same combination of group affiliations [in a second individual] that these particular groups will intersect again.[77]

In the Bruderhof, one is rarely allowed to retain membership in an outside organization. For a while, many ex-Quaker members retained their memberships in the Fellowship of Reconciliation, an international pacifist organization. Finally, even this was abandoned. Even group membership in organizations like the Fellowship of Intentional Communities, was dropped because of the danger of individuals gaining conflicting statuses from two different organizations. All Bruderhof statuses derive from the Brotherhood.

The pattern of everyday life is arranged to facilitate unity. The day is scheduled to synchronize activities. Special events in the individual's life, such as birthdays, weddings, childbirths, are made into group experiences. As we saw in the description of a Bruderhof engagement, everybody from the smallest children to the oldest grandparents, contributes something to the wedding celebration. Therefore everybody is a part of it; it belongs to everybody.

Of course, it is never possible to eliminate disunity completely from communal life. The Bruderhof life is a constant struggle to find consensus in the midst of ever-emerging new disagreements. Policy matters especially are a fertile source of disagreement. As one member put it: 'We all agree on the deepest things, like our confession of faith, and on the trivial. It's on the middle range that we develop disagreements.' It's easy to see why such 'middle range' matters – matters of policy – should be the greatest source of disagreement. On deep and on trivial matters alike, unity is defined as more important than any particular stand on any particular issue. Believing or not believing in the Virgin Birth, for instance, or dining at six-thirty or at seven, are issues that are of far less importance to everyone than that everyone in the community believe the same thing about the Virgin Birth and that everyone in the community dine at the same time. The individual who is socialized to expect his payoff in the joy of the collective behavior experience knows that his interests lie more in belonging to a fellowship of common belief than in being able to hold to any theological principle in particular, more in dining with all of his Brothers than in dining at the time that is most convenient to him.

But this is not the case for matters of policy. Here the issue often is precisely one of how unity can best be achieved. The individual perceives the outcome of the issue as directly affecting his payoff. Therefore unity on policy matters is not enough. Each individual must be assured that the policy decided upon is designed to augment future unity.

Another source of disunity impossible to eradicate from Bruderhof life is that stemming from age and sex classification. The community is aware of this problem. They say that the euphoria at El Arado was much stronger and 'freer' than in other *hofs*. (El Arado was the *hof* in Uruguay which was composed mostly of young adults.) Age and sex classifications give rise to statuses not derived from the Brotherhood. As such, they interfere with absolute control of the Brotherhood over the status system. The Bruderhof attempts to guard against this problem by building justifications for sex and age status differences, such as those discussed in chapter three, into the ideological framework of the life. But these independent status systems have always been, and probably always will be, a source of disruption in the Bruderhof system.

Despite these inevitable sources of disunity, the Bruderhof has succeeded in developing an extraordinarily high degree of unity among its members. When a collective behavior experience breaks down the boundaries of each individual's separate ego, a collective ego can emerge that is exceptionally rich, pervasive, and inclusive. The sense of many individuals directed by a single purpose, which is so common in crowds and mobs, is amplified many times in the Bruderhof by the knowledge that this sense is in fact the real condition of the group in its everyday life.

## 5. *Depth of Participation*

The following is an excerpt from a letter written to me by a social scientist who had, in his youth, been a member of the Bruderhof for eleven years:

> It is no surprise to notice that the Bruderhof ideology bears close resemblance to paranoid delusive structures; the difference being only that it is held by a whole social group, not by an individual, and adopted, not invented. Think of grandeur: to be a member of an elite which has the only true way of life, and thus is superior, even in its meanest members, to all the great of this world; whose communal and personal struggles have not only a worldwide, but also a pan-historical, and even a cosmic significance. Think of the externalization of evil impulses in the Evil Spirits which fight the good spirit. Think of the persecution and martyrdom fantasies, e.g., of H.'s flaming envy of the martyrs of the German resistance movement.
>
> ... explanations of euphoria which restrict themselves to the pleasantness of a cooperative environment, the freedom from individual choice, the sense of shared purpose, or even mild intoxication with religious imagery, seem to me too pallid to do justice to the reality . . . .

As the letter indicates, the intensity of the euphoric experience is a function not only of the collective state of the group, but also of the individual state of each person, and finally of the tension between the two.

The typical Bruderhof recruit is characterized by a low sense of self-esteem. He thinks of himself as lacking in comparison, not to other people, but rather to his ideal self. Some Bruderhof members had been quite successful in the outside world and were aware, and even proud, of this fact. But in almost all cases this success did not begin to measure up to the demands which the individual had placed upon himself. In other words, the self-contempt that characterizes Bruderhof recruits is a product of the impossibly high standards that they set for themselves rather than any objective failures.

The self-contempt of the initiate is the raw material with which the Bruderhof works. It seeks to make the isolated individual ego so distasteful to the member that he will have a powerful incentive for fleeing this state and taking refuge in the collective behavior experience. One ex-member described the pressure thus placed on the individual as involving the following steps:

Your anxiety was real; we intensified it and confirmed it. Your rejection of the world was right; we confirm that rejection. Your rejection of the self was right; we confirm that rejection. Now accept a Good Self (the role as community member) which is also a good world. And continue to reject the Bad World (Bad Parent), which is identified with the Bad Self.

Self-rejection is thus linked to world-rejection and both are tied to community acceptance through the Bruderhof socialization process. In this way, two prerequisites for high individual commitment to the group are engendered: that the individual have a strongly felt need for something obtainable from the group, and that the individual perceive the group as the only possible source of this need gratification.

In order to give something of the flavor of the pressures which this situation places on the individual, let me quote at length from the account of the experiences of one man who considered joining the Bruderhof, but left before becoming a Brother:

I was in the garden. I was working all by myself, weeding straw-berries. And I felt very, very upset. I thought, 'Here my wife and my kids are just crazy about this place, and this stupid Apostles' Creed hangs over me. Oh, if I could only believe what they believe!' And, so, I thought, 'I'm going to pray right now.' I knelt down in the row and I started to pray: 'Oh, God help me . . .' and I thought, 'No! I cannot pray that. I can pray to know the truth. I cannot pray to believe what other people believe.' And, it was a terrible crisis in my life. It was the most severe crisis in my life. Then I got up and I made a very quick decision. It just suddenly came over me – I cannot do that. I want to know what is true. I must try to find out what God's will is for me.

So then the next thing that happened was that I had a dream at night. I woke up in a cold sweat and tossed around. Margaret said, 'What's wrong?' I said, 'I just had a terrible dream.' She said, 'What was it?' I said, 'Well, I dreamt that I had a job to do.' In Celo (a community with an individualist basis they had previously belonged to) we lived in the woods, you know, we cut all our own wood. And when you begin to cut a tree down with an ax, you notch it on one side. I said, 'I dreamt that I had a piece of cutting to do. And my job was to cut my own head off. And I was notching one side and making it bigger, and all of a sudden I could feel the warm blood streaming down my back. And I still was perfectly certain about exactly what I had to do and I ran into the house. And I said, 'Margaret, you've got to come and help me. I'm going to kill myself before I get through with this job, and you'll have to finish it up.' 'Well,' she said, 'that's a terrible dream. I don't know what it means, but I think you should go and talk to the Servant about that.'

So, I went to talk to him. He said, 'How do you interpret that dream?' I said, 'I think I have a fear that I am cutting off a part of my personality – my rationality, my intellectual center. I feel the drive to cut it off, so that I can join the Bruderhof.' He said, 'You're an anxious person. And it's too bad that you're so anxious. You have unreasonable fears, and so on. We don't destroy anybody's intellectuality here.' But then he counseled me to come back if other things bothered me.

Soon I had another dream. Woke up again in a cold sweat. What was it? Well, we were building that great big apartment house, you know the one where the old carriage house was before it burned down. We had been having a big build that day. Our boys had been up on the roof, and all of us together were finishing it up. And I dreamt we were out there building. I was off at the side, and they were putting steel bands around it, fastening them up tight. And you could see the building just shaking inside of the steel bands. And Margaret said, 'Why do they put steel bands around?' I said, 'Why, Margaret, it's perfectly obvious. If they didn't have the steel bands around it, it would all fly to pieces.'

So I told the Servant about that too. And again he had much the same things to say: 'Your fear of external restraint on people is unreasonable. Our commitment here is just as free as water flowing over a dam . . . . There's no restraint.' And so, I would try to think about that.

A little while after that, we went to visit the W's. And they talked a lot about how happy they were in the Bruderhof. And I told them some of the difficulties that I had been having with the Apostles' Creed. And Jack W. said, in his real loud way, 'Oh, I wouldn't have anything to do with that when I was a novice.' I said, 'You wouldn't? But they told me we had to believe it.' Then he had very little to say, but he said, 'They couldn't get me to say that.' His wife had very little to say, except that they all said how nice it was to be there, and how wonderful it was, what a wonderful life.

I went home, and that night I had a dream. I dreamt that all the Bruderhof, all these friends of mine were under the kitchen sink. You know the little place that they have right under a kitchen sink with the pipes coming down? I hadn't noticed them there, and all of a sudden I noticed them there. And they said, 'Come on in. Come on in, Dan. It's so wonderful here. We're so happy.' And I said, 'Well, I will.' And I tried to go in, and I couldn't get in. And I said, 'I can't get under there. I'm too tall.'

Well, I would talk about those things. I was trying to thrash it out. I was hoping that I could become a Bruderhof member. That if I confronted it honestly, then the light would come . . . .

Finally, I made up my mind. I woke up at night one night and I said, 'Margaret, I've got to leave here.' And she said, 'But Dan, we gave all our money.' I said, 'We loaned it to them.' They had said they needed money to build and they were wondering where they could get some, and we had said we'll loan you our money. I said, 'I feel if we have to crawl down out of this mountain, we should leave.' And she said, 'When you do, Dan, I'm going to go too.' It was a very tremendous decision for us. The boys didn't want to leave. As soon as they heard about it, oh! they dissolved in tears. But we prepared to leave. We talked to the Servant and he agreed that we should leave . . . . I think we still had enough money left to get home. So, we left. And as soon as we got to the bottom of the mountain, the boys' tears dried up and they said, 'Well, we're glad we're gone.' They welcomed us back at Celo, and we were very happy we left. And soon, Margaret was very happy she left, too.

For the initiate, the final stage of ego loss comes with baptism. But it would be a mistake to think that the struggle against the ego occurs just once in the life of each individual. Actually, Bruderhof life is an ever continuing struggle between the ego and the collective self. It is characterized by ever-recurring lapses, confessions, and periods of cleansing and renewal, both for each individual and for the entire community.

The collective behavior experience may be likened to a trip from the state of individuality to the state of collective identity. In the section on unity, we saw how the Bruderhof structure increases the frequency of such trips by means of positive reinforcement at the point of destination. Now we have seen how the same goals are also furthered through negative reinforcement at the point of departure. The third inducement will be discussed next – that of making the voyage itself easy, safe, and pleasant.

## 6. *The Interpretive Framework*

The experience of losing individual selfhood and merging into a collective self can be perceived in many ways. Often it is accompanied by feelings of panic and dread. Sometimes, on the other hand, it may bring about a state of lassitude and apathy similar to that experienced by Odysseus' men on the island of the lotus eaters. Neither of these variants of the experience would be functional for Bruderhof life. What the Bruderhof strives for is a collective behavior experience of rebirth and renewal, endowing flagging enthusiasms with the freshness and vigor of their beginnings – a positive experience, and yet one which demands ever renewed effort on the part of each individual.

For this to occur, the Bruderhof must create a spiritual climate in which elements of passivity and activity are delicately balanced. This is accomplished by means of the myth, which was discussed in chapter one, of Man as the battleground between the forces of good and evil – literally, between good and evil spirits. Man, himself, is helpless against either of these forces (hence the passivity). His only ability – and it is a crucial one – is to choose which of the forces will dominate him (hence the activity).

So far there is nothing special about this myth. It is similar to the myths of many of the established Protestant churches. Where the Bruderhof differs from other Christian sects, and shows itself to be Anabaptist, is that the battle between good and evil is immanent rather than transcendent. Neither heaven nor the souls of individual men are the battleground, but rather the earth itself and the community itself. The Bruderhof quite literally believes that the Church (by which it means the living community of men and women and children) is the beachhead through which God may enter the enemy territory – the world.

The writings of the founder of the Bruderhof illustrate the consequences of belief in this myth:

> The Church must be brought to Christ as a pure virgin. The Church's task, therefore, is to wait for Christ in spotless readiness. A Church with the ultimate earnestness, with the holiest task, does not believe *in* people but believes *for* people, believes that the spirit rules over the body through the soul. This can take place only when God's Spirit commands the body . . . .
>
> Where the bride is, the bridegroom is. Where the city-church is, the Spirit is. The one and only way the city-church can come into being is through the Spirit coming to us.[78]

But the Brothers can, at the same time, say:

> We are soldiers in the army of God, fighting to win back a portion of the universe for the Holy Spirit. You may think our life is constant happiness and joy, but underneath there is a constant struggle going on every day among us and within each of us.

The first of these beliefs puts the Bruderhof member in the passive, or responsive, frame of mind necessary to fully 'receive the Spirit'. He feels overwhelmed by something greater than himself, something that will completely engulf him. But he is aware that he has chosen to be so engulfed voluntarily, and furthermore he believes that the force is a benevolent one. Therefore, he may feel awe and trembling, but will usually not experience dread or panic.

The second of these beliefs supplies the equally necessary active or initiatory urge to do something beyond merely feeling and enjoying the experience. Thus the Brothers see the Spirit as a form of energy which they can use in their work. One Brother described his feelings about the *Gemeindestunde*: 'It refreshes you by sort of a dry-cleaning process, calling attention to the big things – this justifies the sweating in the fields.' Another spoke of times when he was especially tired and felt like skipping a communal meal. But, if he forced himself to go, he found that he finished the meal feeling more charged with energy than if he had gone home to take a nap.

The myth of the immanent battle between good and evil serves as an interpretive framework for the collective behavior experience by explaining what is happening, why it is happening, and why it should be happening. The framework ensures that roughly the same external stimuli will touch off collective behavior experiences in all of the community members at the same time: it is therefore also a part of the triggering process.

## 7. *The Triggering Process*

We are concerned with two aspects of the triggering process: first, simply that certain triggering mechanisms exist, and second, that all individuals respond to them in roughly the same way. It should be clear from the discussion so far that, in the Bruderhof, there are no precipitating mechanisms originating outside the system – as is the case, for instance, with collective behavior among lynch mobs or in revival meetings. Any system which hopes to be governed by regular participation in collective behavior experiences must have internal triggering mechanisms.

The search for unity in the Brotherhood leads to euphoria. When it is discovered that the decision on which unity has been reached has not succeeded in solving the community's problems, euphoria is lost. Disappointment provokes tension as the search for unity is begun again. Another crisis may even ensue. A cyclical two phase pattern of alternating periods of struggle and joy is thus perpetuated.

One of the first members of the Bruderhof reminisced about the early years of the community:

I don't know what kept me there through those years. During the first seven years after Eberhard's death, every year we had at least one crisis. [Q: Did you feel after the crisis was over that something had been achieved?] Sure we felt after the crisis that something had been achieved. But it only showed later what had been achieved. We went from one swing of the pendulum to the other.

Perhaps this member wasn't quite aware of what had been achieved. The function of these crises was undoubtedly at least as much to provide the impetus for a new wave of euphoria as to determine policy on any substantive issue. Although subsequent cycles have sometimes lasted longer than a year, the crisis has continued to be the major triggering mechanism of Brotherhood euphoria down through the entire history of the Bruderhof, to the present day.

Here I am in danger of giving a very wrong impression – that euphoria in the Bruderhof is attained only in vast swallows, after crises in which the Brotherhood has ceased to exist. This is indeed one major way in which joy is attained, and I stress it because the contours of the process are clearest on this large scale. But Bruderhof life is actually an intricate composition of many types, sizes, and scales of crisis and joy. The ocean provides a useful analogy. A major pattern of successive waves gives the surf its basic form, but within that form, countless smaller wave sequences create a rich, asymmetrical, constantly varying pattern within a pattern. Each occasion of coming together in unity on a decision in the Brotherhood is an occasion for joy. Each soul-searching before a *Gemeindestunde*, followed by coming together in unity for prayer, is a signal for joy. Each individual's own struggle with his conscience is, in a very real sense, a kind of crisis. And each victory in such a struggle is a signal for joy, not only in the individual himself, but also in his Brothers:

That was one of my troubles, giving up clothing. Certain skirts. One velvet skirt I had [laughing], oh, how I loved that velvet skirt! [Q: Why did you have to give it up?] Well, to give up and not to care about anything particularly – and you see we all had to struggle that way – we were made to feel, in that life, that you shouldn't want something particularly pretty, and that looked well on you, that compliments you. This was pride. And you should in order to really grow . . . in order to be like God would wish you to be, you would give up these things. Well, I remember I struggled with this and finally one day I was able to march over with a few of these things, and my velvet skirt. And I just felt, when I expressed this to them [the Housemothers] A. and L., *they rejoiced with me.*

For some, it is these rather simple joys that constitute the major payoff of Bruderhof life – not at all the big joy. As one ex-member put it:

I'd definitely make a distinction between ordinary joy in the Bruderhof and the joy that came after a crisis. To tell you the truth, there was something about the post-crisis joy that I was never comfortable with. I can't say exactly what, but I know that for me the real joy always came while I was alone, working in the fields, and feeling in complete unity with myself and my Brothers [paraphrased].

It would also be a mistake to present an image of this crisis-joy cycle as something obeying fixed laws in itself. The cycle can be and has been purposely manipulated by leaders. Said one ex-member:

H. was a master at management of the crisis. He knew just when things needed shaking up. He knew how to shake them up. And he knew how far to go.

Another informant was less cynical:

It's not that anyone would consciously say to himself, 'Hmm, things are getting sort of dull. Maybe we'd better have a crisis.' But there'd sort of be a feeling – and I think everybody would get it – that something was wrong, something deep inside that didn't have the power to get out. Then a good Servant could step in . . . .

## 8. *Mobilization for Action*

We have seen how the Bruderhof maintains the structural conditions for and generates the precipitation of a steady supply of joy. Now we must turn to the question of how this joy is turned into a steady and reliable source of enthusiasm for and commitment to the community. The three major functional problems to be discussed are the ephemeral nature of euphoria, its sporadic nature, and the wave-like rhythm of its intensity.

In most of social life there is a rather sharp distinction between modes of institutional behavior and modes of collective behavior.

Perhaps the major factor leading to the ability of the Bruderhof to transform euphoria into useful energy is the lack of such a distinction in the Bruderhof. Now we are in a position to understand fully the functional value of the bearing-witness ideology. By endowing every aspect of the life with sacred significance, the Bruderhof paves the way for the routinization of euphoria. In response to the question, 'When did the joy come?' an apostate Sister, who was also a *sabra*, replied:

It came at different times. It's impossible to say when. I wouldn't especially say in the meetings – some meetings yes – but not always – also not always in the work, but sometimes.

And I recall the statement of the Bruderhof member asked about formal worship:

We have no gestures or forms. What's inside is important. The spirit of life is trying to get in all the time, and when we get it it can either be in a meeting or digging potatoes.

The Bruderhof, then, copes with the ephemeral nature of collective behavior in much the same way that a farmer copes with evaporation of moisture from the soil. The worst sort of soil for this purpose is hard, solid and sloped. The rain tends to stay on the surface and either drain off quickly or collect in one or a few places. In either case, most of it is quickly lost to evaporation. This corresponds to the form taken by collective behavior in the typical town or organization. Because it cannot fit into the fabric of the routine life of such groups, it tends to create its own place in the group life. As in the craze or panic, it may merely run along the surface of the group life, like water running down a hill. Or, as in the cases of revival meetings or the bacchanalia of ancient Rome, it may be able to form a distinct institution of its own. But if it does, the energy produced will be concentrated and intense, like water running down from all sources into a common pool. As such it will have only limited effect on the rest of the group life and will tend to evaporate most quickly.

The best kind of terrain for retaining moisture is softly rolling, its soil permeated with plant roots and other forms of subterranean life. Rain falling on such soil soaks deeply into every part, and the rate of evaporation is minimized. This is what happens to the collective behavior experience in the Bruderhof. Because every part of the life, from the most trivial to the most important, has significance both in the realm of the sacred and the realm of the profane, there is therefore no part of the life that cannot be touched and affected by the experience.

The spreading of joy through all the routines of life also means that the joyful experience will be one of controlled intensity. The pace of the common routine, its task orientation, the fact that the experience is perceived in the context of business as usual – these serve as brakes upon the intensity. Finally, there is the interpretive framework, in which joy is seen, not as an emotional experience, but as an aid to task fulfillment. Thus the euphoric mood is kept from being whipped up into a frenzy which would soon spend itself.

How does this integration into the life make joy less ephemeral? Consider the Bruderhof emerging from a hypothetical crisis. Some people have felt that the community should be doing more social work and political activity in the larger society. This has been the subject of a long and bitter debate. During the course of the debate several Brothers have been excluded, some have voluntarily quit the community, and perhaps there has been a turnover in Servants. Now at last, let us say, the Brotherhood sees the light. Unity of purpose is regained. Stable leadership has been found. The excludees are beginning to see the error of their way and return to the fold. How does all of this affect the community?

On the behavioral level, what has brought about a new wave of euphoria is success in the decision-making process. Because of the very nature of such a process, success comes gradually rather than all of a sudden, and euphoria also builds up gradually. But let us say that there is one particular Brotherhood meeting in which a final consensus is reached. This consensus has extension both into the sacred and into the secular realms. One aspect of it is a concrete decision to spend so much money, during the next few years, on buying land and building up a new *hof* in a certain densely populated area. Another aspect of it is the implicit decision not to spend money on other things which some had felt were more important – perhaps one of these things is college educations for Bruderhof children. A third part of the consensus, and probably that which is most emphasized, is the attainment of a new understanding of the nature of community, of the real (sacred) meaning of the family and parent-child relationships, and of the importance of missionary work.

Around 11:00 p.m., unanimous consensus is finally achieved. What happens next? Certainly there is a feeling of exultation in the air. Perhaps some stirring communal songs are sung. But, in general, it is late; the Brothers are tired (most of them have worked a full day at manual labor), and the decision itself points to many new tasks and sacrifices that will have to be undertaken. There is also a sobering mood in the air. Rather than spending all night in joyous celebration, the Brotherhood goes home to bed. Tomorrow they will have to be up at 6:00 or 7:00 to send the children off to school and get ready for work. Instead of concentrating the intense joy into a single wild celebration, circumstances cause it to spread out instead as a glow over the life.

Everything that the Brothers do in their lives has a sacred significance. Therefore everything is directly affected by the Brotherhood decision. When a husband and wife return from the Brotherhood meeting to their apartment and see their children, they are filled with a special joy, coming from a new realization of the sacred meaning of the family relationship and from the knowledge that they are at unity with the entire community in their understanding of this relationship. They feel the Holy Spirit to be present, filling the relationship with His own sacred light. Similarly, the couple's own relationship is a receptacle for the Holy Spirit. Their love-making is filled with it in a special way. The way that they see their entire relationship is altered and enhanced by the achievement of unity.

The next day at work, the Brothers and Sisters greet each other with fresh remembrances of their common euphoria. Each member throws himself into his work with new vigor. Individuals are moved to spontaneous acts of kindness toward one another. These acts become contagious. Perhaps the children's reaction to their parents' reaction to them the night before has set the stage for a new wave of joy breaking out in the school. This in turn, reinforces the joy of the grownups. Bruderhof guests tend to notice that something special has happened, and respond to it in a very favorable way. This may tend to reinforce the members' belief that the Bruderhof is indeed in the presence of the Holy Spirit.

Because every aspect of the life is accessible to sacred interpretation, it is not necessary even for all joy to originate in the resolution of a crisis or difficult decision. Any interaction at any time, any task, any activity can be the starting point for a wave of joy. This can be the case even while the community as a whole is in a state of crisis, which tends to dampen the contrast between euphoric and crisis stages in the cycle.

Nevertheless, there are quite striking changes in the quality of Bruderhof life as it passes into or out of a great wave of joy. The crisis-euphoria cycle makes this inevitable but, aside from this cycle, collective behavior in general seems always to occur sporadically. How does the Bruderhof cope with this problem?

Unlike its ephemerality, the sporadic nature of collective behavior has not been eliminated by the Bruderhof system. Rather, the system has accommodated to it. The Bruderhof is able to switch between two different modes of existence, appropriate for crises and times of euphoria, respectively. The community calls these modes creative withdrawal and outreach. Each has its own motivating force and its own goals and satisfactions.

The Bruderhof is able to muddle through its crisis times, its periods of creative withdrawal, for several reasons. One is that the community is designed to be able to cut down rapidly on the pressures placed on it. Economic survival takes up only a small part of the energy of the Brothers, in comparison with other, spiritual, concerns. During a crisis, it is completely legitimate, according to the Bruderhof ideology, to retreat inward and concentrate only on the community itself and the crisis problems at hand. This is a function of the supreme value given to unity as a value by the Bruderhof. Without unity nothing of importance can be accomplished. So during a crisis it is permissible to stop publishing, expel all visitors and guests, and cease any social-work activities, in order to work single-mindedly on the problem of regaining unity. At the same time that the motivating force for remaining in the Bruderhof is taken away, the demands of the system on the individual are decreased. This may be perceived by the individual as a form of (comparative) payoff.

During crises, joy is replaced with the 'spirit of the fight', which has a kind of euphoric air of its own. 'We are living for a cause in the same way that the Communists are. This life is a struggle going on every day,' we were told by the Servant of the Word during a recent Bruderhof crisis. During crisis situations the community borrows some of the techniques of *esprit de corps* of a combat battalion or a football team. The euphoria it produces is the euphoria of shared suffering.

Another method of surviving non-euphoric periods is especially necessary for times that are neither joyous nor crisis-ridden, but merely boring. I mentioned earlier that a boring period may be seen as symptomatic of some hidden wrong and may lead to a situation in which a crisis is deliberately provoked. But, of course, this is the exception rather than the rule. Generally, such periods are met with an attitude of expectation or faith. The attainment of a childlike sense of expectation is perhaps the key part of the Bruderhof socialization process. The Bruderhof member is taught about the sporadic nature of the Spirit – 'God doesn't need us. The Holy Spirit can leave us at any time. It's not a possession.' The Bruderhof learns to expect crises and, what is more important, to expect the joyful end of all crises, even when this is nowhere in sight. Here the non-linear conception of time – the myth of the eternal return – discussed in chapter one becomes functional. During a crisis, the Bruderhof member has the feeling that he's been through all this before. It's always turned out right in the past. Therefore it will turn out all right this time.

The periods in which euphoria is absent are perhaps less potentially destructive for a community than are the times when euphoria itself gets out of hand. Collective behavior is dangerous stuff. Observers of the phenomenon know how volatile it can be – how rapidly a boisterous dance can turn into an ugly melee, or a holiday crowd into an angry mob. One of the problems is un-predictability. Another is the apparent wave nature of collective behavior emotions, their tendency to oscillate between extremes. In communities these extremes have often become the extremes of love and hatred, of creation and destruction.

Euphoria is kept from becoming too highly positive through techniques of structured intimacy. There are set forms for express-ing intimate feelings of brotherly love, appreciation, etc. By allowing the Brothers to express these feelings, but only in set forms, the Bruderhof is able to keep the intensity of the emotions within bounds. Heightening demands for self-examination and self-control accompany very euphoric periods. This reaches its culmination in the institution of the Lord's Supper. The Lord's Supper is the highest expression of unity in the Bruderhof. Only when it is felt that there is perfect unity will a Lord's Supper be held. But the preparation for this event involves intense and pro-longed soul-searching on the part of all members, such as is usually only required of the novice or the excludee. Several times, the digging up of old sins during the preparation for a Lord's Supper has provoked a crisis instead.

Dealing with negative emotion released by Brotherhood euphoria is a bit more complicated. The basic mechanism involved is the displacement of generalized anger and hostility onto the scapegoat – usually a Servant of the Word. The Bruder-hof has institutionalized, and the ideology legitimized, a pattern of replacing Servants during times of trouble. For an under-standing of how this works, we must now turn to the general subject of leadership and social control.

> the myth of the golden bough

## *Chapter Five* □ LEADERSHIP AND SOCIAL CONTROL

The Bruderhof attempts to base its system of social control on voluntarism and on authoritarianism at the same time. This combination is by no means rare for intentional communities. Caplow points out that:

> The frequent combination of autocratic headship and democratic election [in the utopian community] is significant. The individual voluntarily assigns to the organization a general right to police him and cooperates in group exercises to make him less resistant to policing. In the successful utopia, the rules are internalized to an extraordinary degree.[79]

One of the strengths of the Bruderhof system comes from a successful merging of near total control at the organizational level and voluntary enthusiastic commitment at the individual level. They are equally necessary. Without the community's ability to legitimate its concern for every aspect of its members' lives, the total involvement needed for the collective behavior process would be progressively weakened. Without the individual's commitment to this totalitarianism, social control would be effective only in so far as behavior was visible.

The Bruderhof member is socialized to respond with methodical compliance to the community's demand for information about every aspect of his life. One ex-Brother told me how it was impossible for him to keep from confessing his sexual fantasies even when these appeared involuntarily in dreams. But no collectivity can rely merely on self-surveillance as a means of social control. In the Bruderhof, self-surveillance and self-correction help to maintain order, but they are buttressed by a tough and practical system of sanctions, legitimated by the Christian ideology.

As long as Eberhard Arnold was alive, he was the final court of appeals for all community disputes. He had a prophetic authority which minimized divisions which otherwise would have been more dangerous. When Eberhard led his flock into the Hutterian Church, one of his purposes was to find a functional alternative to this dependence upon himself as an ultimate court. Even during this present time of coolness toward the Hutterians, the Bruderhof acknowledges the success of this quest and its importance for the Bruderhof's survival after the death of Arnold:

> Our debt to the Hutterites is beyond measure. They gave us the Orders. Before the Orders we had the Spirit but we always floundered.

The Orders are essentially a system of sanctions based on varying degrees of exclusion from the community life and a system of hierarchical distribution of executive responsibilities. Together, these form the basis of the Bruderhof's system of social control.

## 1. *The Exclusion System*

> Moreover if thy brother shall trespass against thee, go and tell him his fault between him and thee alone; if he shall hear thee, thou hast gained thy brother. But if he will not hear thee, then take with thee one or two more, that in the mouth of two or three witnesses every word may be established. And if he shall neglect to hear them, tell it unto the church: but if he neglect to hear the church, let him be unto thee as an heathen man and a publican.[80]

The four-hundred-year-old Hutterian confederation of communities has evolved a workable set of sanctions independent of the presence of a charismatic leader. These sanctions derive their legitimacy from the words of Christ in the Gospel of Matthew quoted above. They range from the mildest of admonitions, through various degrees of exclusion from the communal life, to the severest sanction – expulsion from the community.

Admonishment in the Bruderhof is a formal institution. It is the most common and mildest of the sanctions. If a person has a grudge against, or a criticism of, another person, he is required to go directly to that person and speak to him about the problem. Keeping resentments to oneself or gossiping are, as we have seen, strictly forbidden. Admonishment is seen as a service. As an ex-member put it:

The community life is a mirror – it shows you what you are, and sometimes you don't like what you see. If one member notices that another is dour, lazy, or stubborn, he tells him so, using a judicious mixture of tact and point-blank severity, and he expects him to apologize and change his ways.

The admonisher can be tough and sharp when necessary, but he must also be humble, never superior or self-righteous. The person being criticized must listen patiently, thankfully, and openly. If he haughtily rejects the criticism, he is liable to get into even more trouble for pride, even if the criticism itself proves groundless. Successful admonishment often triggers a warm, mild euphoria in both admonisher and admonished.

If two members cannot resolve a problem themselves, they ask one or two Witness Brothers to help them. If the matter is serious, they may even consult with a larger number of Witness Brothers and, perhaps, a Servant. If the critic, the criticized, and the Witness Brothers still cannot resolve the problem, then it is brought to the Brotherhood. Now it becomes more serious. It will probably require a public confession or perhaps even an exclusion.

An ex-member who read the above account had this comment:

The classical form from Matthew, as you describe it, is accurate, but it almost never happened in quite that form . . . because if something was trivial, usually an admonition was enough. It was kind of rare that anyone would be that stubborn. I think it did happen in one or two cases that I can remember. I remember the one and only new German member that we got after the second world war. He was a Ph.D. in economics and . . . he seems to have been such a case. He stuck his chin out and someone admonished and he wouldn't take it. So they got a little circle which worked on him and he wouldn't take that. So they got him in the Brotherhood and he wouldn't take that. Then the Servant shouted at him, and he got up and walked out and that was it, he left us – the Servant shouting after him, 'Repent! Repent!'

The classical form for admonishment, although rarely followed step by step, is a basis which can be adapted to particular problems.

If a problem cannot be settled by admonishment, the community must resort to some form of exclusion of the sinful party from communal activities. The legitimacy of the use of exclusion, beyond the fact that it is Christ's teaching, comes from the absolute primacy given to unity. Sin is contagious and must be isolated, through admonishment if possible. If not, the sinner himself must be isolated, to protect the community until the sin is gone.

There are various grades of exclusion. The mildest is exclusion from the *Gemeindestunde*, either just once or indefinitely, until reform is demonstrated. For more serious offenses, a person may also be excluded from Brotherhood meetings. (This is known in the Hutterian Orders as *Bedenkzeit*.) Next there is small exclusion (*Kleiner Ausschluss*), in which the Brother is allowed only minimal contact with the other community members during the daily routine; and great exclusion (*Grosser Ausschluss*) in which he has absolutely no participation in the daily life of the *hof*. The most severe form of exclusion is to be sent away from the Bruderhof completely, to make one's own way in the world.[81]

These grades are not rigid categories. Especially after the break with the Hutterians in the early 1950s, exclusion categories became quite fluid. An ex-member who was present during both the Hutterite and post-Hutterite periods reports:

It seemed to me that the form of the exclusion got more liberal as time went on too. To put it extremely, at the beginning of this time there were just about three grades, period: out of the *Gemeindestunde*, small exclusion, and great exclusion (or else being sent away). When you got excluded they read a Hutterian script at you . . . . One of the phrases is, 'Because you have despised God, and because you have put yourself outside the community,' . . . . Later, things that were formerly a matter of rigid rule, became a matter of functional adjustment, to see what would help this person the most . . . . From one point of view it was good that these exclusion rituals were made more flexible. But then it made you think maybe these rituals never meant so much in the first place.

Most problems can be settled by one of the three milder forms of exclusion. Which one is chosen will depend upon a subjective evaluation of the needs of the sinner. A mild grade of exclusion is distinguished by the fact that the sinner makes a sincere confession at the *beginning* of the exclusion. He is forgiven, and the matter is considered closed, but it is felt that the sin was serious enough that he should have some time to think it over. This time is known as 'distance'. An ex-member described the process of a mild exclusion:

The thing is already settled, but you have to make a statement about it anyway. You describe in the Brotherhood, in very general terms, what happened. In particular, they want an accurate description of what you did in terms of personality traits: I allowed myself to be (proud, selfish, jealous), I fell victim to a sense of resentment, something like that. Then you apologize. Okay, it's cleared, because it really was clear even before that, that you'd reformed. There were gradations of this. In the most serious, your distance would not be merely a passage of time, but would require that you took the initiative, and went to the Brotherhood, and said, 'Okay, I think I'm ready to be received back.'

The milder forms of discipline are used even with guests who are seriously seeking the novitiate. In his book on Chinese thought reform, Robert Lifton speaks of the technique of softening the subject by extending privileges, thus intensifying the shock when the privileges are withdrawn.[82] Goffman cites similar tactics in his essay on total institutions.[83] In the Bruderhof, a guest who has indicated a serious interest in becoming a member may be invited to participate in the *Gemeindestunde*. One such guest was the man whose dreams of self-mutilation were described in chapter four. Later, because of his dreams and other matters, he was asked to stop coming to the *Gemeindestunde*. Although this would not formally be looked upon as an exclusion by the Bruderhof, its effects are much the same. This man said:

It seemed to me that a person was not allowed to doubt in the Bruderhof. I felt that I couldn't believe unless I could doubt and express my doubts. And, as soon as a person had doubts, they put a *tremendous* pressure on him by asking him not to go to the *Gemeindestunde*. Once you had gone to *Gemeindestunde*, and then couldn't go, you were like a leper. I mean I felt that way .... I felt people talked to me less, I felt like an outcast.

A popular form of mild sanction that doesn't fit into the formal exclusion system is known as giving a person a 'change of scenery'. That is, transferring him to another job and/or another *hof*. This technique was also quite popular in the Oneida Community. It may be one of the reasons for Caplow's observation that successful utopian communities tend to belong to federations of communities. A 'change of scenery' is often quite disruptive of the routine of the daily life. The Bruderhof doesn't mind this. The exigencies of work must always give way before the 'inner needs' of the community members.

For really serious offenses the Brother is subject to one of the three types of exclusion that require ritual avoidance. In the 'small exclusion', the Brother continues to work at his community job, live with his family, and eat in the dining room. 'He is not supposed to converse with anyone beyond "Good Morning" and "please pass the salt",' according to one informant. In the 'great exclusion', the Brother is completely isolated. He is usually sent to stay by himself in a cabin or cottage on the outskirts of the community. His food is brought down to him. Once a day, or so, a Servant or Witness Brother comes and talks with him. He spends the rest of his time reading and meditating or sometimes doing some therapeutic craft work. The reading will be from the Scriptures or other inspirational writings.

The most serious offenses require expulsion. These usually involve power, sex, or unusually recalcitrant cases of pride. Although in ordinary times it is rarely used, the threat of expulsion hangs heavily over the heads of all. It is the real teeth of the exclusion system. A person can be sent away for any length of time at all or for an indefinite period of time. He can be sent away with his family or without his family, with money or without money. The community can decide to maintain a certain amount of limited contact with him during his expulsion or it can sever all contact. For everybody, but especially for parents with small children and for those born in the community, the prospect of being thrust out into the alien 'outside' is extremely frightening.

Even in the severest of its punishments, the Bruderhof never totally ends relations with a Brother. An ex-member reports:

Sometimes they would send him away and put him in a definite place where they had friends .... They would say, 'You go and be a bookkeeper for this company for a while. You have that talent. You can earn your own living, and we'll keep in contact with you.' .... and if it got worse, then they'd say, 'Get out of here Brother, and if you want to hear from us again, you take the initiative to get in contact with us. We really hope that you will. But, for the time being, we're not going to do anything. We're not going to take care of you. You take care of yourself.'

Although many expulsions are, in fact, permanent, the Bruderhof maintains that this has been made so by the attitudes of those expelled. From its side, the door always remains open, and hope remains that even the most hard-hearted sinner will repent and return.

Unanimous consensus in the Brotherhood is required in order to exclude or expel. When I first heard this, I was puzzled. How then would it be possible to exclude a deviant group? An ex-member explained:

Factions just aren't allowed to organize. It might be that they would exclude ten people at a whack, but this would be ten individuals; it wouldn't be a party composed of ten members, and they wouldn't dream of supporting each other [paraphrased].

If a Servant or a group of Brotherhood members are threatened with exclusion, the situation is less clear. Sometimes a husband and wife will support each other. No informant has been able to delineate clear rules for such circumstances. Even such patterns as emerge are hard to understand unless one grasps the fact that the sacred dimension of the Brotherhood really exists in the minds of all of its members. In almost all cases, inability to find unity with one's Brothers is, in itself, a prime symptom of guilt. Thus, a group of people, a husband and wife or even a group as large as ten, will almost always leave the meeting if asked to by the rest of the Brotherhood. If they were to refuse, a crisis would ensue. The Brotherhood would no longer exist. Help would have to be obtained from 'outside' (i.e., another *hof*).

None of my informants could imagine a situation in which a group as large as even ten would disobey a decision of a *firm and decisive* Brotherhood. A firm and decisive Brotherhood is one with confidence in its leaders, with no vocal opposition within the ranks, and above all, one that *feels* sure of itself. This last condition is the crucial one. If the Brotherhood feels certain that it is speaking the will of God, it can almost always convince any other Brother that this is the case. On the other hand, if a group of ten is firm and decisive, and the rest are wavering, the former may be able to dictate decisions to the latter.

The only time that the exclusion system and the unanimous decision policy do come into conflict is when the exclusion of a Servant is at issue – especially a powerful Servant who has been in office for a long while. If the entire Brotherhood were to oppose a Servant, the Servant would, sooner or later, accept the Brotherhood's decision. But if 75 per cent of the Brotherhood were to oppose a Servant, and the other 25 per cent were to side with him, then a crisis would occur. In practice, most exclusions of Servants have been accomplished either through crises or through the intervention of other Servants.

Forgiveness occurs after the Brother has 'had time to think it over', has repented, and has made a public confession. Often this will be done in the *Gemeindestunde*:

> P. was in some difficulty. At *Gemeindestunde* he got up. He said he had been blind and was mistaken and he was eager to be taken back. Often people would make this sort of apology during *Gemeindestunde*.

For 'misdemeanors', a simple confession in the *Gemeindestunde* or in the Brotherhood was followed by reinstatement. For more serious crimes, a certain undefined waiting period is required. The Servant meets with the Brother in exclusion until the two of them together are convinced that the Brother is ready to be taken back.

In the most severe cases, a Brother may be asked to stay away for months or a year before coming back to be reconsidered. The Bruderhof has in the past worked it out so that many such serious forgivenesses will occur around Easter time.

Exclusion happens to just about everybody at some time or another. One ex-member remarked that many of the old-timers in the Bruderhof, particularly among those who had never achieved a position in the hierarchy themselves, liked to mention that some great and respected Servant 'had had his troubles too, a while back'. Functionally, the exclusion system serves as the great equalizer. Everyone's been through it and everyone may well be through it again; so one refrains from feeling or acting superior to a Brother who is currently 'having his troubles'.

This does not always work out in practice as it is stated in theory. Especially if a Brother fell from a position in the hierarchy, he 'will be watched for a while' after he comes back. Also, of course, he will have to work his way back very slowly, if at all, to his former position of authority.

## 2. *The Hierarchy*

The following sympathetic description of leadership in the Bruderhof comes from a recent article by Robert Friedmann:

> At the head of the Society stands an elder or *Vorsteher* whose guidance together with other trusted leaders is accepted as a matter of fact by all full members of the group. Such an authoritarian set-up could easily be felt as a real barrier to man's full application of his freedom of decision, and actually now and then it was felt this way. On the other hand, however, does not love belong also in the very center of such a Christian community? Hence authority together with love provides a rather wholesome though disciplined atmosphere on such a Bruderhof, very different from the atmosphere of our secular society with its overemphasis on individualism. For the latter there is no room in a Society intent on the realization of 'primitive' Christian values.[84]

In reality, the authority structure of the Bruderhof is much more complex and less totally benign than Friedmann's description indicates. A more accurate model of the Bruderhof authority structure would consist of a series of concentric circles. Any number of gradations among these can be found, but in general, nine distinct circles at least should be delineated: (1) the elder or *Vorsteher* (sometimes called the chief of the Servants or chief Servant); (2) Servants of the Word; (3) Stewards, Witness Brothers, Housemothers; (4) married Brotherhood members; (5) single 'decision-making' Brotherhood members; (6) 'non-decision-making' Brotherhood members; (7) novices; (8) older teenagers and long-term guests; (9) children, guests, and excluded members.

For a long while there was a question in the Bruderhof as to whether or not there should be a *Vorsteher*. The Hutterian Orders call for a Bishop to preside over a group of *hofs*. At the time that they admitted the Bruderhof into the Hutterian Church, the elders appointed Eberhard Arnold Bishop for Germany, although there was only one *hof* in Germany at that time. When Arnold died, the office lapsed. During the nine-*hof* period there was some speculation about whether the office needed to be revived in the era of the Bruderhof as an international social movement. But this was not done, and it was not until after the great crisis that Brother David became the second Bruderhof *Vorsteher*.

Below the top level, the structure of offices and statuses has remained quite stable since the reorganization into the Hutterian order in the 1930s. The *Vorsteher* spends much of his time traveling among the various *hofs*. Although Brother David's main residence is at Woodcrest, he does not act as Servant there. All *hofs* have two Servants. These are not equal in rank; one is said to assist the other. At Woodcrest, in 1966, D. and M. were the Servants. M. was said to have the job of assisting D., although his title was full Servant, not Assistant Servant. Having two Servants per *hof* is the norm rather than the inflexible rule. Sometimes not enough Servants with proper qualifications can be found. In this case, the Bruderhof will never lower its standards. Instead, some *hofs* will have to make do with only one. Sometimes, if one of the Servants is engaged in much traveling, or is working on a special project, a *hof* may have three Servants. There may also be various retired Servants, lapsed Servants, and excluded Servants. At Woodcrest in 1966, there were five Servants, in addition to David. Two of these were active. Another was the retired former Servant of Woodcrest. He continued to attend all inner circle meetings and take part in high-level decisions. The other two, A. and G., were either lapsed or excluded.

The Witness Brothers, Steward, and Housemothers occupy the rank below that of Servant. At Woodcrest in 1966 there were five Witness Brothers (all male). Six is the norm, although with much greater variation according to need. There are rarely fewer than three Witness Brothers, however, nor more than seven. Tradition calls for the Witness Brothers to be chosen from among those involved in the practical work. This was more important formerly, when various work departments needed to have representation of their needs in the inner circle, than it is today. Nevertheless, the tradition continues. Two of the Witness Brothers in Woodcrest in 1966 were maintenance men. One was an assistant production foreman in the shop. Another was shipping manager, and the fifth was men's work distributor.

There were six Housemothers in Woodcrest in 1966. These included Brother David's wife, who was *the* Housemother, the wives of the two Servants and the wife of the Steward. Wives of Servants and Witness Brothers traditionally have a better chance than others of becoming Housemothers.

The Witness Brothers serve as the Servants' liaisons to the work departments. The Housemothers do the same for the women's work departments. The Steward acts as financial advisor to the Servant. He is the Servant's right-hand man in matters of the instrumental sphere. Servants, Witness Brothers, Housemothers, and Steward meet together frequently. They form a kind of executive committee for the Bruderhof.

When I speak of 'the hierarchy' in this book, I will usually be referring merely to the top three grades, *Vorsteher,* Servant, and Witness Brother-Housemother-Steward. Actually this is just a third of the entire hierarchy. There are also three grades of ordinary Brotherhood members and three grades of non-Brotherhood members. These may be referred to as the middle and lower hierarchies respectively. Henceforth, reference to 'the hierarchy', without qualifying adjectives, should be taken to mean the top three grades only.

The three grades of Brotherhood member are distinguished by their degree of access to information and the scope of their participation in decision-making. Some very sensitive information regarding personal problems of members is subject to pastoral privilege and never gets beyond the circle of the upper hierarchy. All information that does reach the Brotherhood is accessible to married members. Single members do not ordinarily get information dealing with sexual problems or marital relations, nor do they participate in decisions regarding these matters. When sexual material comes up on the agenda of the Brotherhood meeting, single people will be asked to leave until it has been dealt with. In all other respects single members are treated the same as married members, except, as was noted in chapter three, there is greater prestige attached to being married.

Non-decision-making Brotherhood members are those who are in good standing but who, for some reason, must be 'protected', from the 'burden' of difficult decisions. This may be either a permanent or a temporary status. It includes members who are feeble-minded or senile (which by no means disqualifies a person from high status in the *gemeinde*), members who are emotionally unstable, and members in a generally weak physical condition (such as a severe heart condition) that renders them unable to bear the burden of decision-making. It also includes, on a temporary basis, members who have some need to rest other than one requiring exclusion. Recuperation from a serious illness, shock due to death in the family, fatigue due to overwork, or a temporary state of emotional turmoil are some of the situations that may lead to temporary occupancy of a non-decision-making status in the Brotherhood.

In terms of decision-making, there is no distinction between the non-decision-making Brother and the novice. Both may attend some, but not all, Brotherhood meetings, at the discretion of the Brotherhood. In fact, the novice may often have access to more information than the non-decision-making

Brother. However the latter is ranked higher because of his higher sacral distinction and because more Brotherhood meetings are open to him than to the novice.

Only very rarely will anyone below the level of novice attend, let alone participate in, a Brotherhood meeting. These are the undeclared, who have made no commitment at all to the community. They are part of the household but not the *gemeinde*. An exception, of course, is the class of Brothers in exclusion. Excluded Brothers are not really in the hierarchy at all. Most often, but not always, those under the more severe grades of exclusion are treated like those in the lowest level. The lower part of the hierarchy includes guests and children. A distinction is made among the former on the basis of the potentiality for commitment, and among the latter on this basis plus that of age. Often a key indicator of one's rank among the undeclared is whether or not one is allowed to attend the *Gemeindestunde*. This privilege is often opened to serious guests and older teenagers. Serious guests and older teenagers will also often be given more information about what is going on behind the scenes than other undeclared residents of the community.

## 3. *The Power of the Servants*

The Bruderhof has always guarded against even the slightest manifestation of human power in the community. But no group of people has ever been able to thwart the eventual development of control relationships among its members. At the Bruderhof, the office of Servant in particular has always remained structurally conducive to the accumulation of power, often despite the sincere wishes of the office-holder.

The primary qualification for the job of Servant is a combination of the ability to evoke the cosmic perspective and the sensitivity to perceive the roots of personal and interpersonal problems. This is known as the 'gift of the discerning spirit'. It involves both the passionate charisma of the prophet and the empathetic perceptivity of the psychoanalyst. It evokes both love and fear. One ex-member said of the current *Vorsteher:*

David sometimes was kind and gentle, but when he got angry he had within him the wrath of God. I saw him once when he disagreed with something that was said in a meeting and he stood up and said, 'We won't even listen to you' – shouted – and walked out, and everyone walked out with him.

All Servants have strong personalities, and the ability to be 'sharp' when the occasion requires it. Excessive tenderness is and has been grounds for disqualifying a nominee for the Service:

The name of W. came up. Everyone agreed that he was spiritually in good standing, was emotionally stable, was not power-hungry, and could be relied upon. But then somebody wondered whether W. could be tough enough for the job. Somebody else recalled that, as a Witness Brother, he had been too willing to accept people's excuses where more drastic action was called for. So we discussed this for a while, and finally we decided not to make W. a Servant, but to allow him to continue as a Witness Brother [paraphrased].

Once a Brother with a strong personality and the 'discerning spirit' has been made a Servant, his occupation of the status itself greatly magnifies and enhances his natural power. In addition to being an administrator and a spiritual leader, the Servant also serves as a communications nexus. This role is much more important in the Bruderhof than in most other organizations. This is because, as we have already seen, the voicing of opinions against a person through informal channels invalidates such opinions at the Bruderhof in much the same way that collecting information by wiretapping invalidates the use of such information in our society. Even if a group of Brothers have a reason, which in itself is legitimate, for meeting informally, the very fact that they have done so makes the meeting and any decisions reached at the meeting illegitimate. So there are no legitimate channels of communication which by-pass the Servant. He is privy to all recognized information about personnel.

The Servant's role as communications nexus ensures that all information available to other members of the hierarchy is available to him. His pastoral role ensures that a great deal of information will be available to him that is not necessarily available to any other member of the hierarchy. A Brother or a novice in any sort of trouble comes to a Servant or a Witness Brother to talk about it. Unless it is quite trivial, the Witness Brother must communicate the subject of his meeting to the Servant, but the Servant may use his discretion about whether to communicate pastoral problems downward to the Witness Brothers. He may keep the information to himself, he may speak to a few Witness Brothers (or Housemothers), he may speak to all of them, or he may bring the matter directly to the Brotherhood.

Take a typical horrible case, which was rather rare, an adultery case. As I say, these were rare. The guy goes, he confesses to a Servant. Right away the Servant feels, 'This is too much for me to bear alone.' So he goes and calls his other Servants together to talk with the guy and they get the full details. They may or may not confide all this in the Witness Brothers. Maybe they will get the Witness Brothers together to hear the guy. If it's a sticky thing, it might have consequences and there are decisions to be made and so on . . . . Then the Servant will call a Brotherhood meeting. He'll tell the people, not everything that he's heard, but certain things. The Servants would suggest an exclusion, and they would decide what grade of exclusion was appropriate, since they had information that other people didn't. Novices would be given a version that was a little more expurgated . . . . Then guests would be told, so-and-so has had to be excluded. They might be told it was a sexual matter or they might not be. Then the kids would hear, probably from the guests. They had a grapevine going. In fact they heard things before Brotherhood members heard them sometimes, which was a bit of a standing joke among us, 'Three forms of communication: telegraph, telephone, and tell-a-schoolchild.'

It is ironical that the Bruderhof, which bases so much of its life upon spontaneity and openness, should feel compelled to be so secretive about matters of personal sin, especially sexual sin. It is this rather Victorian tenor of their life which keeps them from even questioning the validity of the classification of information. Even an ex-Servant who felt most strongly the need to bring more democracy to the Bruderhof had this to say:

Suppose this person has done something morally wrong. O.K., you could broadcast all the news in the group. This might be very hard on the individual. And it might be really objectively not desirable to do it . . . . But that means the Brotherhood has to trust actually a small group who are trusted with the confessions. There's a certain validity in that. But this at the same time gives a tremendous power to the Servant and the Witness Brothers. Because he always, if he wants to get something through, can say, 'I'm sorry, I don't feel I can give more details. These are confidential.' What are you going to say? The main facts, of course, were always given, but not always details.

Another ex-member told of the following specific case:

Like there was one case where we had a guy that got involved with some woman or other, and it really wasn't her fault. She wasn't at fault at all. He was making passes at her all the time. This had been going on for a while. She was in great conflicts about this. She thought, 'This isn't right.' He was a Servant at the time. She struggled for a definition of the situation in her head: 'Is this guy making passes at me? I can't be right because he's a Servant.' Finally she comes to the conclusion, 'It isn't right. I don't care who he is!' So she goes and confesses this. Because she was felt not to be at fault, nobody ever heard, except two or three Servants, who that was. I don't know who it was. *It would have made her life very impossible*, and she had nothing in particular to repent of [emphasis added].

The theme of the balance of power between the hierarchy and the Brotherhood has run all through Bruderhof history since the death of Eberhard Arnold. No stable pattern has ever been achieved. The balance continues always to shift from one side to the other. The members of the hierarchy in a single *hof* gather together in what is called Morning Meeting several times a week. The functions of this Morning Meeting have shifted through the years between the extremes of being an exchange center for important executive information and being the effective government of the *hof*.

Now we also have been in Morning Meetings in the past – R. was a Servant and I was a Housemother. When we visited Woodcrest [from Paraguay] we felt that the Morning Meeting had become in Woodcrest, more important than in any other place. There was always a tendency of that danger though. It had become more and more the actual body. They decided what had to happen. After it was all worked through in the Morning Meeting, and they had all had a chance to lay out the points and have their say, then it was presented to the

Brotherhood in such a way that the Brotherhood actually couldn't say much any more.

The ability of the hierarchy to control and utilize information often startles the new recruit. The guest or novice comes face to face with what it means to live in (even a voluntary) total institution when he encounters the total lack of confidentiality of low-level conversations. The following story was told by a long-term serious guest who never became a novice:

M. [who was a Brother] had been my partner in business before we both came to the Bruderhof. He came to visit me one afternoon. He said, 'How are you getting along?' And so I told him. I was real frank, you know. I told him about all the doubts I'd been having, and other things. And that afternoon I was called in to the Servant of the Word and he repeated everything that M. had said to me, and everything I'd said to him. Well, that shocked me. I knew that they were Brothers, and there were no real confidences, but I wasn't emotionally prepared for it, and I felt as if I'd been betrayed.

Their position as communications nexus, their pastoral functions, their membership in Morning Meeting, their ex-officio membership in all committees of special expertise, the fact that their wives are often Housemothers, their frequent communication with Servants in other *hofs*, all contribute to a tremendous concentration of information, and therefore a tremendous concentration of power, in the hands of the Servants. But the Servant possesses still more power as a result of his position as head of the sacred hierarchy. In a voluntary society which is itself élitist, the rank and file will generally have a personal stake in investing an aura of sacredness in those who lead, and therefore embody, this group. This dignity is often in excess of that desired by the Servant himself. One ex-Servant remarked that he was amused at noticing the great weight that was suddenly put on his words when he became a Servant. Another ex-Servant reported:

The power of the Servant is often subconscious. I didn't realize – I was flabbergasted – when E. told me, 'You know, B., you have tremendous power.' I said, 'What do you mean, tremendous power?' He said, 'Well, when you say something, people pick it up and say,

"You know B. says, etc., etc".' I said, 'Really? I never knew that. I'm glad you told me about it.'

The Hutterians carry the dignity of the Servant much further than is done in the Bruderhof. A Hutterian Servant must never take his meals with the regular Brothers. His meals are brought to his home, and they are often better quality and consist of larger portions than do the meals of the ordinary Brothers. This is not done in the Bruderhof today although it was in the 1940s. The Servant eats in the main dining room with everyone else. He does not have a special table but sits wherever, and with whomever, there is room.

Another source of the power of a Servant's position is that general agreement and contentment with the Servant is a major symptom of unity in the Bruderhof. A person will think twice before challenging that unity which is the source of his major payoff as a member. If he does challenge, the other Brothers will, aside from the merits of his case, be inclined to be annoyed at this person 'bringing in a disturbance'. If a Servant is intent on holding onto his power he can use this resentment against this Brother to have him excluded for having a 'wrong attitude' or a 'divisive spirit'. Two anecdotes illustrate the use of this technique. The first is told by an apostate who was a member in Paraguay only:

In 1957 we held a world conference of all our nine *hofs*. Z. started off in Germany, went to Wheathill [in England] for a while, then he and the Wheathill Servant went to Woodcrest and stayed a while there, and then they came down to us [in Paraguay]. So Z.'d been around. And he proceeded to give his report, not only on his own community but on these other places as well . . . and one Brother protested about this in a sort of mild way. He said, 'Well, I respect Z. a great deal, but we'd like to hear from somebody else.' And Z. got very annoyed about this . . . pulled a Michelian oligarch technique: 'Choose between me and him, this guy is challenging me.' He forces a total decision, not just on this issue but puts his whole authority on the line. So naturally this guy gets bashed . . . he had to repent and make a statement regretting what he had said. He really didn't mean it, or he did mean it but he had bad motives, is what he had to say.

The other story also told by an ex-member refers to conditions at Woodcrest during the last few years:

> Who dares to tackle a Servant? I'll tell you something: several people in Woodcrest have tackled David. One after another was sent away. D. has been away. The W.'s have been away – and made to leave on an hour's notice – Why? Because they have criticized David. C. has been away because he has criticized David. All Witness Brothers! K. has been away because he criticized David. He hasn't gone back and he's not going back. Now these are just a few who I tell you. These are all from the closest circle which David had around him. They dared to stand up. Now these were Witness Brothers. Then the other Witness Brothers sided with David and it was brought to the Brotherhood and they were sent away, one by one.

## 4. *Choosing and Deposing Leaders*

The conclusion might be drawn from the foregoing, that changes in leadership are relatively rare in the Bruderhof. Nothing can be further from the truth. One of the great strengths of the community throughout all of its history, according to a man who has been a close friend of the Bruderhof for many years, is their willingness and ability to 'break even the most respected and competent general to private when he starts getting too interested in power.'

Even more remarkable – and, in my opinion, even more contributory to the Bruderhof's success – is the built-in recognition that leaders may eventually fail, that power always eventually corrupts. The Bruderhof theory is to choose a strong man, use him as long as he can hold up, then support him and give him a rest when he fails. This theory has been put into practice many times with Servants and with Witness Brothers. Even the highest have eventually fallen, temporarily if not permanently. One Brother has been in and out of the hierarchy at least a half dozen times. He came out of exclusion a little over three years ago, and is now, according to some rumors, working his way up again. The current *Vorsteher* was knocked out of the hierarchy once, long ago. Although today he holds an unprecedented amount of power, there is no reason to doubt that he too could eventually fall and need to be given 'a rest.'

I have observed no minimum requirements of age or member-ship seniority in the selection of Servants. In 1966, the ages of the Servants ranged from thirty-seven to sixty-six. It is rare, however, for a Servant to be chosen who is under the age of thirty or has been a member less than two years. The job is closed to women, but aside from that, the only considerations seem to be fitness 'both spiritual and practical' for the job.

In choosing a new Servant, both the Brotherhood and the hierarchy play a role. A special Brotherhood meeting is called for the purpose. Where practical, Brothers from all nearby *hofs* also attend this meeting. Choosing a Servant is inter-*hof* business. Anyone can nominate a candidate for the job, but the nominees of those in the hierarchy get more attention. The nominees are often Witness Brothers. Whoever they are, they are not supposed to indicate eagerness for the job, in fact, a certain reluctance, as in American politics up to twenty years ago, is considered to be in good taste.

Nominees and their wives are asked to leave the meeting. Their personal characteristics are then minutely discussed. Sometimes a meeting will 'find' two Servants, sometimes one, and sometimes none. It is never a matter of voting for the best man. If none of the candidates meets the qualifications, the community will have to temporarily make do without a Servant – a situation that is not rare in Bruderhof history.

The choosing of a Servant requires complete unanimity, like any other Bruderhof decision. If a Servant is 'found', he first serves a sort of probationary period as an unconfirmed Servant. After a period of time ranging from six months to two years, he is confirmed in the Service. Confirmation does not affect tenure in office. A confirmed Servant can be demoted as easily as an uncon-firmed Servant. Usually the new Servant will spend some time assisting a more experienced Servant before going on to the job of running a *hof* by himself.

The election of Witness Brothers is similar to the election of

Servants, except that this is a matter concerning only the *hof* in which the Witness Brothers will serve, and a joint Brotherhood meeting is not felt to be needed.

Deposing a Servant is, in theory, just the obverse of choosing one. In practice, of course, it is much more complex. The crucial difference is the risk factor involved in suggesting a demotion. As was discussed earlier, it is almost impossible for an ordinary Brother, unsupported by anyone in authority, to call for the removal of a Servant without getting himself into trouble. An ex-Servant recalls:

> In . . . Paraguay I worked with several others in the direction: We must have a Brotherhood who can express freely what they really think. And if they have something against us, let them talk it out. Let us not get people in trouble if they say something against our leading people because if we do that we never will have a free community.

In practice, there have been times of greater or less openness in the Bruderhof. During certain periods, ordinary Brothers feel free to express themselves on any matter. During others, timidity and conformity prevail.

How then is a Servant removed from office? There is no yearly review. Service is for life unless there is a demotion. One informant reports that over half of the Servant demotions that he recalls also involved exclusion. Sometimes it happens that a Servant confesses to a sin, or perhaps merely asks for a rest and to be relieved of the office. But the same informant also reports that, in his recollection, 'a majority had to be shot down.'

The Servant intent on holding onto his office, however, often proves a formidable target. The case of Z. is an example. Z. was never really a *Vorsteher*, but he occupied the unofficial position of first among the Servants during the quarter century between the two *Vorstehers*. He proved particularly difficult to depose. At the world-conference in 1957, he would not even tolerate mild criticism in the Brotherhood. He insisted that the group make an immediate choice, to censure him or the critic, knowing very well which it would have to choose. Two years later, at another Brotherhood meeting, another incident occurred which an ex-member recalled:

This guy got up and he presented a bill of particulars. He said, 'I'm not satisfied with the way Z. is performing.' This was one of those new Woodcrest Americans. He had a little more brass and maybe a little more democratic presupposition than the average member. He said, 'Z. doesn't listen to people. He cuts them off when they're trying to say something in the Brotherhood. He decides things himself. He's sarcastic with people. He makes nasty remarks about various members of the Brotherhood. And this is just not right.'

Of course, the protester was quickly reprimanded. But this time, the mood was different. (This was at the early stages of the great crisis – The Year the Servants Fell.) Other *hofs* heard of the incident and began to talk about it. Eventually, a group of leaders from other *hofs* went over to investigate, anti-Z. sentiment mounted, and he was eventually removed from office. But before the protester was allowed back in good standing, he had to make a statement that even though it had turned out that he had been right, his attitude had not been proper.

Although no general pattern for removing Servants from office exists, it is usually the case that a single isolated Brother does not simply propose a demotion. An ex-Servant said, in answer to this question:

I tell you I haven't experienced it once in all the thirty-five years that I've been a member, that a Brotherhood member stood up in the Brotherhood and said, 'I want that he should be no more a Servant.' I have not seen that. It usually goes via Servants, or via Witness Brothers, and then the Brotherhood comes in too.

Or say, what could happen is, if a Servant did something wrong to an individual, this individual might go to another Servant and say, 'Look, that and that happened.' In this case the individual might stand up, if he has proof. But generally it is not so easy to remove a Servant, except if that Servant is so honest that he would not put up a big fight.

Interestingly enough, however, the very Servant who made the above statement had been removed from office, while he was absent at another *hof*, in exactly the way he said never occurred:

One night in the Brotherhood meeting my wife said that a certain Servant had a lot of pride and that his children were given special treatment. That night, no one agreed with her – she was reprimanded. The next night there was another meeting. Several Brothers started speaking about the same thing. By the time the meeting was over, he was no longer a Servant.

This story indicates the difficulty of making any definite generalizations about Bruderhof practice. However, it must be said that the Brother who told the story had no way of knowing what was happening in the inner circles. It might have been that the top leaders were planning the demotion, and therefore welcomed this suggestion from the rank and file.

Lesser leaders, of course, could always be demoted at the instigation of greater leaders. An ex-member recalls:

We had a guy in Uruguay one time. Apparently, being co-leader of the *hof* went to his head a little. He got so he'd sit around and drink all day – he had drunk before that. This came to a head and they said, 'No more liquor!' And he didn't have any more either. He went into exclusion, because it wasn't just drinking. It was that he was lying around and playing the grand pasha all the time. He had this sort of attitude that he was some big thing.

Sometimes two Servants of approximately equal stature come into conflict. When this happens, there is a crisis until the Brotherhood unites behind one or the other. This happened in 1940 when Z. opposed the Arnold brothers. 'The Brotherhood ceased to exist' when the members were unsure of whose leading to follow. Eventually they united behind Z. and the Arnolds were sent into exclusion. Even the highest are not immune.

## 5. *Setting Policy*

The basic goal of the Bruderhof, as described in chapter one, is to bear witness to the Holy Spirit and the Kingdom of God by living the life prescribed by Jesus in the Sermon on the Mount. This has not changed over the years. However, this basic goal is sufficiently broad to allow many different interpretations. During its earliest years, the Bruderhof suffered a serious schism over the question of economic realism as opposed to an economics based on faith. Both sides were able to justify their positions as in harmony with the Bruderhof's stated purpose in life. The matter was finally settled by Eberhard Arnold's fiat in favor of an economics based on faith. Those who could not accept his decision, a large majority, left the community.

Since the death of Arnold, the Bruderhof has continually had to struggle to reach consensus on necessary definitions, priorities, and modifications of the ideology in the light of concrete circumstances. There have been basic divisions on three major areas of Bruderhof policy which have been themes throughout all or most of the community's history. The first division concerns whether to emphasize a spiritual-emotional or a legal-rational approach to building community. The second concerns whether the Brotherhood should be organized on democratic or oligarchical principles. The third is a matter of orientation to the outside world. It concerns whether the community should put its energies into reaching out for new members and involvement in the world's problems or into self-examination and community purification.

These controversies, in various combinations, have been at the root of many of the frequent crises and power struggles which have marked Bruderhof history. But the Bruderhof also has a peaceful method of changing policy which, if it has not been able to eliminate the necessity for periodic crises, has at least lessened their severity. This is the method which Joseph Eaton, in his study of the Hutterians, has called 'the technique of controlled acculturation'.[85] In a sacred society, even mundane customs are given a sacred significance. They cannot readily be altered without the danger of a crisis of confidence in the entire system. But policy changes, and therefore changes, in customs, must always occur if a community is not to stagnate. The technique used by both the Hutterians and the Bruderhof is to allow a slow and fairly constant evolution of customs, simultaneously maintaining feelings of progress and of cultural continuity. The basis for an old policy can thus be eroded while the foundation of the new is slowly being laid. When a new policy is adopted, everybody will feel as if it has really grown organically out of the community's life.

Another factor that has lessened the severity of policy crises is that the three major ideological splits have tended to cross-cut, rather than reinforce, each other. It might be imagined that a conservative-liberal split would occur in which a legal-rational outlook, oligarchy, and a desire for withdrawal would be part of a common set opposing the set of spiritual-emotional outlook, democracy, and a desire for outreach. But this has never happened. All possible combinations of these positions are found within the Bruderhof. Furthermore, an examination of the accompanying table indicates that no two decades of the Bruderhof's history show the same policy orientation on all three issues.

HISTORICAL CHANGES IN THE THREE MAJOR CONTROVERSIAL AREAS OF BRUDERHOF POLICY SINCE 1920*

| Policy | 1920s | 1930s | 1940s | 1950s | 1960s |
|---|---|---|---|---|---|
| Legal-rational vs. spiritual-emotional approach to community | S–E | L–R† | L–R | L–R | S–E |
| Democracy vs. oligarchy in the Brotherhood | Democratic centralism | Oligarchy | Oligarchy | Democracy | Democratic centralism |
| Outreach vs. withdrawal | Outreach | Outreach | Withdrawal (involuntary) | Outreach | Withdrawal |

†In the 1930s, the Bruderhof mixed the two approaches until Eberhard Arnold's death in 1935, whereupon it began to move more in the direction of the legalism of the Hutterian forms.

*The division by decades is not as contrived as it looks. By coincidence, most major Bruderhof policy shakeups—joining the Hutterians, the exodus to Paraguay, breaking with the Hutterians, the great crisis—occurred at the beginning of decades.

In 1931, the Bruderhof was incorporated into the Hutterian Church, signalling a change from the original spiritual-emotional approach to community typified by the years in Sannerz to a legal-rational emphasis typified by the exclusion system and the hierarchy (the Hutterian Orders). Along with this change came a change in the procedure of Brotherhood meetings. These meetings in the 1920s could not really be described as democratic. Eberhard

Arnold was the ultimate authority. But Eberhard Arnold was also a great man, and one who knew the importance of allowing each person's voice to be heard. Everyone's opinion counted, but in the end Arnold would often take all of these opinions and synthesize them into a policy which then was binding on the entire community. This system is similar to that known to social and political scientists as democratic centralism. This gave way to a more oligarchical system, especially after Arnold's death, where many Brothers (and especially Sisters) would hardly ever venture a serious opinion, and real decision-making was increasingly concentrated in the hands of a few who held positions in the hierarchy.

These were revolutionary changes, and one of the reasons that the Bruderhof was able to adapt to them so well is that they came gradually rather than all at once. Chapter two describes the spontaneous evolution of the need for some semblance of hierarchy in the late 1920s, even before contact with the Hutterites. The original adaptation to Hutterianism was therefore partly justified to the die-hard Youth Movement people as something evolving out of the common life experience. Furthermore, for the first five years of Hutterianism, Eberhard Arnold was able to maintain a subtle balance between the spirit of the old and the spirit of the new. It was really only in the late 1930s, after Arnold's death, that the oligarchic organization of the Brotherhood began. Finally, a number of Hutterian forms, such as the prohibition against smoking, were never really accepted in practice. This gave the Youth Movement camp some feeling, at least, that the capitulation had not been complete.

Twenty years later, another major revolution in the direction of Bruderhof policy occurred, this time in connexion with the break from the Hutterian Church. This split, too, did not come about all at once. Many Hutterian taboos and customs – forms of dress, prohibitions against dancing – had virtually disappeared by the time of the formal break in 1950. Others, like the repression of women, were rapidly crumbling under the assaults of the new American members. The major revolutionary change of the 1950s was the change from an oligarchic to a democratic Brotherhood. The change from a withdrawal orientation to an outreach orientation was also important, but it was not revolutionary because the withdrawal of the 1940s had been involuntary, an unfortunate result of the war and the Paraguayan exile. In the other area, a legal-rational approach continued until the time of the great crisis. The legalism of the Hutterian forms was discarded, but it was replaced with a reliance on intrinsic Bruderhof *know-how*, a belief that the Bruderhof had found the way and could go on now to save the world.

There was considerable opposition to the Hutterite split. This was diffused because the split took place gradually. Even after the formal split, certain Hutterian customs lingered for a while. Beard styles and costumes were slow to change. One informant reports that women, as in many other traditional societies, were the most conservative: 'The first time a woman appeared in slacks – oh my, there were some eyebrows lifted!'

Because of the gradualism of the Bruderhof's controlled acculturation, the sacred legitimacy of the community was not damaged by the Hutterite split. Predictably, there were many outraged opponents. Their spokesmen protested that this was a direct betrayal of the leadership of Eberhard Arnold, who specifically said that the goal of the Bruderhof should always be unity with as much of the larger Christian community as possible, and who specifically led the community into the Hutterian Church with this goal in mind. They pointed out that Arnold, himself, had said that this unity was more important than the music or the dancing that the Bruderhof would have to give up. But because the movement away from the Hutterians had happened gradually, this argument could be countered by pointing to the fact that it had been a long time since real unity had existed between the Bruderhof and the Hutterians, and to all the changes that would have to be made to achieve this unity. Opponents to the split could thus be portrayed as advocates of change, while those who engineered the split could picture themselves as conservatives. Furthermore, the opposition was divided in its opinions as to the fruits of the split. Some who abhorred what they thought was a betrayal of Eberhard Arnold, were pleased with the movement toward democratization. Others, made uneasy by democracy, were won over by the argument that de-Hutterization would help the community's efforts toward outreach.

A sudden jarring of the members' world-views, which in other societies has often led to a jarring of the entire structure of faith, was avoided. How important this is to the maintenance of order can be seen by examining a situation in the Bruderhof in which change came about less gradually – the rapid expansion of the 1950s which led to the great crisis.

The 1950s saw the flowering of liberalism at the Bruderhof. After the enforced isolation of the 1940s, the community was hungry for new members and was willing to make compromises in order to get them. For the first time since the Arnold era the Bruderhof abandoned its insistence on a uniform confession of faith (centering around the Apostles' Creed) as a precondition for membership. As a result, a good number of members with fairly broad-minded, Quakerish beliefs were admitted. Intoxicated with the stirring power of its life, the community began to make extravagant claims to prospective converts in order to get them to make a visit to the Bruderhof, on the theory that once their hearts had been captured by actual exposure to the community life, they could safely be introduced to the hard realities of what the Bruderhof calls 'the price of community'.

In one sense, the strategy worked. The Bruderhof gobbled up hundreds of new members, sometimes even taking in whole other intentional communities at a gulp. For the first and only time in its history, the Brotherhood, at least in North America, became neither democratic centralist nor oligarchic, but something of a true democracy. The value of unity was never given up, but more and more it was left to the Holy Spirit to somehow pull all of the many strands together. By the late 1950s, the Bruderhof was plunging headlong toward becoming a world-wide, liberal, semi-democratic social movement.

When Brother David and the Woodcrest Brotherhood saw which way the wind was blowing they panicked and stepped on the brakes hard, with disastrous consequences. There was no time for controlled acculturation, they felt. If the community was to be saved, drastic action had to be taken immediately. The traumatic results – the great crisis and the schism – have been discussed in chapter two. Interestingly, the reaction against liberalism centered around the only element of the liberal set which had not been articulated during the 1950s – that is, a withdrawal from cold-hearted legalism and rationality, and a return to the spontaneity and emotionalism of the days of the German Youth Movement.

Hundreds of people left the Bruderhof during the great crisis, disillusioned with community forever, largely because the change happened so fast. Behind every successful social movement there is a myth, and behind every myth there is, inevitably, a certain amount of self-deception. Sacred belief is a fragile belief and, once torn open and laid bare, it often can never be put back together again. Even those who stayed felt the strain from which, ten years later, the community is only beginning to recover.

The great crisis was the only point in Bruderhof history at which the community reversed poles on all three major policy issues. A spiritual-emotional approach to community building replaced the legal-rational approach with a vengeance. The community plunged just as headlong into pietistic withdrawal in the 1960s as it had into evangelical expansionism in the 1950s. However, reversal on the third pole was incomplete. The Brotherhood did not switch from democracy to oligarchy, but rather tried to revive the democratic centralism of the Eberhard Arnold days. Indeed, in some respects, the Brotherhood today is much more democratic than during the years in England and Paraguay. But Brother David is not Eberhard Arnold, and it has reportedly been rather dangerous in recent years for members to express their sincere opinions if they are too far out of line.

It should be noted that, even during the great crisis, the cross-cutting of the major Bruderhof policy divisions mitigated the severity, at least of the post-crisis recovery, if not of the crisis itself. The abandonment of outreach and democracy was not accompanied by the denial that they are virtues. Quite the contrary, the Bruderhof takes every opportunity to stress the longing with which they all desire that a period of outreach might again occur. Great stress is constantly placed on the responsibility of each Brother to voice his opinion on all issues, even at a time when it is exceptionally dangerous for him to do so.

Bruderhof policy disputes do not all center around the three major issues. There is the traditional problem of adjudicating among the demands of the various work departments, which used to be one of the major functions of the Servant of the Word. In Paraguay, the Servant never did manual work but he was expected to be conversant with costs, budgets, and the needs of the various departments. Now, with the community on a single-industry economy, the Servant has almost ceased to concern himself with such matters. When a decision with moral implications had to be made, as was the case in a recent controversy about whether to engage in soft-sell or hard-sell advertising for Community Playthings, the Servant still concerns himself. But the day-to-day, and even the year-to-year, management of the economy has come more and more into the hands of men such as the current general manager of Community Playthings, who does not even have an official title in the Hutterian hierarchy.

The prohibition against 'kitchen brotherhoods' makes it difficult for policy changes to occur as they most often do in a democratic society – at the behest of an emerging interest group. An ex-member tells this story:

> We had a little gang of us who were interested in publishing work. We used to get together and bitch about how the Brotherhood wasn't making the necessary decisions to get the stuff moving. But we never thought of standing up for our position, although there were about six or eight of us. We knew we were wrong. We knew they would tell us that we were allowing our enthusiasm for a partial goal to interfere with the whole. What can you say about such frustrations without having your attitude attacked simply because you've gotten excited? You can't have an interest group. They consciously prevent that.

However, the method of controlled acculturation keeps hope alive. If you can't organize an interest group, at least there's the possibility that the community itself will eventually come around to your point of view. In fact, fifteen years later, the community finally did get around to a major push in the direction of publishing. A woman member, now an apostate, told how this policy of gradual change kept her spirits up:

> They asked me to part my hair down the middle. They said this was the custom in the Bruderhof. This was done by the Hutterian women in the Middle Ages. I said, 'No, I would look plainer than ever. It would be too depressing.' And I didn't do it. But I did wear this traditional Hutterian head scarf all the time, even in Paraguay in the tropics because I was a Brotherhood member and we were supposed to wear them always.
>
> What was good was that we discarded it. Always, when you were getting a bit depressed about something, there would be a crisis, and we'd clear things up. You always felt, 'Well, there's hope. We will change. We are changing.'

## 6. *Personal Deviance*

Bruderhof life is a continuing struggle between the ego inclinations of the individual and the call to a Christian communal life. Most of the effort of the Bruderhof system of social control therefore goes into correcting deviance. It is important to realize that the Bruderhof considers deviance natural and universal. Nobody escapes it. Sanctions are seen then, less as punishment, than as a service to the one sanctioned, to help separate him from his sin. In order to deal effectively with the problem of potentially universal deviance, the community must first identify the deviance as it occurs, judge the deviant, sanction him if necessary, and finally rehabilitate him.

*Identifying deviance.* The Bruderhof is much more concerned with an individual's underlying attitudes, in most cases, than with his overt behavior. It follows from this that 'good' behavior may be rebuked if the underlying attitudes are wrong and that 'bad' behavior may be condoned if it is thought that the behavior is not indicative of a bad attitude. An example of the former is reported by a woman who was a long-term serious guest at the Woodcrest Bruderhof. She was told that her behavior was too perfect. The Brothers felt that she was a sharp observer of, and adapter to, her environment. They asked her if she wasn't just noticing what sort of actions would evoke favorable responses, and then exhibiting actions. When she admitted that she had been doing that, she was told that she would never advance in the life in that way. 'Something has to happen inside you, of which these actions are only the natural reflection,' is the sort of thing said under these circumstances. Although such a case is rare in the Bruderhof, it is common for neutral behavior to be admonished. One cannot be sure of avoiding sanction just by staying out of trouble.

The opposite case is quite common as well. As we have seen, the community emphasizes the childlike spirit, which may be accompanied by a good deal of mischievousness – even naughtiness. If pranks are done in a spontaneous, childlike way, they are very likely to escape punishment. They may even be praised as being the sign of a lively spirit. This is especially the case with children. If a child does something wrong, the first thing to be investigated is likely not to be how serious was the crime, but in what spirit was it done. Even minor transgressions carried out in a premeditated, calculating way are considered very serious. Much more serious crimes committed without thinking will often be passed over lightly.

This manifests itself with adults in a tolerant attitude toward lapses of temper. Even the most serious blow-ups, in the heat of a debate in the Brotherhood meeting for instance, are often disregarded. In the case of serious behavioral transgressions, adults are, of course, expected to take more responsibility upon themselves than children, but punishment for even the worst of behavioral crimes can be lessened due to attitudinal considerations. An informant told of an adultery case which illustrates this phenomenon:

... This guy brought it out himself, nobody knew about it. This happened with a girl who was sort of a shaky novice . . . . He came and accused himself . . . and this was one favorable thing. He told me afterwards, he said, 'I felt, when I came and confessed, that I was already most of the way back.' I think this is important. He was received back into the Brotherhood in the space of about six weeks.

[Ordinarily, adultery exclusions have lasted six months, or a year, or longer.] When he came back in, you could tell from the statement he made at the time, something has happened to this guy. Previously he had been a sort of weak Brotherhood member; you had trouble with him, and couldn't really rely on him, and so on. Afterward he really was strong and very responsible, and altogether a different personality.

The attitudes desired in evaluating a person are generally those tending away from concern and identification with the self, and those tending toward concern and identification with the community and the collective indentity. Pride is therefore the epitome of bad attitude. Simplicity and childlike expectation (optimism) are the foremost signs of good attitude. Tendency toward any subgroup loyalty, to clique, to spouse, or to one's own children, is linked to concern for self, and is therefore bad attitude.

Obviously, a system of social control which focuses on the attitudes of individuals is dependent upon the voluntary co-operation of the members in making their attitudes public. A typical prison, for instance, would find it impossible to function if it tried to evaluate the inmates on the basis of their attitudes rather than their behavior. At the Bruderhof, any means of investigation, any way of obtaining information, is considered legitimate. A range of methods is used, from the unsolicited confession at one extreme, to the formal interrogation at the other.

The less pressure that has to be brought to bear upon the individual to make his attitudes known, the more highly esteemed is the method. Thus, the unsolicited confession is the most highly preferred means of information gathering. We saw this in the case of the self-accusing adulterer described above. The Bruderhof socialization process is designed to make it a torment to withhold information about oneself on any matter. Moreover, there is a Bruderhof norm which requires the public assessment of one's feelings upon request. Secrets about dreadful sins have been kept for many years, but this is the exception rather than the rule. During the time of preparation for the Lord's Supper, one is especially required to go back over one's past life to see if any long-standing sins have gone unconfessed. Several may be unearthed at these times.

As powerful as the technique of enjoined expression of attitude is, the Bruderhof does not by any means rely on it alone. One reason is simply that individuals are often not aware of their attitudes and feelings. Since the aim of the Bruderhof system of social control is more to anticipate and prevent deviance than to sanction it, it becomes important to discern potentially deviant attitudes at a fairly early state. Another reason for stronger means of information gathering is that the weaker ones would not work as well if not backed up by the more severe.

Two intermediate methods of information gathering are the required participation of all individuals in a program of pastoral counselling by members of the hierarchy who are skilled diagnosticians of attitudinal failings, and the constant observation of all individuals by these same members of the hierarchy, and by everyone else in the community. Behavior is important as an indicator of attitude. For instance, if a person stays away from communal meals, after a while this will be investigated. It may be that the person has some good or innocuous reason for not wanting to be with people for a while. In this case, the matter will be dropped. But it is often the case that this sort of behavior is indicative of some deeper disturbance, of which the individual may not even be aware. If it is there, counselling will help elucidate it. Of course, one of the disfunctions of this sort of counselling is that the probing process itself may create disturbances where none previously had existed.

The Servant of the Word who is second in command (the Servant's Helper) has special charge of personal counselling. In Paraguay he worked with sexual problems, mainly masturbation, among unmarried men. Other problems that he specializes in include incompatibility of married couples, women who are poor housekeepers, and children's problems, especially those of parent-child relationships. The Servant of the Word, the Witness Brothers, and the Housemothers also are particularly concerned with counselling and surveillance. Women's sexual problems are generally discussed with Housemothers rather than Servants or Witness Brothers.

It is curious that the Bruderhof is able to extend its net of observation so thoroughly over the community without giving the impression at all of being a totalitarian society. As a visitor, I had the impression of great freedom from surveillance. I felt that nobody watched or cared about my movements, whether I came on time or slightly late to work, how much food I ate, etc. I also perceived this as true for everybody else. To some extent, it is true. The atmosphere of the Bruderhof is very relaxed; no one tries to present an appearance for the benefit of others. People do not work as if they had somebody watching them. Yet, coexisting with all of this, is the consciousness that one's actions, and even one's thoughts, are somehow public. A man who spent his teenage years at the Woodcrest Bruderhof, while his parents were members there, told me the following:

> I was constantly on the lookout, constantly doing things for the look, for the effect .... To me it was two different lives. When I got to school [Kingston High School] I acted one way. The second I got on the bus to go home, I changed myself and acted a completely different way.

Almost always, the use of pastoral counselling or surveillance techniques suffices to make salient information public. On those rare occasions when it is not, however, the Bruderhof is not averse to giving an individual the (purely verbal) 'third degree'. During the great crisis, some of the members were required to write repeated confessions. A woman described how she would write a confession and take it to the Servant. The Servant would read it and say, 'But there's nothing new here. I know all this already. Go back and dig deeper.'

Another incident involved three nine-year-old boys who were accused of some minor sexual misconduct. The boys were isolated from each other, and each one was interviewed separately by a Witness Brother. One boy described his interview. He and his father and the Witness Brother were in a room together. Suddenly the Witness Brother shouted at the boy, 'Why did you do it?' The boy said, 'Do what?' 'You know what I mean,' replied the Witness Brother. The boy was told that there was no use denying anything, because his two friends had already confessed, and said that he was also involved. Eventually, the boy started crying and admitted that he had done it. But when he got home with his father, he said that he had not done anything, but was just willing to say anything to avoid further interrogation. Eventually, charges against him were dropped. When I spoke to this boy, seven years later and long after he and his parents had left the Bruderhof, he still maintained that he had not been involved in any of the things that he had been accused of.

Information evoked through interrogation generally results in punishment of the individual. Most likely, the Brothers will consider his resistance to ordinary forms of information collection more serious than the crime itself. Secretiveness is a crime against the all-important inner life, whereas a mere physical or material crime is merely a threat to the external structure.

*Judgment.* Every member of the Bruderhof may be considered a judge in the sense that each Brother has a right, and even a duty, to discern and admonish wrongness in any other member. In practice, judgmental relationships are determined to some extent by one's place in the hierarchy. It is rare for anyone lower than a Witness Brother to bring a serious admonition against a Servant. An ordinary Brother may bring a complaint against a Witness Brother or Housemother, but he will be considerably more hesitant to do this than to bring a complaint against a Brother or Sister of equal rank.

Another restriction is set forth in the 'First Law in Sannerz'. This is the important qualification that judgment must always be made directly to the person being judged, either in private or in the company of Witness Brothers. Gossip is strictly forbidden, and this rule is rigidly enforced. Technically, the anti-gossip rule also includes an anti-tattling rule (i.e., going to a Servant or Witness Brother with a complaint against another member before confronting that member himself). In actuality, this rule is often circumvented. One need only present one's complaint to the counsellor in the form of a petition for advice. 'There is this strained situation between me and Joe. Is there something that I am doing wrong, or should I go and speak to him about it?' Either the counsellor will decide to act on this information himself, or he will advise the person to speak to Joe himself. However

, in the latter case, the member can admonish Joe with much more assurance having, for all practical purposes, cleared it with the hierarchy. In the rare case when an ordinary Brother brings a judgment against a member of the hierarchy, he virtually always clears it first with another member or members of the hierarchy.

In all judgments, whether informal or part of the exclusion system, the Brothers consider, not that one human being is undertaking to judge another, but that the Holy Spirit is manifesting itself through the judge to help and correct the judged. This lends an air of infallibility to judgments made by Bruderhof members and sometimes leads to excesses. An ex-member commented:

... what the group will do, you wouldn't do as an individual. You'd be ashamed to do it. What I did as a member of the Bruderhof, I would be ashamed to do as an individual now.

*Sanctions.* Probably every society uses ridicule as a means of social control. At the Bruderhof, this is the most informal and light-weight means of sanction. It is employed where behavior is extremely annoying to some people, but clearly within the right of the individual to exercise. A good example has to do with beards.

The Bruderhof is now in a state in which relations with the Hutterians are cool but may be changing. In such a situation, it would be extremely impolitic for the Brotherhood to make any blanket policy concerning beards – either to prohibit or to require them. Nevertheless, beards continue to delight some members of the Bruderhof and offend others, much as in the larger society. Usually, this conflict remains at the level of a cold war, but occasionally it bursts into open battle. A recent beard battle is described in the following poem written by two fifth-grade Woodcrest girls:

> One day Dwight and Glen
> Decided to grow some Beards.
> Some of us were against it
> But others were not.
> One supper time there was
> A parade against

> The bearded men
> Who were young in age.
> But old ones over 50
> The women have said,
> 'A beard on you looks quite true.'
> But on the young they said,
> 'A beard on you does not look true.
> So instead it must go to shreds.'
> So up went their signs
> And the signs all said
> 'Now ban the beard.'
> And 'A Man with a Beard
> is Quite Greatly Feared.'
> One also said, to make Glen dread:
> 'A Man that Does not Quite
> Properly Shave
> Belongs in a Great Big Dark
> Black Cave!'
> And now all the beards are coming in style,
> Some are shaved off and some don't look real.
> But on Glen and Dwight
> Their beards look quite true,
> > They do, they DO
> > THEY DOOOO!

Other signs in the demonstration included: 'Beards can be wiped out,' 'People find it scary to meet a man who is hairy,' and 'Beards are a fire hazard.' Not all Bruderhof members are as courageous as Glen and Dwight, however. One single man in his early twenties endured a constant stream of practical joking and teasing for about two weeks before finally giving in to pressure and shaving. It must be said in his defense that a single man arouses even more indignation than a married man by growing a beard, and Glen and Dwight are both married men and fathers.

When ridicule doesn't work or is not appropriate, the Bruderhof will often try to ignore deviance if it is not deemed a threat to the system, or to handle it through a kind of therapeutic counselling if it is a threat. Admonishment and exclusion are used only reluctantly, as a last resort. It is important not to confuse the rigid formalism of the exclusion *system* with the way this system works in *practice*. The community likes to have the system present in each person's mind as a latent warning. But each individual case is treated as unique. What is good for the community and what is good for the individual will be considered, never merely what legalism requires. The following is a description by an ex-member of a case in which public admonishment was used in an (unsuccessful) attempt to create a psychic rebirth in a particularly phlegmatic Brother:

One time a rather older, thirtyish single Brother and a thirty-fiveish single Sister – it got to be seen that they used to meet at noontime when the kitchen was relatively deserted, they'd come in there and have a little chat. In the kitchen, in the middle of the *hof*, yah! So they got each of them separately. The Sisters lectured the Sister and the Brothers lectured the Brother. I was at the Brothers' meeting . . . . They said to him, 'Look, there is a way to do a courtship. You're becoming a public spectacle. The kids are seeing you. They're talking about it. They know you've got a thing on this woman. This is just not proper. Now, do you want to marry her?' He said, 'Well, I'm not sure.' They said, 'That's a nambypamby attitude. I'd have more respect for you if you said, "Yes, I do want to marry her." You can go to the Servant and say it the usual way. But just fooling around this way is infra dig. This is not done.' He was sort of speechless and kind of wilted at all this. Z. was at this meeting. He said, 'Brother, ever since I've known you, four or five years, you've been sort of a nonentity. We never hear anything from you. You're not active. You just do your work and you go along and you never say anything. Now how come?' In other words he says, 'Now we've got you by the collar.' This is interesting. He was going to make a kind of crisis out of it, through which the guy could be shaken out of a kind of rut. [This] happened in another case . . . where the guy had come back . . . a big ball of fire . . . a really very valuable person, as he had not been before. Z. hoped this would be a [similar] kind of conversion experience. 'Now we've got something where we can get at you.' It didn't particularly happen that way.

Bruderhof sanctions, however harsh they may become, are always based upon love, never upon retribution. It is true that retributive motives may be operating subconsciously and may be rationalized by the community as acts of love. But far more often, the sanction is genuinely an act of love – 'the love that is sharp'.

This is sometimes difficult to understand because the love that the Bruderhof has towards its members is toward what they see as the Holy Spirit in each of them. They hate what they see as evil spirits in a person, and attempt to kill them. Thus, if an individual identifies with a part of himself that the Bruderhof considers a manifestation of an evil spirit, that individual will perceive hatred coming from the community, rather than love.

*Rehabilitation.* In a close community such as the Bruderhof, a system of rehabilitation is extremely important. Since there is no anonymity, the taint of crime would be impossible to erase if there were not some such process. This is seen clearly in the case of a man who had committed adultery, upon whom, for some reason, the rehabilitation process did not take:

> ... he always had this beaten look about him, all the time. His kid ridiculed him. His son, who was twelve, he used to talk about his father as 'the old sinner'. It was kind of pitiful.

A person's chance of being readmitted to the Brotherhood, without the taint of his sin upon him, depends mostly upon himself. If he has really forgiven himself for the sin, the chances are that the Brotherhood will also really forgive him. If he retains strong guilt feelings, these may prove contagious and be picked up by the others. The man mentioned above, who was ridiculed by his son, is an example of the latter type:

> I think it depends more on how the person himself perceives it afterward. [This guy] was always thinking, 'I am a sinner.' And he acted like a sinner. He went around with a sort of 'kick me' sign on him. So, in a way, his subsequent reputation was his own creation.

For those who are not conquered by guilt, rehabilitation is usually a fairly easy process. Except for the worst crimes, there is usually no underlying resentment against the individual. In very extreme cases, the person may be moved to a different *hof*, to give him the feeling of a fresh start. In general, all that is needed is to be plunged right back into the center of the life, probably with a job that requires a good deal of strenuous manual labor. Pretty soon the person fades into that amorphous mass of those who 'have had their troubles', which includes virtually everyone.

## 7. *Managing Tension*

Tension, in a closed community like the Bruderhof, is a natural by-product of the life. To minimize tension is not a satisfactory solution. It must be kept at a high enough level to function in the collective behavior generating system described in chapter four. At the same time, it must be kept from getting so intense that it begins to destroy the community.

The major technique for dealing with everyday tensions is centered around the norm of openness. If one is feeling angry or resentful toward another person, whether justifiably or not, it is permissible to 'share' this feeling with that other person. This is not the same thing as an admonishment. Often it is more like a confession (e.g., 'You know, I just wanted to tell you that the reason I was so short with you this morning was that I didn't get much sleep last night because two of our kids have the flu, so I was sort of irritable at your loud happy singing in the hall.') In any case, it creates a feeling of closeness between the two people and releases one from the pressure of secretly feeding his gripe.

A more aggressive way of releasing trivial tensions is by teasing and practical joking. The large role that these activities play in Bruderhof life has already been discussed in chapter one. Since the Bruderhof is a rather quietistic community, a tease or a joke with a violent dénouement (such as throwing someone in the water or putting pepper in the teacher's sandwich) is especially valuable as a release of aggression as well as tension. Many Bruderhof jokes are of this harmlessly violent kind.

A more ritualized form of teasing occurs in the skits performed at Bruderhof celebrations. The following is quoted from an unpublished term paper on the Bruderhof written by an ex-member:

... it could be argued that the satirical skits, invariably presented at engagement celebrations, represented a subtle kind of propaganda effort. It was customary to impersonate and caricature the future bride and groom. Since engagement negotiations were carried on through the Servant, in high secrecy, he was a natural figure in the stage plot, and his looks, mannerisms, and favorite phrases were lampooned at liberty. One must say, however, that the satire on the Servant never expressed partisan viewpoints, nor was anyone else really ridiculed in a controversial sense. The function of the skits was probably to allow potential resentments, particularly those against authority, to be vented in a socially approved setting.

These techniques, of course, while helpful in coping with the ordinary frictions of life, are totally inadequate for dealing with large-scale tensions built up as a by-product of the communal process. In chapter four, I discussed the apparent wave nature of collective behavior intensity. The collective behavior process seems to generate extreme degrees of both positive and negative affect. In chapter four I discussed some of the mechanisms for coping with over-intense positive affect. I will now discuss means of dealing with over-intense negative affect.

Historically, societies have used, with great success, two social-psychological techniques for coping with the build-up of negative emotions and negative affect. One is the catharsis, or cleansing process. As described by Aristotle, this is the process of following a tension-producing situation through to its logical and deepest culmination in the tragic sense of life. Aristotle held that this was the function of the tragic theatre for the ancient Athenian. The other, which we associate more with the Judaic than with the Greek tradition, is the scapegoat ritual. In this ritual, all of the sins (tensions, neuroses, evil spirits) of the group are psychically attributed to one being (inanimate, animal, or human) which is then sacrificed or driven away, taking all the evil with it. The Bruderhof possesses functional equivalents to both of these processes.

Catharsis is obtained in the Bruderhof through participation in the communal crisis followed by the 'clearance'. It is crucial for the success of this technique that the difficulty that provokes the crisis not be muddled through, or circumvented, or compromised. People who have been in or acquainted with the Bruderhof often criticize it for lacking mechanisms for compromise. 'You're afraid to ever disagree with anything, since any little disagreement can cause a full-scale crisis,' they say. Certainly, if the community is not strong enough to survive the crisis, they would be right. But given a community like the Bruderhof, which is strong enough to survive crises, these people miss the functional significance of this taboo on compromise. One function, the suppression of dissent, has been discussed. The other function is the attainment of a catharsis of (or cleansing from) a source of tension, which can only be achieved by following it to its fullest expression and its fullest implications. I know of no adequate theory which explains why this is so, but much of psychoanalytic theory and practice has been based on this same premise.

Even the most serious problems can be cleansed by the technique of crisis. Once, during the early years of the Bruderhof's existence, a person began complaining of continuing severe headaches. The Brotherhood decided that these complaints were due to excessive self-concern and they reprimanded this man and insisted that he continue working. Soon afterward he died of some sort of brain damage. This is the sort of event that could have left the community paralyzed by guilt that would eventually eat away at its very foundation. Instead, the Brotherhood had the matter out – thoroughly, and then-and-there. Everyone was forced to face up squarely to the enormity of what they had done. It was seen that changes would have to be made, and changes were made: since that time, the community has made more use of trained, professional medical and psychiatric diagnosis. This type of solution is known in the Bruderhof as 'having a clearance'. It comes at the end of a crisis when it has become clear that things have to be changed. The same rules apply to a clearance as to forgiveness of an individual's sins. Once the clearance has taken place, the matter may not be mentioned again.

Sometimes, as in the case just mentioned, the need for a crisis and a clearance is immediately obvious to everyone. This is the exception rather than the rule. Usually, there may be a vague uneasiness in the air – or not even that. Sometimes, externally, things may seem fine to most or all of the Brothers. In such cases, it is the special function of the Servant to discern the need for a crisis and to precipitate it. This is one of the Servant's most crucial duties. Though it is mentioned last in this chapter, this

talent is probably more essential to a good Servant of the Word
than any other.

The great crisis was precipitated in this way by a Servant of the
Word. He discerned in a situation which, if not tranquil, was at
least no more disturbed than usual, a deep and fatal wrongness.
Few other organizations would have been willing or able to
endure the risk and the torment of those three years in order to
face up to a problem that had not even been evident to the large
majority of its members. Without making any judgment as to the
rightness or the wrongness of these actions, it can be said that the
Bruderhof has emerged from that crisis greatly strengthened, at
least in internal cohesiveness.

Crises also serve another purpose. They release people from
the burden of secret feelings and resentments, which come to the
surface during crises even if the individual has not previously had
the will or the courage to express them. A present-day hippie
community in California has an institution which they call the
Withholding game. Every week, the group has a meeting in
which this game is played. Each member, in turn, speaks out all
of the resentments and annoyances that he has accumulated
during the week. Everything that has been withheld comes out.
The person to whom an attack or criticism has been directed at
this meeting is required to respond by saying, 'Thank you.' This
is the only comment that he can make. This institution is similar
to the synanon game practiced by the Synanon community, and
to mutual criticism, as practiced by Oneida. It points to the
necessity of some means of expressing secret feelings in the
intentional community.

In the Bruderhof, such release from secrecy occurs in crises,
rather than on regularly scheduled, institutionalized occasions.
Because of the way in which the Bruderhof is structured, much of
the secret resentment and hostility tends to be directed toward
members of the hierarchy – particularly the Servant. Because he
exercises so much authority in decision making and policy
setting, he naturally also bears much of the responsibility for its
success or failure, and the Brothers tend to look on him as a
father figure. Furthermore, the ordinary channels of communica-

tion and admonition are difficult to use between an ordinary Brother and a Servant. Since an unusually great amount of tension may often build up between the Brothers and the Servant, the Servant acts, quite involuntarily, as a focus for the accumulating hostilities and aggressions of the group.

Now we are in a position to see one of the major functions of the Bruderhof pattern of rapid turnover in leadership and of electing leaders with the expectation that, sooner or later, they will fall. The Servant, in falling, becomes the scapegoat of the community. Tension is released. Secret hostilities come out of hiding. Months or years of pent up aggression are dumped on the poor guy's head. A Servant now in exile reports:

Usually it was the leaders who got into trouble you see. All through the years we had a leadership problem. Oh, we had so many changes in Servants .... Many times Servants were in exclusion, or had some troubles, or something, and then the people came out: 'Yah, I had a feeling against him.' ... 'Yah, I had something against him.' ... 'Yah' ... 'Yah.' But they didn't dare speak out when he was not in trouble....

In actual fact, because I knew how it had gone all through the years, before I left Paraguay I asked everybody, 'Now please, if you have something against me, will you please say it here and now before I go? Not after I have been up to North America, and maybe one day I get into trouble, and then you say, 'Yes, yes, I had the feeling.' [Q: What did they say to that?] Yes, they promised to do it. But I still got one or two letters later.

The great crisis required the expulsion or resignation of almost a dozen Servants, some of whom have never returned. Usually, however, the deposed Servant merely needs a little rest, preceded by a short time in exclusion. Then he spends a period in the ordinary manual work. After a while, he begins to work his way up in the hierarchy again, unless his spirit has been broken by the scapegoat experience. If this occurs, the deposed leader generally leaves the community. Rarely does an ex-Servant stay in the Bruderhof as an ordinary Brother if his path to reinstatement seems blocked. There are, however, several notable exceptions to this rule.

The Bruderhof system of social control places extraordinary demands upon leaders and ordinary Brothers alike. An ex-member summed it up in this way:

There is a drastic difference from the demands on the personality made in civil life. There, only outward conformity is demanded. I think that few total institutions demand so much conformity down into the private recesses of feeling. In a concentration camp, officer candidate school, even POW camp *cum* brainwash, you still can gripe, provided you obey – and if not publicly, then privately, and if not gripe, then at least *feel* opposed. It is difficult to convey the degree to which the Bruderhof demanded and got conformity in the most private attitudes and feelings.

It is obvious that the average person could never tolerate such a system, no matter how great his motivation and how great the rewards. As the Brothers themselves often say, 'Something has got to change. Something old has to die in you, and something new be born, before this life is possible.'

## *Chapter Six* □ LEAVING THE OLD SELF BEHIND

### 1. *Who joins the Bruderhof?*

It is not that this is a group of exceptional people – they are for the most part quite ordinary people – coal miner, peasant farmer, optician, doctor, teacher, social worker, alcoholic, tramp, local Paraguayan Indian, chemist, people on the verge of mental breakdown, business-man, minister, Protestant, Catholic, Jew, Marxist, atheist, agnostic, and all manage to live together in unity and harmony because they don't rely on their own strength but are given the strength.[86]

One of the remarkable things about the Bruderhof is the heterogeneity of its population. Walking up the hill to the reservoir on a warm Sunday afternoon, one might see the wife of a former millionaire business executive sipping tea with a grizzly-faced former hobo from Germany and a former Italian Catholic juvenile delinquent from the Boston slums. Further up the hill, perhaps a Midwestern schoolteacher and a Paraguayan peasant are working in the garden together. In the face of all of these differences, it is easy to lose sight of the fact that what has brought most of these people together is a discrepancy between their previous actions and their aspirations.

The Bruderhof was founded by a band of people tormented by the need to do more than they had been able to do about the misery of the world. This element still predominates in the pre-conversion histories of the majority of Bruderhof members. In some, this can be identified as neurotic guilt, in others, saintly compassion. For most, of course, it falls somewhere between these poles.

A charming thing about the Bruderhof as a community is the presence of all age groups, from tiny babies to septuagenarians.

14.5

Population statistics are meaningless since the colonies are constantly in flux, but the accompanying table gives a snapshot picture of the number of people in the various age-kinship categories that can be identified at the Bruderhof. In the last thirty years, the proportion of adults in Bruderhof colonies has steadily declined. In 1941, adults comprised 56 per cent of the population of Primavera. By 1950, this figure had dropped to 44 per cent. In 1965, fewer than 40 per cent of the residents of Woodcrest were adults.

POPULATION OF WOODCREST IN DECEMBER 1965
BY AGE-KINSHIP CATEGORIES

| | | | |
|---|---|---|---|
| Grandparents* | 3 | Third Graders | 11 |
| Parents† | 74 | Second Graders | 5 |
| Singles | 26 | First Graders | 7 |
| Collegers‡ | 24 | Preschoolers | 7 |
| High Schoolers | 41 | Kindergarteners | 6 |
| Eighth Graders | 8 | Baby House: | 21 |
| Seventh Graders | 11 | Threes | 6 |
| Sixth Graders | 9 | Twos | 5 |
| Fifth Graders | 8 | Ones | 4 |
| Fourth Graders | 8 | Old Babies | 4 |
| | | New Babies | 2 |
| | | Total | 269 |

*Membership in this category is not strictly defined. I have used it for these people whose children are grown up and married and have children of their own. It probably would also include very old childless couples, or even very old single people, but there were none of these at Woodcrest when I was there. For most purposes, it would not include younger grandparents, some of whose children were still in school.

†The Bruderhof calls them the Mommies and Daddies. For many purposes it includes childless couples, especially if they are not too old and take an interest in children. But if there had been any newlyweds at this time, they would have formed a category of their own.

‡Only fifteen of these were actually attending a college.

The ethnic diversity of the Bruderhof is great, giving the community a rich cultural mix. However, this diversity has declined since the great crisis. During the nine-*hof* period, over twenty nationalities were represented in the Bruderhof. In Woodcrest during 1965, only seven nationalities were represented, two of them by only one person each. The accompanying table lists the population of those at Woodcrest who were over the age of twenty-one in 1965, by number and percentage in each nationality background:

| | | |
|---|---|---|
| American | 63 | 59% |
| German-Swiss | 26 | 24% |
| English | 10 | 9% |
| Dutch | 4 | 4% |
| Swedish | 2 | 2% |
| Canadian | 1 | 1% |
| Austrian | 1 | 1% |
| Total | 107 | 100% |

Of the seventy-seven married adults, three had professional degrees beyond the college level; thirty-five had completed college; eighteen had not completed college, and about the remaining twenty-one I have no information. Of this group, the largest number, fourteen, had been Quakers (nine by birth and five by conviction); the next largest group was eleven Methodists. Twenty-five others had been members of various Protestant groups, including six from the Church of the Brethren and two former Hutterians. There were two Jews, two Catholics, and the remaining twenty had had no specific religious background or one that I was not able to discover.

It is possible to recognize several typical career patterns in the pre-Bruderhof lives of members. The following descriptions are composites which do not necessarily depict the career pattern of any particular person:

A. was a member of the German Youth Movement. Once he went to hear a speech given by Eberhard Arnold, who was then general secretary of the Christian Student Union. A. was so impressed with Arnold's message that he began and kept up a correspondence with him. When he heard that the Arnolds had started a venture in communal living, he decided to go for a visit. Once there, he was so impressed with the rightness of this way of life that he decided to stay.

B. was a young English Methodist of lower-middle-class background. B. was a pacifist who became increasingly alarmed at the progressive deterioration of European politics during the 1930s. He rejected revolutionary responses, but he, himself, criticized pacifism as being too negative. He joined a discussion group of similar-minded people who were searching for a positive alternative to our war-torn social system. One evening this group had a speaker from the Bruderhof. B. was motivated by this talk to go to the Cotswold Bruderhof for a visit. After several visits and much hesitation he decided to join the community.

C. was an American Quaker who graduated from college in 1941. He married a Quaker girl who had attended the same college. Both were extremely idealistic pacifists. When the United States entered the war, C. was drafted. He refused to serve and was sent to a detention camp in Idaho. There he and his wife met several other young couples with similar ideas. After the war, a group of these young families formed a nonsectarian intentional community. This floundered along, not too successfully, for about eight years, continually struggling to make community work. Then they began to correspond with the Bruderhof in South America. They urged the Bruderhof to set up a colony in the United States. The Bruderhof sent some missionaries to the United States who stopped at C.'s community for a while. C. and the other members were very impressed by the Brothers although they did not like their narrow sectarian attitude. After the Bruderhof founded Woodcrest, the two communities continued to correspond quite often. Eventually, C. and his wife, along with several other of his fellow community members, became convinced that nonsectarian communitarianism could never work. Rather than give up completely, they decided to try the Bruderhof. They came for a brief visit and have been there ever since. C. is now a Servant of the Word and his wife is a Housemother.

D. was a college-educated career woman from New York City. She came from a sophisticated liberal background and was an agnostic. D. had majored in sociology in college and had always been interested in social movements. When somebody told her about the Bruderhof, she decided to go to Woodcrest for a weekend to observe a real utopian community. She was completely flabbergasted by her experience. Something for which she had no words seemed to call her to the community. She came back for several more visits and finally, a completely changed person, decided to join.

## 2. *Hearing the Call*

The Bruderhof message is not particularly exceptional or sophisticated. 'Talk is cheap,' according to the Brothers. One wrote, in a letter to a noted Protestant theologian at Yale Divinity School:

> ... What troubles me most [about our talks together] is the great intellectual effort and keenness, the theological emphasis. Somehow we never seem to meet as simple human beings sharing our needs and hopes, our experiences....
>
> Do you really feel J. that what this world needs is a more up-to-date theology? ... Don't you feel that the world hungers for the deed of love, for true bread, and that the world religions offer stones?...

The Bruderhof asks to be evaluated not on the basis of its theology but on the basis of its actions and its style of life.

In this it has been remarkably successful. Many thousands of people have visited the Bruderhof colonies in the United States since the first was started in 1954. A number of these have been moved strongly enough by what they saw, even on a first visit, to consider changing their entire way of life to join the community. The Bruderhof seems to have a special ability to strike people forcefully on first impression. 'The joy: it hits you first thing if you're at all open – this exists nowhere else on earth,' according to one ex-member. Exposure to the Bruderhof often evokes extravagant responses:

> I have had a remarkable experience this past summer. Would it be too presumptuous if I said that I stood in the midst of the same stream of spiritual power that broke into the world at Pentecost? ... its close approximation in both spirit and form to the primitive Christian

Church-community pictured in the first chapters of the Book of Acts is striking.

It has also elicited extremely negative reactions:

[It] gave me the creeps. I suppose it's a good life for children ... but the adults looked as if they wouldn't even say boo without asking permission. You get the impression they're holding a lot back ... not letting you in on everything that goes on.

And, of course, there are many neutral responses:

It's an interesting life, very quiet and peaceful. The people seem quite happy. I imagine you'd get bored after a while, though [paraphrased].

Sometimes the first reaction is an aha! experience for the visitor:

... may I confess something which I did, and which I knew I was doing at the time [of my first visit] but couldn't do anything about it? That was that I actually over-idealized Woodcrest. I sort of blinded myself to the fact that the people at Woodcrest would be people – just like you and I. I expected to find angels who would fall over themselves as soon as we arrived, in order to look after my comforts. Egotistical of me! But they didn't do that. Instead they *loved* me, and let me discover my protruding ego the hard way. It was 'ouch' on Wednesday of that first week when the light came.

A large minority of Bruderhof converts have had no previous attachment to religion. A current Bruderhof Sister told me the story of her joining: Initially her attitude had been extremely hostile. She was certain that she would not like the place. She was an atheist, and very hostile to piety, principles, and goodness. 'I wanted to do what was wrong and bad,' she said. Her immediate reaction, she reports, was 'as if I had walked into the New Testament. I kept waiting for pious meetings but there were none.' She purposely wore a flashy red dress for the first visit to test their reaction. She was dismayed to find that this was not criticized. This woman returned from the Bruderhof to her home in New York City, 'shaken'. But she tried to forget the experience and resume her old life. She couldn't do it. Nothing was the same. Formerly she had enjoyed music very much. Now when she went to a concert she could see only the misery of the musicians. This woman had undergone a genuine religious conversion experience from a previous position of hostility to religion.

Many who come to the Bruderhof either hostile or indifferent to religion are drawn by interest in socialism, pacifism, communitarianism, toy-making, etc. A frequent Bruderhof career pattern is to experiment with various forms of social protest, become disenchanted with their segmental nature, try various forms of communitarian living, see all of these fail, become intrigued by the apparent success of the Bruderhof community, and finally, join the Bruderhof. A favorite Bruderhof aphorism, 'We're Christians because it works,' illustrates the pragmatic orientation of many Bruderhof converts.

Many converts experience an immediate feeling that they are faced with a major decision upon coming in contact with the Bruderhof. One ex-member wrote when he was a novice:

I could just say that I felt even in the first days a very vital challenge. I had planned to stay here for a year and then return home and decide but I couldn't. Everything I had ever done or could do was challenged by the answer of these people and their way of life, and in 10 days I gave a feeble 'yes' which has grown since then to an absolute conviction.

Often the histories of Bruderhof converts record some important turning point. For many it was either the first or the second World War:

During the flight from the approaching armies at the end of the war, several times I experienced a preservation from death and injury which I could not explain naturally . . . . Then I began to think about life and realized that a life which consisted merely of work and earning one's living had no meaning or content and could never satisfy. About this time I met some young people who were really convinced about Christ and were seeking for some deeper content to life.

It is often tempting to assume that everyone who ascribes to a deviant subculture must be motivated by the same simple set of stimuli. Evidence about the Bruderhof shows that this is not true. The Bruderhof attracts both the contented and the discontented, the seekers and the non-seekers, idealists and cynics, religious and irreligious. And its effect on these people can be immediate or delayed, violent or effortless, temporary or permanent.

## 3. *The Death and Birth of the Self*

A positive response to the Bruderhof, no matter how enthusiastic, is only the beginning of a difficult struggle, culminating in baptism and full membership in the community. This period has been known to last a few weeks or several years. Normally, however, it varies between six months and a year. For most applicants, it is divided into two stages – the time spent as a guest and the novitiate. It is an extremely difficult time in the relationship between the applicant and the community. Both defer gratification and look to the future for reward. The novice is subject to the most severe of socialization processes. He usually does not understand what is being done to him, but must accept it on faith. As one would guess, the dropout rate is extremely high. Without any figures other than anecdotal evidence on which to base an estimate, I would guess that, of all those people who visit the community with thoughts of considering joining it, over 90 per cent never reach baptism. (This figure excludes those who were born or grew up in the community.)

Nevertheless, enough people do last through this difficult process to comprise a significant part of the Bruderhof population. At Woodcrest in 1966, 55 per cent of the adult population had been recruited from the outside world within the previous eleven years.

The novitiate is a time of symbolic death and resurrection. Words cannot adequately describe it. In talking about the death and rebirth of the self we are speaking of an event that occurs at the very depths of human experience. As any lover knows, this movement within the heart is not subject to scientific analysis. All we can analyze are the environmental circumstances in which this change takes place.

The sociologist can study courtship patterns without ever having been in love, can study revival meetings without ever having experienced salvation. Similarly, it is possible to study the process of world-view resocialization which occurs during the Bruderhof novitiate, without understanding the deep inner feelings which begin to well within the heart of the novice, and which alone make Bruderhof life possible.

I define world-view resocialization as one of three levels on which the individual can experience change. First, his behavior can be changed. This is the most superficial sort of change and can be accomplished through sheer coercion. Second, his attitude toward something can be changed. This is a somewhat deeper process. Generally, simple coercion will not suffice, and persuasion is needed. Still, we know of many cases in which attitudinal change has been accomplished without the compliance of the individual involved. The third type of change is the most profound and by far the most difficult to accomplish. This is the change of a person's entire 'world-view', his total attitude toward and conception of the universe. So difficult is it to effect a change in a person's world-view, that it is commonly believed that such world-views, once fixed by childhood socialization processes, become unalterable. It is often assumed that one remains a liberal, or a mystic, or an optimist all of one's life and that opinion or attitude change is possible only within the confines of that perspective.

This assumption is incorrect. Change of world-view is possible, although rare and difficult. It can occur in a religious conversion and in psychoanalysis. Both of these processes are undergone voluntarily. Classic thought reform, on the other hand, is an involuntary method of changing a person's world-view. I am going to compare the Bruderhof novitiate with the thought reform process in order to locate the points of structural similarity which are common to all systems of world-view resocialization, whether voluntary or coercive, religious or secular.

All forms of world-view resocialization have in common the attempt to penetrate to the deepest recesses of the person's inner feelings and beliefs. Robert Lifton says:

This penetration by the psychological forces of the environment into the inner emotions of the individual person is perhaps the outstanding psychiatric fact of thought reform. . . . All of these steps revolve about two policies and two demands: the fluctuation between assault and leniency, and the requirements of confession and re-education. The physical and emotional assaults bring about the symbolic death; leniency and the developing confession are the bridge between death and rebirth; the re-education process, along with the final confession, create the rebirth experience.[88]

Lifton describes an eleven-step socio – psychiatric process of world-view resocialization. These eleven steps can be grouped, for simplicity, into three stages as follows:

A. The Stripping Process
    (1) *the assault upon identity*
    (2) *the establishment of guilt*
    (3) *the self-betrayal*
    (4) *the breaking point*

B. Identification
    (5) *leniency and opportunity*
    (6) *the compulsion to confess*
    (7) *the channelling of guilt*
    (8) *re-education: logical dishonoring*
    (9) *progress and harmony*

C. Death and Rebirth of the Self
    (10) *final confession*
    (11) *rebirth*

Speaking in terms of an eleven step process, it may be hard to avoid the impression that the Bruderhof novitiate is an obstacle course which people are pushed or guided through. Nothing could be further from the truth. There is no set or normal time that any of these steps is supposed to take. Each individual goes through them at his own speed and in his own way. For each, the steps are experienced differently, nor does every novice experience all of the steps. The model is not something imposed on the novice by the Bruderhof from without. There are uniformities because of the psychological uniformities that exist among human beings, especially among human beings with a common heritage of Western culture.

The most familiar of the stages in Lifton's model is the stripping process, simply because it occurs most often. Many institutions such as schools, boot camps, prisons, hospitals, monasteries and growth centers, utilize the stripping process for its own sake.[89] The individual is stripped of the symbols of his identity. His name may be replaced by a number, his clothing for a uniform. At the same time he is made less and less capable of satisfying his own most basic needs without aid from the institution.

In most thought reform centers, the prisoner initially spends some time in solitary confinement. He may be physically weakened through beatings, lack of food, and lack of sleep. Then begins the psychological assault upon his identity. Lifton writes:

> From the beginning, Dr Vincent was told he was not really a doctor, that all of what he considered himself to be was merely a cloak under which he hid what he really was. And Father Luca was told the same thing, especially about the area which he held most precious – his religion . . . . Each was reduced to something not fully human and yet not quite the animal, no longer adult and yet not quite the child;. . . This undermining of identity is the stroke through which the prisoner 'dies to the world', the prerequisite for all that follows.[90]

At the Bruderhof, the serious guest is not isolated spatially; he takes full part in the life of the community. Physical coercion, of course, is never used, although many recruits come to the Bruderhof unused to hard physical labor, which may serve partly as a functional equivalent. However, the guest is kept a psychological isolate. In 1962, two families came to the Bruderhof with the intention of becoming members. One of these families was immediately sent to another *hof* so that they would not be able to lean on each other for support. Family units themselves are not broken up this way, although a certain amount of emotional isolation is created even between husband and wife. One man told me of his surprise when one day his wife suddenly asked for the novitiate. He had been thinking of leaving. She had thought he was ready for the novitiate but was holding back until she was ready. Both were shocked at the failure of communication between them, and felt somehow that the Bruderhof had caused this, although neither could point specifically to anything that the community had done.

The Bruderhof novice is concurrently isolated from his past and from his distinctive roles in the outside world. A woman with psychological training was criticized every time she discussed something in psychological terms. She was told that this was going to be a major barrier for her to overcome. She was also not allowed to have very much contact with a Sister who had gone to graduate school with her. Even traces of Christianity must be eliminated. One member told me (a Jew): 'It's better not to have a conventional Christian upbringing. You think you have something when you don't.' A woman with an exceptionally beautiful voice was in the habit of bursting into song while sitting alone out of doors or at work. The community made her stop this in order to chastise her ego. After she was able to give it up, she was allowed to sing again, and later made head of the choir.

Weakening of the identity is furthered by deprivation of choice. While he is on the *hof,* the applicant's freedom is sharply restricted. The community decides for him what work he shall do. He has, at least after taking the novitiate, no money of his own. He must ask even for simple necessities like toothpaste or shampoo. People take their meals at set times during the day, nor is there ever any choice in the menu. The day itself is broken up into many small units so that one is constantly being interrupted in one's job by the call of some communal function. An ex-member noted the similarity of this to monastic practices:

> In the monastery they have prayers seven times a day; here it was the mealtimes that multiplied. Something would be thought wrong with a person who wanted to keep at his hoeing or his machine and not sit down with the others at second breakfast.

The establishment of guilt is the second step of the stripping process. Lifton writes:

> Gradually, a voice within them was made to say, ever more loudly: 'It is my sinfulness, and not their injustice, which causes me to suffer.'[91]

In the Bruderhof, this step is not that important because the candidate generally comes already equipped with an ample supply of guilt. Nevertheless, mechanisms do exist which bring the individual to spend more of his time thinking about and

feeling his guilt. Bruderhof novices are encouraged to scruti-
nize their feeling states often and deeply. The novice is told that
'something is going to start changing within you' and is urged
to watch for it carefully.

Some members undergo a relatively painless transmutation of
their guilt into relief upon surrender to Christ, but, for many
others, guilt must first become a preoccupation. The following is
a typical anecdote about a recruit at this step – knowing that she
is guilty, but not yet being certain of what:

The Servant asked W. about a book he'd been reading. He said it
was non-essential reading and that while we were here it was assumed
that we would read things that would bring us closer to the life. The
book was Plotinus. So I asked him if he'd ever read it and he said no,
but he knew it was a Greek philosopher. Then W. explained that there
are a lot of people who feel that Plotinus is a sort of pre-Christian
Christian, and we asked how, by looking at a title, they could judge
the contents of a book.

Then everybody had a bad taste in their mouths. We sat in silence. I
felt that my husband was right, but the silence was so oppressive that I
almost had the feeling that we must have done something terribly wrong.
You sort of get the feeling like in Kafka's, *The Trial*, where you know
they've got you for something but you don't know what it is [para-
phrased].

By the time the guest is ready to enter the novitiate, he will
already have a well developed sense of his own guilt. The novitiate
can then foster this and make it more specific. An ex-member
describes the novice's education:

He would have to be confronted with the personal presence of God
in all his purity, majesty, and righteousness, and realize that his previous life was a filthy tatters. He would have to step down from his
pride, bury his old self, and let God live in him. For some the experience
could be gentle and gradual; for others it was shattering. Eventually
the novice would realize that the Bruderhof demanded a life-vow from
him: demanded not only that he give up personal property (an easy
matter) but also personal preferences, pride, self-esteem, cherished
activities and ideas, even in the most secret recesses of his thought.

The third step of the stripping process is that of self-betrayal.
World-view change, unlike coercion and persuasion, goes so

deep that eventually the subject himself must become a willing partner in the process. Self-betrayal is important in enlisting the subject as an ally. Lifton writes:

> ... the more of one's self one is led to betray, the greater is one's involvement with his captors; for by these means they make contact with whatever similar tendencies already exist within the prisoner himself – with the doubts, antagonisms, and ambivalences which each of us carries beneath the surface of his loyalties ... turning back becomes ever more difficult.[92]

Self-betrayal is bitter medicine for the thought reform victim. It often results in feelings of disgust and self-loathing severe enough to present the danger that the victim will be lost completely through a nervous breakdown. In the Bruderhof, it need not be traumatic, first because the recruit arrives with an initial predisposition to break with his old life, and also because the ideology has prepared him for it gradually. Because pride itself is the cardinal sin, whatever one takes most pride in is precisely, for that very reason, the greatest obstacle to progress. A man who has been active in socialist politics must learn to deny such activity as hopelessly ineffectual idealism. The psychologist mentioned above had to concentrate specifically on her 'problem' of viewing interpersonal relationships psychologically. One woman described her renunciation of a belief in the efficacy of health foods, around which much of her past life had revolved, as 'like cutting out an eye'. Yet she experienced great joy in being able to give this up for the sake of a greater good.

The stripping process culminates in what Lifton calls the breaking point. This is a situation of impasse. The individual is brought to the point of total conflict from which he sees no escape. Lifton says:

> He is not totally estranged from the environment, because even antagonism is a form of contact; but he is totally cut off from the essential succor of affectionate communication and relatedness, without which he cannot survive. And at the same time, his increasing self-betrayal, sense of guilt, and his loss of identity all join to estrange him from himself – or at least from the self which he has known. He can contemplate the future with only hopelessness and dread.[93]

During this period, the individual is brought face to face with what Lifton calls the basic fear, a fear which he describes as, 'similar to what Erikson has called, "an ego chill . . . the sudden awareness that our nonexistence . . . is entirely possible".'

The breaking point of the Bruderhof novice is not allowed to happen until the recruit is judged spiritually strong enough to handle it. The mood suddenly changes from one of love and helpful (though firm) guidance, to one of sharp impatience and impossible expectation:

I had the feeling, after a while, that no matter what we did, at the Bruderhof, that we were damned if we did something and damned if we didn't do it. If our children were quiet it wasn't good and if our children were noisy it wasn't good. Until you repent and ask to be part of it, you're just judged in this way. You're seen as evil, and you're selfish.

Although many recruits become bewildered and angry at this point (and some even leave), the change is actually a sign that the novice is drawing near to his goal. A similar procedure is used in Zen monasteries. As the Zen novice approaches *kensho*, he will be given various impossible tasks and riddles. This induces the state of complete helplessness which is necessary before enlightenment.

Such a harsh approach to basic resocialization may be necessary, but it inevitably results in a certain number of casualties. The Bruderhof has had people break down and go away embittered after being subjected to the severity of this process. One girl who was born on the Bruderhof and left with her family when she was a teenager discusses such a case:

We just wanted to forget the whole thing, really. The worst part of the community is the way they torture people's minds. Like they can actually make you believe that you're bad, brainwash you. That's what they did to my sister. When she came out of there, she really believed that she was evil . . . . When you hear nothing else all day . . . . When our parents came back, my sister was close to a nervous breakdown. She was just crying and crying all day and we couldn't stop her. She used to get up at twelve o'clock at night to talk with my parents. She couldn't sleep.

Thought reform plays out the stripping process against a background of prison cells and torture. The Bruderhof novice, in all probability, is surrounded with the greatest joy and the deepest love that he ever has or ever will experience. Thought reform plays on the subject's desire to be a part of the glorious political state, which exists sometime in the indefinite future. The Bruderhof holds out the offer of participation in a glorious but difficult life in the present – which the novice can see and touch, and which he longs to be a part of. Yet these differences do not seem to matter much. In both cases, the person clings to his old ways with all the tenacity he can muster, and in both cases it requires all the skill and patience that the collectivity can spare to break this grip on the past. So manacled is the average individual to his mother-culture, that all the desire and will power in the world are of little aid in freeing him from its rule.

The second major stage is that of identification. The stripping process is responsible for the destruction of the old, the identification process for the creation of the new. There are institutions which carry resocialization through the second stage but do not then proceed to the third stage, of death and rebirth.[94] The process is essentially complete after stage two, except that it has not jelled. The new world-view, in most cases, will persist only as long as there is pressure from an external environment. When the subject leaves he will, after a reasonable period of readjustment, be able to see his transformation more objectively, as a temporary psychological reaction to extreme social pressures. He may, however, still have guilt feelings about it.

The identification stage begins in a state of impasse between the group and the individual. Then, suddenly and unexpectedly, a door opens for the novice. He is offered a choice: 'There are two ways for you to go: one way leads to life, and the other to death. If you want the road that leads to life, you must take our way.'[95]

The Bruderhof also emphasizes the importance of this basic choice, In fact, the above quotation might well have been taken verbatim from an interview with an ex-member. The following poem, by a Bruderhof Sister, illustrates the community's presentation of this choice:

### The Gate

No one compels you, traveller;
this road or that road, make your choice!
Dust or mud, heat or cold,
fellowship or solitude,
foul weather or a fairer sky,
the choice is yours as you go by!

But here if you would take this path
there is a gate whose latch is love,
whose key is single and which swings
upon the hinge of faithfulness,

and none can mock, who seeks this way,
the king we worship shamelessly.
If you would enter, traveller,
into this city fair and wide,
it is forever and you leave
all trappings of the self outside.

In the Bruderhof, there is no sudden and dramatic switch to leniency and opportunity such as Lifton describes. The novice is aware from the beginning of the choices open to him, and generally spares himself part of the torment of the stripping process by accepting the right choices early and gracefully. Leniency and opportunity at the Bruderhof is not a specific step in a process, but can be used whenever the community feels that the novice needs some bolstering. This bolstering will often take the effect of assuring the person that his own strength or lack of strength is irrelevant to the struggle, and that by depending upon God's strength he can be assured of victory.

A woman's report of a conversation with the Servant illustrates this. This is the same woman who, as described above, had reached the point where she felt that she was 'damned if she did something and damned if she didn't':

They said, 'How can we find the right way with you? Do you think we'll find the right way with you?' I said that I hoped that they would. They asked if I thought I could be of help in this. I said, 'Yes.' *And they said, 'That's the wrong answer.'* What I should have said is, 'Only with God's help.' It showed that I was putting myself and my will before God, and that's why I answered these things wrong. They felt I was in grave danger of being willful [emphasis added].

The stick, however, is never used without the carrot. The candidates's own impotence is contrasted with God's omnipotence. Sometimes the novice becomes so discouraged by the stripping process that he finds it difficult to believe that even God can help him. Here it becomes important for the Bruderhof to emphasize that God can do anything, and will, if asked in the right way: 'But,' an ex-member puts it, 'if one asked properly in prayer, God would always give the strength to behave right. He wouldn't be nasty enough not to.' At this stage, distinguished old Bruderhof members will often confide in the novice stories of their own early struggles. The novice is made to see that his own situation, as dismal as it might appear, is nothing more than the universal human condition, and that all of the Bruderhof members, with God's help, have won through similar struggles.

God, of course, does not do this work automatically. The novice must open himself up, as completely as possible. Thus the foundation for the later confessional steps of the identification stage is built. The novice is taught to seek help with his problems. An ex-member recalled:

Once the Servant and I talked about my husband. He had been a social worker before we came. His job had been to help other people with their problems, and now it was hard for him to reverse his role and ask for help.

The Servant pointed out that social work is merely patching up the system while at the Bruderhof, they were seeking an entirely new order – the Kingdom of God. He said that we couldn't ever possibly reach this by ourselves, so that we shouldn't think of coming for help as being like a welfare recipient coming for aid. He said that he could see that my husband and I were so used to solving our problems by ourselves that this was going to be a special problem area in our case. We needed to start feeling really free to come in at any time and talk about anything that happened to be on our minds [paraphrased].

The next steps in the stage of identification, Lifton calls the compulsion to confess and the channelling of guilt. During the former, the subject learns to identify with the two major roles: the repentant sinner and the receptive criminal. It is at this time that the subject takes over from the collectivity the major responsibility for his own continuing transformation:

[The repentant sinner] in effect says: 'I must locate this evil part of me, this mental abcess, and excise it from my very being lest it remain to cause me more harm.' This leads directly to the second identity – that of the receptive criminal, the man who is . . . not only beginning to concur in the environment's legal and moral judgement of him, but also to commit himself to acquiring the beliefs, values, and identities officially considered desirable.[96]

The subject develops a compulsion to confess but does not yet know what he must confess. His guilt must be channelled. Lifton says:

Once the compulsion to confess is operating, the prisoner is ready to learn a more precise formula – thought reform's conceptual framework for his expression of guilt and repentance . . . . His sense of evil, formerly vague and free-floating, is now made to do specific work for reform . . . . What was most prosaic, or even generous, must now be viewed as criminal.[97]

At the Bruderhof, once the novice understands that his condition is universal, that all of the others have been through it and can comprehend, the compulsion to confess typically manifests itself as an enthusiastic desire to spill the beans. The Bruderhof has an advantage in this regard in that almost all of its candidates have been suffering under enormous burdens of guilt to begin with. There is an exhilarating sense of relief in the realization that there is no longer a need for secrecy even about one's innermost evil. Everyone is a sinner. Everyone is in the same boat. This exhilaration is similar to that reported under similar circumstances in encounter groups, in Synanon, and in the early days of Moral Rearmament.[98]

An ex-member told me that he never felt more loved and protected at the Bruderhof than when he was confessing a sin. Indeed, as we have seen in chapter four, so much of the Bruderhof life is based upon periodic tension and release from tension, that the entire structure of the community acts to develop in the novice the compulsion to confess. Bruderhof confession is a ritualized procedure which almost always triggers a glow of joy; and joy, of course, is the major payoff of the life and the chief symptom of being in a state of grace.

The Bruderhof novice thus has little trouble quickly developing a compulsion to confess. Confession is a way of life at the Bruderhof, not only for novices, but for distinguished Brothers and Sisters of thirty years' good standing. Learning just what he is supposed to confess is sometimes trickier. An ex-novice who quit before baptism reported:

They had some way of knowing which things were bringing us closer to the life and which things were leading us away. It was like playing that game, when you're a child ... you know, when you hide something and someone says, 'Now you're hot, now you're cold.' We felt like we had all of these sensitive thermometer-people around us, and we wanted to be allowed to stay, so we would follow all these little signals that say, 'You're getting hot, you're getting close,' rather than the opposite.

They picked this up. One of the Servants talked to us and said that he had the feeling that we wanted methods. This was no good. We had to feel free to find our own way. I felt this was good advice, but I almost said to him, 'O.K. Now what's the method for not doing this' [paraphrased].

The chief vehicle for teaching the Bruderhof novice to channel his guilt correctly is the community's ritualized form of expression (jargon). As with George Orwell's Newspeak, only feeling states for which categories in the vocabulary exist are recognized as legitimate. For instance, an individual cannot feel justifiably annoyed with the community about its stand on one particular issue. Even to attempt to express such a sentiment defines a person, ipso facto, as 'unclear'. An ex-member said:

If you as a guest or novice insist on opinions about pacifism, sex, vegetarianism, the virgin birth, that vary from the Bruderhof's, but you are nice about it, they will say that you are 'not yet clear' about those things. The right opinion is there and you will see it as soon as your vision is no longer blinded by ego. Obey the challenges that you *do* 'see clearly', and soon the rest will become clear; clarity will be given to you.

There are many such standardized feeling expressions in the Bruderhof vocabulary. From the point of view of novice socialization, one of the most important is the definition of attitude as *haltung* (the way one holds oneself). This definition makes it impossible for the individual to escape responsibility for any of his past or present actions. The community allies with the most tyrannical parts of the novice's guilt-ridden self. Any inadequacies, real or imagined, in his life and work, are seen as the result of his prideful refusal to surrender to God's omnipotence.

Very often, people come to the Bruderhof feeling guilty about the wrong things. A common problem is the socialist guest who sees the Bruderhof as a potential escape from competition and capitalism. As a novice, this person must be taught that capitalism is only a symptom rather than a cause of the world's ills. He finds that Community Playthings itself is inevitably caught up in the competitive economy. Concurrently, he learns to feel guilty instead about his own deep-seated selfishness, which is at the root of capitalism, but which goes much deeper.

An element of hypocrisy is often exposed by such rechannelling of guilt. Perhaps a socialist comes to the Bruderhof feeling smug about the progressive way he has run his business enterprise. He feels comfortably superior to his associates, and even more so now that he has decided to forsake all and join the Bruderhof. During his novitiate, the community unerringly ferrets out his own manifestations of selfishness – perhaps in the way he treats his wife and children. The novice soon sees himself as being just as bad as the worst of his business associates – worse in fact, since his sin is compounded with that of false pride.

Nowhere is the structural similarity among all types of world-view resocialization more clearly indicated than in the next step in the process of identification, that of re-education through logical dishonoring. According to Lifton, this step revolves around the strengthening of negative identity through the cultivation of existential guilt:

A priest's negative identity is likely to include such elements as the selfish man, the sinner, the proud man, the insincere man, and the unvigilant man. As the reformers encourage a prisoner's negative identity to enlarge and luxuriate, the prisoner becomes ready to doubt the more affirmative self-image (diligent priest, considerate healer, tolerant teacher) which he had previously looked upon as his true identity. He finds an ever-expanding part of himself falling into dishonor in his own eyes . . . . He is confronted with his human limitations, with the contrast between what he is and what he would be. His emotion may be called true or genuine guilt, or true shame – or existential guilt – to distinguish it from the less profound and more synthetic forms of inner experience . . . The one-sided exploitation of existential guilt is thought reform's trump card, and perhaps its most important source of emotional influence over its participants. Revolving around it are issues most decisive to thought reform's outcome.[99]

The one-sided exploitation of existential guilt is also the Bruderhof's trump card. The Bruderhof speaks not of positive and negative identity, but of the good self and the bad self. In a sense, the entire Bruderhof novitiate can be seen as a process of sensitizing the novice to the difference between his two selves, urging him to 'take his stand' in his good self, and showing him how, left to his own devices, he inevitably drifts back into his bad self. An introspective ex-member, whose perspective may be typical, describes this as a regression to infantile wishes:

In ordinary life, as an adult, one can never be wholly the good self. Other people are always somewhat frustrating to the infantile demand to be loved exclusively, alone, and without interruption. One finds oneself resenting this and hating them.

The disparagement of the individual's positive identity is called 'logical dishonoring' by Lifton because it is presented to the subject not as a reason for despair, but as a logical consequence of the world situation, and a logical reason why he should embrace a utopian ideology as his and the world's only hope:

A prisoner's inconsistencies and evildoings are related to historical forces, political happenings, and economic trends. Thus, his acceptance of his negative identity and the learning of Communist doctrine become inseparable, one completely dependent on the other .... The buildup of his negative identity, along with his developing acceptance of Communist doctrine, provide the first contours of something new.[100]

The Bruderhof ideology provides a means whereby the novice, once having accepted his negative identity, can learn to externalize it and thus make it tolerable. The ideology shows how the bad self is merely the natural self, in the absence of the Holy Spirit. The good self comes to be defined as 'member of the Brotherhood'. Regaining self-respect then becomes the equivalent of becoming a Bruderhof member – leaving the old (bad) self behind. An ex-member social scientist commented upon this phenomenon in a letter to me:

Regardless of an individual's status within the Bruderhof, as a Bruderhof member he is élite. He is given a rationale that allows contempt for all non-members plus a masking benevolence toward them. The individual also gains a sense of power-gratification from the assumption that the Bruderhof way of life will eventually be forced on the rest of the world. Christianity is the one true way of life. We have faith that one day the world will live in Christianity. The world is going to pot for lack of Christianity. The world will be destroyed if it refuses to accept Christianity [paraphrased].

Robert Lifton speaks of the final step of the identification stage as one of progress and harmony. During this time the new self gets the emotional support it needs to survive. It is hard to see such a step in the Bruderhof socialization process. The novitiate is, after all, not a coercive process like thought reform. Except during times of severe personal crisis, the novice generally participates in the joyful experiences and loving relationships of the community. Feelings of progress and harmony are thus interspersed throughout the novitiate, rather than constituting a specific step.

This leads us to the third, final, and most rarely practiced stage – which is also the least understood. Evidence from thought reform centers, from psychoanalytic case histories, from monasteries, and from institutions such as Synanon, indicates that a death and rebirth crisis can occur after the identification stage, to internalize the new self and make it permanent.

As a last, desperate line of defense, the individual perceives his crisis as tantamount to his own physical death, and all of his organismic impulses to survive are called into play. If the third stage is to be achieved, the way must somehow be prepared for the individual to accept what seems to him to be his own death. Religious institutions often specialize in helping people cope with the idea of death, and it is for this reason that, in general, only religious institutions have been able to bring people successfully through this third stage. In recent years, non-religious institutions such as thought reform centers and addiction treatment programs have been able to substitute precise psychiatric understanding and technique for the power of traditional religion.

Unfortunately, these final steps of the conversion process, which are by far the most important, are also by far the most difficult to analyze, or even describe. This phenomenon has been observed in other studies of religious conversion; no words can be found to describe the experience of the actual time of the conversion itself. Some of my informants, however, have struggled to give some sense of what happened to them:

> The metaphor or simile or whatever you want to call it that came to me was, can I jump over this cliff? I said to the Servant, that he was over here and I was over there. I had to jump over this cliff and there was this chasm to get to where the people in the Bruderhof were. And I couldn't jump. I absolutely couldn't. Or into the chasm. Anyway, I had to jump over a separation, over the chasm or whatever you want to say. And I couldn't. I couldn't let go. I said to myself, 'What the

hell am I holding on to? I'm holding on to this stupid, impoverished ego.' I knew it, and I still couldn't do it. So there you are. To be able to let go, this is called faith – to believe in the impossible, to go ahead.

Those that make it through to the other side, likewise have little ability to describe what they have experienced. A great sense of joy and a deep sense of peace are part but not all of the experience. No doubt it is experienced differently by different people. Always the previous suffering will be spoken of as an inevitable prerequisite: 'This feeling of release and redemption, it starts with this feeling of being so miserable.'

One of the best descriptions of this crisis, as well as of the preparation for it, comes from Rodney Collin's description of schools of esoteric knowledge. I think that the following long passage is worth quoting:                          *Gurdjieff*

> The next part of the work of a school is the gradual breaking down of the old personality among its more intimate pupils. This work also may touch in stronger or weaker degree quite a large number. And in an individual the process may go on for years, or even for all that remains of a lifetime.
>
> This process may be compared with the drying out of nuts in preparation for shelling. When a walnut, for example, is green, it is impossible to remove the shell without seriously damaging the kernel. Shell and kernel then form an inseparable whole. After a suitable drying-out process, however, the shell becomes brittle and separated from the kernel, at which stage a comparatively light tap will split it, revealing the kernel in its perfection.
>
> All those entering a school from the outside may be regarded as 'green': while those who honestly expose themselves to school influence, after a certain number of years begin to approach the state when essence and old personality have become loosened from each other, and a comparatively light blow is sufficient to separate them. This loosening of personality from essence is one of the chief purposes of school discipline. Different methods, ranging from violent reproof to an example of complete humility, may be used by the teacher, according to his nature, to produce the same result.
>
> While this effect is being produced in the pupil by school influence, his own inner work is that of self-purification. Put in another way, this means that he strives to eliminate from his organism everything that

he does not want to keep permanently. Such things will include dis-harmonious physical states and bodily sickness: harmful emotions and uncontrollable attachments and longings: malicious, fearful and self-centered thoughts. Physical purification is not absolutely essential, but if it is ignored, the suffering of the learner at a later stage is greatly in-creased, and a tremendous strain is put upon his will in order to over-come physical inertia and pain. One of the effects of physical purification is to eliminate unnecessary suffering.

During this period of preparation, the pupil has also to learn how to make himself do difficult things and how to carry out certain painful or repetitive exercises, which will later be necessary to fix a certain state in him. He should not carry them too far at this stage, because he does not want to fix anything. At the same time, he must master them so that they will be quite familiar at the moment when he needs to use them intensively.

All this preparation leads to the point where it is time for the old personality to die or be killed. This death depends upon many things and it may come about in many ways. It may be the deed of a teacher, either gradual or in one terrible assault. It may perhaps be induced by some overwhelming pressure from life, which the pupil has voluntarily accepted or invoked. Hardship and sacrifice, spread over many years of preparation, may have reduced personality to a powerless wraith. Pain, prison, starvation, torture, abandonment or ruin – swallowed and not rebelled against – may equally destroy it. As in the analogy of the nut, if dessication is complete, any blow can split the shell which will fall away of its own accord.

What is left has no position, no money, no family, no acquaintances, no ambition, no power of acting for itself. Many of these things may return to the pupil later in a different way. But at this moment – whether in school, in prison, or on the battlefield – he finds himself without anything and without any past. It is as though his body were placed naked on a desert island where it had no previous connections of any kind. For a little while he is as a newborn child.[101]

This final stage of the thought reform process has two parts: the final confession and the rebirth. The subject empties him-self in one last all-encompassing confession which serves to 'fix' in him his new personality:

Both Dr Vincent and Father Luca took part in an agonizing drama of death and rebirth. In each case, it was made clear that the 'reaction-ary spy' who entered the prison must perish, and that in his place must arise a 'new man', resurrected in the Communist mold. Indeed, Dr Vincent still used the phrase, 'To die and be reborn' – words which he had heard more than once during his imprisonment.[102]

In the Bruderhof, the purgative confession is only one of many means of triggering the rebirth experience. For many there is instead a powerful personal experience of Christ – an actual physical recognition of his presence. For others there is nothing dramatic, but only a gradually strengthening realization of being called to a new way of life, of being redeemed. In these cases, the novice may one day become aware that a new energy, a new perspective, has begun moving within him, almost without his noticing that anything has changed.

The final stage of Bruderhof socialization is also the Bruderhof member's first lesson in ego loss and collective merging. As was described in chapter four, this is an integral part of the joy-producing experience. Probably this training is essential if the Bruderhof is to be able to rely on the controlled collective behavior experience as its major source of commitment and energy. Although rarely as dramatic as in the novitiate, periodic collective deaths and rebirths will punctuate the career of the Bruderhof member for the rest of his life.

The similarities between Bruderhof socialization and involuntary means of world-view change raise disturbing questions about the compatibility of freedom and community. If community is dependent upon the collective behavior experience, and if the collective behavior experience is dependent upon openness to the death and rebirth experience, and if this openness can only be achieved through a process similar, if only structurally, to thought reform, then one is forced to confront a serious question. Is community beyond the grasp of modern man? Is it attainable only at a price that no reasonable man would be willing to pay?

There is a danger, however, in making structural comparisons among totally different processes. A fault of the comparative method is that there is an inevitable tendency to stress similarities and neglect differences. As I mentioned earlier, thought reform and Bruderhof resocialization are poles apart phenomenologically. One is coercive, rigid, and exploitive. The other is voluntary, flexible, and loving. Thought reform sacrifices its victims for the sake of future generations. The Bruderhof, although concerned with the future, offers its members a deeply rewarding life in the present.

Sometimes the third stage just doesn't happen. There is nothing inevitable about the process I have described: it can break down at any point. Sometimes a recruit goes through a lengthy and painful training period and then finds that he can't make it over the final hurdle. Such people aren't allowed to linger on indefinitely. They will be given every assistance, but, if nothing moves in them, they will finally be asked to leave:

It just shocked us to hear them [tell us we had to leave]. We felt, if we could only stay a little bit longer. But their feeling was, no, that we'd been there long enough, in fact longer than they usually let people stay. They felt, to put it bluntly, you have to shit or get off the pot. They didn't say that, but this is the way I interpreted it. This is one time you don't just float on the waves, baby. You've got to make a decision. You're either going to take this step and trust what happens next, or you don't, and then you have to go away . . . .

Some people [at the meeting] didn't feel clear that we should leave. They felt real close to us, some of these people, and they expressed this. They said, 'But if the others feel this so clearly, we'll go along with it. But we have the feeling that, maybe you don't see it, but you're really very close to us.' They were sort of trying to make it happen right there, but not wanting to push us. It was done very very beautifully, I think.

We didn't feel any resentment. We felt real love. I cried because I hated to leave and there were so many things there that I cried at the thought of leaving. I cried halfway to California. I don't think it was until we got to Wyoming that I noticed sunsets and stuff like that. I was really – because this was a thing I had longed for so much; and yet to have to make that jump! And yet they were quite right! Because, you see, this was the reality element. We'd been living in a dream world. But there is something [in the Bruderhof] which is much more serious. It's an all or nothing thing. So they were really helping me to get down from the clouds. I was really grateful. They did the right thing.

Occasionally, a person is baptized without ever having the

rebirth experience at all:

> I was baptized without ever really having a redemption experience. I believed in it. I wanted it. But I never had it. At the time I sort of simulated it. Later, when I was a Brother, it came to me [paraphrased].

In general, however, the novice goes through the entire three stage process and then is considered ready for baptism. The baptism ceremony itself is an awesome experience. The prospective member takes lifetime vows at this point (see appendix A). All of his material possessions become the property of the Bruderhof forever. Even more important, he binds his entire life to the will of the community without qualification. He must promise to put loyalty to the community ahead even of loyalty to his spouse and family. The candidate is asked a series of questions at the baptism ceremony. Great attention is paid to his answers and to the way in which he answers. It is not unknown, although it is rare, for a candidate to be disqualified (and sent back to the novitiate) at the point of the baptism ceremony itself.

Baptism marks not the end, but the true beginning, of the individual's struggle with his weak and evil self. He soon learns that the old self has not permanently died but must continually be kept in its weak state. When he was a novice his job was to learn that he had no power to do so, but only God, acting through the community, had this power. Now that he is a community member he must strive continually to remember this. Admonishment and the exclusion system are there for his lapses.

## 4. *The Special Case of the Sabra*

In following the chronological development of the Bruderhof member's career, we ought next to discuss the ways in which the new self is maintained. But first it is necessary to digress to a subject which complicates the model: some Bruderhof candidates are born in the Bruderhof and enter the novitiate directly from 'membership' in a Bruderhof family.

One of the major differences between the Bruderhof and almost every other communitarian group is that the Bruderhof does not try to hold on to its children after they have finished school. Naturally, each parent hopes that his child will decide to join the community. But this natural parental desire is never allowed to influence community policy. On the contrary, Bruderhof children are encouraged to train for and to experience the outside world. If they then decide that they want to join the community, this is fine, but the requirements for membership are no lighter than for any stranger coming from outside.

This is one of the Bruderhof's major strengths. Other communities that have survived for more than one generation (e.g., Oneida, the Hutterians) have found that the second generation never had the enthusiasm or the ideological fidelity of the first. There seems to be a law of spiritual regression. Even the appallingly thorough socialization program experienced by Hutterian children has not served to retard that group's rapid devolution from intentional community to ethnic subculture. But the Bruderhof takes only those of each generation who are 'called' to the life – in recent years approximately 75 per cent.

The Bruderhof *sabra* has no 'birthright' to membership. But neither is it quite accurate to say that he is treated just like a recruit from the outside world. For one thing, the Bruderhof has not been able to eliminate the mystique surrounding the *sabra* – 'our product'. By virtue of his birth and upbringing in the community, the *sabra* has a head start. In childhood, he is kept purer and more innocent than is possible in the outside world. In this cohort group, from Baby House through college, he has experienced many intimations of what community life is all about.

This brings us to the second major difference in the treatment of the *sabra*. He does not have to be resocialized. His socialization process has been going on since his birth. By the time the *sabra* has reached the novitiate, he has already passed through the first two stages of the resocialization process. He need only prepare and wait for the redemption experience. On the other hand, the *sabra* experiences difficulties unknown to the outside recruit. He has no deep understanding of what the outside world is really like. It is difficult for him to feel *called* to a life into which he instinctively feels that he has been *born*.

Bruno Bettelheim has spoken of the difficulties experienced by *sabra* children in the kibbutzim, in trying to live up to the heroic image of their parents, the pioneering founders of the movement. One Bruderhof child who left the community asserts that the situation at the Bruderhof is similar, but even worse:

So if the kibbutz has brought up this passive kind of person, they were more successful than we were. Because, you see, there is no vow demanded of a kibbutz high schooler, at least not that I've heard of, in which the kibbutz person, the kibbutz teenager says that 'I have discovered completely, independently, for myself, and only for myself ... that this way of life is right, not because my parents live it', and so on. Which is the point to which we in the Bruderhof have to get before we're even considered for full membership. We cannot say, 'This is the way of my fathers and my friends, and it's the way I love, and therefore I would like to stay.' That's not enough in our community and that's the frightening thing.

That's where you're put through a goddam head test. Is your head with Christ? you know. And you wonder, 'Now who the hell is He?' Now our parents say they know who He is, because they have been lonely, and they have, through their religious searching, founded and built a Christian brotherhood. They've read all the books and so on. Why read Plato? It's all in the Bible. Well, they found that out, perhaps, that all wisdom, say, is contained in very few words, you know. But then they prevented us in many cases from following that same journey.[103]

The life of a Bruderhof child is extremely sheltered. Until high school he has very little unprogrammed contact with the outside world. This was the case even more in Paraguay than in America. The story is told in the Bruderhof of the child in Primavera who, upon seeing a stranger asked, 'Is that a Paraguayan, or a Mennonite, or a real person?' This was not regarded as a healthy sign.

The Bruderhof child's life is full and happy despite lack of contact with the outside world. Every *sabra* that I spoke with remembered his or her (pre-teenage) childhood with pleasure:

Actually I think the community is very good for children .... You're with your own age group all the time. You're away from your parents except for at night. You're not constantly with your mother

. . . . Even in South America, it was a so-called primitive country, but for a child it was ideal. It was like a farm, and we were always outdoors, playing outside.

Relationships between children and the adult community members are close and warm. Most community children grow up with a sense of safety, of being surrounded by love, without developing excessive dependence upon the father and mother. A Primavera *sabra* recalls early childhood memories:

. . . your parents . . . kissed you goodnight and said, 'O.K. now, daddy and mummy have to go to dinner,' . . . and it would be, 'Who's on watch tonight?' and so on, 'Do you think she'll tell a story?' and stuff like that . . . .

But of course here the personality of the watch came very much into play – and of course I always wanted the young girls particularly. This is probably where one's first erotic kind of thing came, when somebody other than your sister came and cuddled you and told you a story. She was an older girl, probably a senior teenage girl or usually a young woman. But anyway then the next night it could be an old lady, some battle-axe, you know, and you had to just take that. You'd just know that when you saw her coming, you know, 'Pssh' and you lay dead-still in bed. And this was so with all the kids. You had your favorites and you talked about which ones.[104]

But the most important relationships for Bruderhof *sabra* children are not with adults, but with the child's own peer group. Just as with the adults, collective singing plays an important part in developing peer group solidarity from a very early age:

Almost as soon as the children learn to talk they are singing the simple 'Hallelujah' round of which they never tire. And throughout the early years as toddlers and on into the kindergarten years, to sing about what they experience in nature is just as natural as to talk about it. Can't you just imagine them going for a walk in the rain, all donned in their colorful raincoats and hats, splashing in the puddles and singing, 'Pit, pit, pat go the little wet feet?' Or singing any of the dozens of early spring songs as they discover the slender green shoots of a crocus, the tiny buds opening on a bush, or a Johnny-Jump-Up in bloom?[105]

As the children grow older, the cohort continues to serve as the child's *gemeinde* within the larger community. Only slowly, and in many cases reluctantly, does he begin to emerge out of this smaller fellowship to take his place in the community as a whole. The Primavera *sabra* quoted above speaks of this:

> The age group. You've always been in your age peer group, you know, and you know each other inside out, but you never really expressed cross-sexual affection very much. That's because the community ethic, just like the kibbutz, was against it. Not that you didn't have feelings – my God! – but you never really showed them. But you had a kind of brotherly, sisterly respect which we fought against for many years, say between ten and fourteen. Because at the age of fourteen you realize that you're soon going to be apart, you're soon going to have to go to work in different departments and see much less of each other. Maybe some are going to leave the community for training outside.[106]

The children's cohort even gets a taste of Bruderhof power struggles. The following was told to me by a *sabra* girl whose family had left the community. Her father had been a Servant of the Word and her mother had been a Housemother:

> My father was always the leader. Whoever the leader was, their children always turned out to be leaders in the school, in your group .... The children turned you into leaders. Like they would always come to you, always leave the decision up to you. If two children had a fight and you had nothing to do with it they'd come to you, tell you about the fight, and you were supposed to resolve it. [Q: So the children knew whose parents were leaders?] Oh, yes. And it had an effect on them socially. But I didn't mind it. Sometimes they would pay you back for it, you know. So you would get the whole group against you. Not the *whole* group. You'd have your best friends with you. But sometimes the whole group would throw it back in your face when actually it isn't your fault ....
>
> Because our mother was always a Housemother, they always thought we got better things. There's one thing I really noticed when I left the community, the relief of jealousy ... this looking out, like on birthdays, to make sure that we didn't get more than the other children. I really didn't like it. I resented it, and often I wished my mother wasn't a Housemother because of it.

The purity of the children's groups is guarded closely by the adults. A modified form of the exclusion system is even used. A child felt to be a bad influence may be separated from his peers to avoid spreading the infection. One child reported a six-month isolation which he experienced when he was about nine years old. He and some other children had been accused of some minor sexual transgression. He would not confess to this and so he was sent to live with one of the single young men of the community. He was able to have only limited contact with his family and no contact with the other children. He was given private lessons instead of attending school. Part of his daily routine included working in the shop alongside the man with whom he was living.

As with the adults, punishment for sin is matched by complete forgiveness once the child has repented. One Sister remarked that 'it sometimes comes at the child like a knife to find so much forgiveness after being so naughty – and to be forgiven again and again'. Thus the essence of Bruderhof life takes root early.

Graduation from the eighth grade is an important turning-point in the life of a Bruderhof child. With much ritual, fanfare, and teasing warnings he is cast into the cold hard world of the public high school. Actually, every attempt is made to see to it that the experience of change is not too drastic. A Sister who teaches eighth grade in the Woodcrest school, writes the following:

We are very grateful to the high school for their understanding help and their concern for all the young people who come under their care. This going out has not meant any abrupt change in our children, nor in their relationship to their community home. They meet many challenges in high school and have to find their own way and stand on their own feet. They remain children who are slowly and naturally becoming young adults. They can, if they are determined, remain free from the corrosion of a false social pressure to become 'counterfeit adults', and from the forced preoccupation with sex which has spread like a sickness throughout American high schools . . . .

The wish of the community is not to hold the children at home, but rather to give the uncertain every chance to be away, to see the community life at a distance, to make a free decision as to where and how they wish to give their lives.[107]

After high school, most young people go on to college or advanced vocational training. Some decide to leave right after high school. Some decide to go directly from high school into the life of the community. In the old days, when education stopped for most at the age of fifteen, it was possible, although rare, to become a Brotherhood member at fifteen. Nowadays one almost never finds a full member below the age of eighteen.

At some point in his life, usually during his early twenties, the *sabra* must make up his mind whether he wants to join or leave. Although each case is handled individually, prolonged indecision is usually not tolerated. The young man or woman who continually says that he cannot make up his mind will eventually be told to leave for a while until he is clear about what he wants to do.

The novitiate of a *sabra* is likely to be a good deal less stormy than the novitiate of an outsider. There is much less likelihood that he will encounter any earthshaking surprises. But it is not necessarily any shorter. The redemption experience comes at its own pace whether a person is a *sabra* or an outsider. There are cases of outsiders' receiving baptism after a month and cases of *sabras* who have had to wait many years. I asked a twenty-four-year-old *sabra* whether she had decided to stay in the Bruderhof. She replied that she wanted the life but that it was not up to her. She had not been baptized but she was waiting and hoping for this. When I asked a younger *sabra* at Woodcrest why she had become a member, she spoke of the world being in such a bad state and the need to do something about it. She said that she supposed that if her parents had not been here she wouldn't be a member, but that she's glad that she is.

There is no difference in the vows of the ceremony of baptism for the *sabra* and for the outsider, except of course that the *sabra* has no material possessions to surrender. After baptism, any trace of distinction between *sabra* and non-*sabra* disappears. No differentiation of any kind is made among Brotherhood members according to their past backgrounds. All must continually struggle to maintain the weak self.

## 5. *The Maintenance of the Weak Self*

Baptism is probably the major rite of passage in the Bruderhof member's life. Before baptism the individual has few rights. His every action may be publicly scrutinized by any Brotherhood member. His voice in the decision-making process is by invitation only. His opinions are listened to as indications of his spiritual progress, more than as opinions. He is not eligible to be engaged or married.[108]

Precisely because entrance into full membership in the community results in such a sharp rise in status, it is important for the functioning of the community that there be no relaxation in the suppression of the individual ego. The individual must never get the impression that the struggle is over. The struggle to maintain the weak self is never over. Even those revered elders who have been in the Brotherhood for over forty years are not free of it. We must ask the question then, how is the weak self maintained after a person becomes a full community member?

The most important mechanisms for maintaining the weak self in the Bruderhof are just those which help create the weak self during the novitiate. The changes that take place in a person's life when he becomes a member are important. Just as significant, however, are those things which do not change. I spoke of the novice's isolation – physical, interpersonal, and from his former life. The full member experiences similar isolation. He is rarely allowed to maintain membership in outside organizations, or to leave the *hof* for any length of time without permission. Deprivation of choice and preference continue after baptism. An attitude of dependency, and the definition of the self as evil and the community as good continue to be strongly encouraged. The major difference is that, prior to baptism, the individual undergoes resocialization administered from without. After baptism, as long as he remains in good standing, he is more largely responsible for his own self-discipline.

The main danger that baptism presents to the maintenance of the weak self is that the individual may think that he had gained certain rights by achieving the status of full member. This usually manifests itself in the desire to have a career, or in the feeling that now one 'belongs' in some permanent sense to a human material community and a web of interpersonal relationships. The Bruderhof needs mechanisms to expunge both of these false expectations when and if they occur.

One does not enter a career when one enters the Brotherhood. There is no path of advancement from anything to anything else. One may gain a certain sacral prestige from accumulated seniority, but never promotion in actual office. Young people as well as old may become part of the executive hierarchy. Old people as well as young may be found as shop workers or laundry workers. Moreover, there is no pattern of advancement. One person may be a worker, then a Witness Brother, then a Servant. Another may be a Servant, then a Witness Brother, and then a worker. Still another may be a Servant, then a worker, then a Witness Brother.

Even on the job, one is not permitted to become ego-involved with one's creative work. I have discussed, in chapter one, the taboo on praising or taking pride in one's work. The periodic Bruderhof crises are functional in this regard because they provide continual interruptions in task activity. Bruderhof theology prescribes two attitudes which one must maintain toward one's personal and collective fortunes. These are described by an ex-member:

(1) *Erwartung* [expectation]. One is to expect everything from God. To do one's damnedest, but be constantly aware that one's own effort avails nothing. Symbolically, even the way hands are held [in prayer], upraised, separate, and open, expresses Expectation .... Expectation is called an aspect of the childlike spirit: the child asks and is given everything from its father. What the child does is not work for the fulfillment of his own plan, but obey a directive and leave the results up to the discretion of the father.

(2) *Gelassenheit* [hanging loose]. The ability to take frustration with calm equanimity when it comes, and the attitude that is prepared to accept anything. A translation might be 'playing it cool', à la beatnik or organization man. It has similar protective functions, but playing it cool involves withdrawal of loyalty, which at the Bruderhof is not allowed.

Community members must also guard against the false impression that they have a right (if not individually, then at least collectively) to a share of the physical community and that they have a right to be loved and taken care of by their fellow community members. Many of the ex-members from Paraguay that I interviewed were indignant that the community that they had built with their own hands had been sold by the Bruderhof, and that this decision had been made largely by Brothers who had not participated in building the community. These people have certain legitimate grievances about the way the dissolution of Primavera took place, and particularly the role of personal power struggles in the decisions. But in addition to this legitimate criticism, I often sensed the feeling that these communities were the personal (collective) property of those who had built them – a natural enough attitude, but not one consonant with the Bruderhof world-view.

Even more common than possessiveness about the communal plant is possessiveness in interpersonal relations. It is repeatedly stressed that Bruderhof love is *agape* rather than *eros*. The love is automatic, no matter what one's personal characteristics, as long as one is committed to the life. But the love is just as automatically turned off if one leaves. And for a person in disgrace, the positive expression of this love is turned off in favor of 'the love that is sharp'. Many Bruderhof members have found this impossible to understand, even after having been members for many years. It is ironic that people don't find it hard to believe that a whole village of people can immediately fall in love with them at first sight, but many are dismayed to find out how quickly this love can be turned off when they fall into disgrace.

It is not only in the receiving of love that the Bruderhof member is in danger of losing his weak self; it is in the bestowing of love as well. In so far as love is *eros*, the ability to love is the ability to have autonomous feelings and to express preferences, both of which are ego-building activities. It is therefore all the more important that Bruderhof love be *agape*. In *agape*, one does not love so much as one participates in a love experience. God loves, using you and other people as transmitters and receivers.

In addition to the mechanisms discussed above, the Bruderhof stresses the importance of a continual struggle to maintain the weak self. An ex-member commented:

If one's ego isn't involved, then whatever the decision is, that's the decision of the group. But where we are, our little egos are involved,

and we think the decision ought to go one way or the other . . . .
This is the kind of thing you have to struggle with the rest of your life.
There isn't any way that you're able to say, 'I've achieved it,' because
you haven't. An hour maybe, or for two hours, or a day, but whatever
is happening has an effect. This is where you have the ups and downs.

The Bruderhof is always on guard against any traces of pride or
complacency, either in an individual or in the entire community.
When one person wrote to a friend in another *hof*, 'I take comfort
in the knowledge that we are an outpost of the Kingdom of God,'
this helped start an inter-*hof* crisis. One is not supposed to feel
that one has arrived, but rather that one is continually falling
short.

Such a life may seem masochistic in the extreme. Perhaps for
some it is. But it is important to remember that the rhythm of the
Bruderhofer's life differs from that of most people. It is based not
on tranquillity and equilibrium (or the search for these), but on
the continual oscillation of struggle and joy, of tension and
release. The Bruderhof member's lot cannot then reasonably be
judged according to the criteria of a different culture. We must
judge it, if we judge at all, by its results.

## 6. *Effects on the Individual*

To me, the most significant aspect of Bruderhof life is its richness.
A favorite Bruderhof aphorism is that the personality flourishes
in the absence of the ego. This seems, from my observations, to
be valid. There are no 'grey' people at the Bruderhof. After I had
been there only a short time, each one stood out sharply in my
mind as a unique and colorful personality. Undoubtedly, a great
deal of this has to do with the selection effect. People who pick
up stakes to go and join the Bruderhof must be somewhat unusual
to begin with. But the point is that participation in the resocialization process that results in the death of the self at least
does not destroy this uniqueness. And according to the members
themselves, including many ex-members who are otherwise quite
bitter, it is even enhanced.

A crucial factor in accounting for this seems to be the focussing effect of Bruderhof life, a result of the single-mindedness with which the communal goals are pursued:

> We felt we were perceiving things with greater clarity. I mean one thing is, you're away from the telephone, the doorbell, having to go out and shop, and all the things that impinge on your life when you're out in society. At the Bruderhof you're protected from all these outside forces that take your life in so many directions. You can really concentrate on relationships. Time becomes TIME. Trees and walking in the woods become really enjoyable activities, because you're walking for the sake of walking, not to get to work in the morning. There was a lot more time with the family, like having tea in the afternoon with your own family. You see your husband a lot more. There are lots of aspects – the children looked differently to me – I saw them more clearly – I was seeing all of us more clearly. And we had common experiences, like the whole family would hear the same story together at dinner or hear the same music. The children in school would often be discussing the same things the adults were. There was a unified aspect of the wholeness of life, that way.

Another significant property of Bruderhof life is its simplicity. This is more of a mixed blessing. In some ways the emphasis on simple joys and pleasures is touchingly beautiful. Bruderhof people, adults as well as children, get tremendous pleasure out of weaving flowers into a garland, making or lighting a candle, or bursting out into a song. As one woman put it:

> This business of the losing of the self, when you have lost all desire, and all sense of wanting anything for yourself, it's true that the most wonderful things can happen to you. When you're not wanting anything, then whatever happens is a gift.

One Brother told us how much he enjoyed the simple pleasure of having a room of his own for several weeks when he and his wife stayed at the Mother House after their child was born.

On the other hand, the urge for simplicity sometimes leads the Bruderhof into an almost morbid avoidance of some of the more difficult aspects of life, particularly the area of sex. All intentional communities have had difficulties with the problem of sex, and the Bruderhof is no exception. But the Bruderhof is unusual in its reluctance to admit the existence of this problem. This, more than anything else, brings an atmosphere of awkwardness and stiffness into Bruderhof life which is just the opposite of the intended spontaneity and simplicity. I know of at least one single Brother who left the community after ten years because he found this condition finally unbearable.

It seems to me that the Bruderhof children suffer most under this system. It is true that some of the young teenagers radiate an air of purity and virgin serenity which is genuinely beautiful and which is virtually unknown in ordinary American society. This, no doubt, is what the Bruderhof is aiming at with all of its children. Unfortunately, many Bruderhof children grow up with just enough knowledge of sex to get the impression that it is the source of an awful lot of trouble. Youthful experimenters are hit the hardest. Those children unlucky enough to be caught kissing or petting are punished severely. I spoke to one boy who had been caught necking with a girl in the woods when he was about twelve years old. Unfortunately, the girl happened to be the daughter of the *Vorsteher,* although the results probably would have been much the same no matter who she had been. The reaction of the community to this incident so traumatized this boy that now, at the age of twenty, he reports that he still has great difficulty in relating to girls, although it has been over six years since his family left the Bruderhof.

While at Woodcrest, I observed that a number of Bruderhof children were always getting into some kind of mischief. At a Woodcrest guest meeting, a Witness Brother was asked why the Bruderhof does not take a more active part in the outside world, as they did in the early days. The Witness Brother replied that one reason was that they had their hands full trying to cope with their children. 'Our kids may look like angels when you see them playing together on the lawn, but believe me, some of them are the worst little brats you've ever seen,' he said. It would be absurd to attribute this situation entirely to the problem of sex. Undoubtedly, the large size of the families, the constant influx of all manner of guests, and the periodic crises and euphoric episodes all have a lot to do with the situation. But the combination of the great intimacy of boys and girls in the cohort group and the Victorian prudishness of the community certainly contribute to the situation.

Perhaps the most fundamental of all questions to be asked about the effect of the Bruderhof on the individual concerns the loss of freedom. One of the most frequent comments made by visitors is that the life seems almost ideal in all respects except, of course, for the total loss of freedom. Certainly, from a common-sense point of view, one loses all vestiges of personal freedom in joining the Bruderhof. From the sociological point of view that the individual in society is also under many constraints, the issue is much less clear.

Another problem is philosophical. Just what is freedom anyway? Durkheim's analysis of the state of *anomie* points out that one of the effects of 'freedom' from any external controls is the eventual inability of the individual to act so as to satisfy his needs.[109] And while the Chicago School of sociologists asserted that the expansion of action alternatives made possible by the city was tantamount to freedom, urban sociologists in our time speak instead of alienation and the 'one-dimensional man'. We can be sure that the concept of freedom has something to do with the concept of will, since it is meaningless to speak of a being without will as being free or unfree. But the situation is further complicated by lack of ability to locate this will. And opposition between natural will and rational will and between long-range will and momentary will further increases the confusion.

I shall discuss freedom in the Bruderhof in terms of two dimensions: (1) the ability to decide to do something and then go ahead and do it; (2) the ability to change one's mind at any moment as to one's goal, and to act effectively to implement that change. Both of these seem to me to be important elements of freedom. The Bruderhof incorporates much of the first and little of the second.

To make a plan and carry it through to completion is always a difficult task. This is especially the case if the task is prolonged over several months or a year. If the task is to last a lifetime, the odds against success must be enormous if the task requires any considerable amount of concentration and perseverance. Most people who undertake ambitious tasks also take steps to insulate themselves from distractions. The business man has a secretary to protect him from callers. The professor has office hours to protect him from students. The writer or artist has a hidden retreat to protect him from human contacts. In one sense, these mechanisms may be said to inhibit freedom. But if they are adopted voluntarily, in pursuit of a more important goal, they usually will be considered to implement, rather than detract from, freedom. The isolation and constriction endured by the Bruder-hofer may be seen in this light as insulating mechanisms. In part they insulate the member from distractions from the outside world. But mostly they insulate him from his own tendency to distract himself from the goal which he has set himself. As long as the Bruderhofer has chosen this goal voluntarily, it seems to me that whatever mechanisms he uses to help him reach it should be seen also as aids to his freedom.

The other dimension of the problem concerns the ability of the individual to change his mind. This is not easy to do in the Bruderhof. Psychically it is not easy since one has taken vows of lifetime fidelity which are very serious to the sort of person who joins such a community.

Nor is it easy economically for the individual to change his mind. One surrenders all material goods to the Bruderhof, irrevocably, upon becoming a member. The Bruderhof often does give people who leave a certain amount of money, but it considers itself under no obligation to do so. The fact that lack of birth control results in unusually large families in the Bruderhof makes this an even more difficult problem.

Leaving is also very difficult for social reasons. All the people that matter to you will be cut off from you forever. A member is often not even sure if his own spouse will come with him. Several apostates told me that they had been thinking of leaving for a long while before daring to say anything about it to their husbands or wives. The reason for this, of course, is that even conjugal conversation is not privileged in the Bruderhof. If a man tells his wife that he is thinking of leaving, she must either take this

information to the Brotherhood or a Servant, or else be impli-
cated in the guilt herself.

One ex-member speaks of still being very much interested in
living in community. But he says that he will never again have a
community of goods because this makes cowards out of men –
they become afraid, if not for themselves, then for their families.
These sentiments are shared by at least half the apostates with
whom I spoke.

In summary, all that can be said is that the two dimensions of
freedom that I have discussed may be somewhat incompatible
with each other, at least as far as the goals pursued by the
Bruderhof are concerned. To shed further light on this problem,
we shall now turn to a discussion of those who do manage to
change their minds and leave.

## 7. *The Apostate*

When you see the renegades, when you read their old letters, it seems
they're all going around with a piece of old Bruderhof clothing –
some got a shoe, some got half a pant leg. Something they're carrying
around that belongs to that, and hanging on to it too.

The above quotation, from a conversation with an apostate
who had been a Bruderhof member for eleven years, symbolizes
the one most constant theme that runs through the lives of ex-
Bruderhof members – the inability ever to completely break away.
Of course no one is likely to forget any way of life once practiced
for a number of years. But the failure to break away is more than
an inability to forget. In those in whom the resocialization
process really took, it seems as if a segment of the Bruderhof
always remains, shaping and judging the person's actions, long
after the person has left the Bruderhof – perhaps for the rest of
his life.

The first stage of re-entry into the life of the 'outside world' is
often one of extreme shock. One man told me how he immediately
went home to his parents, loyally tried to justify the Bruderhof to
them, and then spent two months doing nothing but watching

T.V. fourteen hours a day. A couple who had been members of the Bruderhof at Woodcrest for six years reported the following:

We felt as if we were severing relations with God. Since we weren't in unity with the Bruderhof, we weren't in unity with the church or with God. We were out for two years before we even dared to consider going to a church [paraphrased].

The above examples are of people who joined the Bruderhof after having grown up in the outside world. At least they were going back to a life that was familiar to them. The readjustment process can be even more traumatic for those who were born in the Bruderhof. There have been several cases of mental breakdowns. One *sabra* girl who left the Bruderhof as a teenager describes her comparatively mild acculturation:

... the hard part was that [in the Bruderhof] we were always ... the leaders, and then you got there [to public high school] and you were nothing. Nobody knew you. We made friends with the lower or the less popular kids at school. We didn't make friends with the kids that were in everything, the in crowd, till I'd say my tenth grade. Then I got to be a cheerleader. We all got to be cheerleaders at the end, which really made us feel great. You know how it is in high school. In college it's nothing but in high school it's everything. I cut my hair in the end of the ninth grade. In the tenth grade I started wearing makeup, and slowly getting the kind of clothes they wore. At first we wore the bobby socks and the shoes that little girls wear, shoes that you tie, but we changed pretty soon.

Another *sabra* apostate reveals a more common phenomenon: the inability to let go of community ties and standards:

You see, there's an incredible embarrassment between me and my own peer group that are in the community, that have stayed in the life. There's a feeling, a mutual feeling of being sorry for each other, but you don't know who really feels sorriest, you see. Probably I feel sorriest for myself because I know that they still have somewhat of the tribal thing and they look upon me as somewhat lost, and there's very little to communicate except the past . . . .

So for me I still feel cheated, because I'm still looking for the heroic act. I've made it outside, individually, and nobody praises me, nobody. My sister says to my parents, 'When I think of brother, I feel so sorry for Phil. He's still floundering, he's still in the jungle, he can't just simply accept.' And I just wish that I would get one word of encouragement for all the lions and all the dragons I have tried to kill.[110]

A striking aspect of many conversations with Bruderhof apostates is the combination of expressed bitterness toward the community with an apparent need to justify it and defend it. The bitterness is expressed in many degrees, from a sarcastic, 'Are they still playing a lot of our symphonic records?' to a malicious, 'We really got to hate them. Don't you think they're Communists? They're Communistic. They're dogmatic.'

Ambivalence about the Bruderhof is often expressed more subtly. Perhaps the essence of this attitude is most poignantly revealed in a statement made by an ex-member, not about the community, but about God. I asked him if he now believed in God. He sighed and said, 'Yeah, I still believe in Him. I still see Him there, but I hate his guts.'

Also, the Bruderhof apostate typically justifies every Bruderhof mechanism of social control, decision-making, or socialization as necessary for the community's survival. Many of the apostates correspond with one another often and call themselves a 'Bruderhof in exile'. Many of them long for some sort of community. There is frequent talk among the exiles about starting a new community. But these plans never get off the ground because, basically, the apostates cannot conceive of any other community but the Bruderhof being at all worthwhile. Sometimes ex-members defend control mechanisms that the Bruderhof itself has since discarded. For instance, one apostate had heard that prosperity at Woodcrest had meant that many food items were now in unlimited open stock. He was worried because he remembered the sense of childlike expectation and joy engendered by the shortage of supplies in Primavera, and the role this played in helping the individual struggle against his bad self.

In talking with apostates, I frequently brought up a subject of great interest to me – other intentional communities. On three separate occasions, with three different people, I noticed the identical strange and dramatic scene. (I must note here that the Bruderhof sometimes speaks of other communitarian experiments with the greatest condescension.) I would be describing a particular intentional community that I had visited or heard about. All of a sudden, there is a dramatic change. My informant's voice takes on a different tone (in one case a German accent even suddenly appeared). He seems to hold himself in a different manner. For a moment, he becomes the Bruderhofer once again, ridiculing this particular community as not having the faintest chance to succeed. I noticed this same phenomenon also in cases where an informant became very involved in explaining to me how some aspect of the Bruderhof life worked. All of a sudden, just for a moment, he would be an autocratic Witness Brother explaining the life to a novice or a guest.

I do not mean to be flippant in speaking of the apostates. These are for the most part a tragic group of people, in the fullest sense of the word: those that have dared to overreach themselves, those that have striven mightily and failed, conquered not by what is worst in human nature but by what is best, broken by the inability to bend.

Certainly there is pathos among the grief and anger of the apostates. There is a very human desire for a relationship which they know very well would negate all that the Bruderhof stands for:

Why can't we really feel, 'Well, we're trying to do something and you're trying to do something. Now we don't agree with some of your ideas. Nevertheless, we still respect you.' But why should there be this feeling of being outcasts, you know? Why can't we have the feeling that, we lived together for twenty years and there is some bond between us, and that, in a sense, can't be broken?

But there is also tragedy, which can be read between the lines of the following statement made by an ex-Servant of the Word in exile:

My wife and I had to tell them very plainly that for us the debacle of 1961 meant a final cut with community, that we could not condone all the things against which we protested already then, and that we could not return to a small closed group where an idyllic sense of communal euphoria was gained from time to time between crises at the cost of so much suffering.

The Bruderhof is a community based upon obedience and brotherly love. Some visitors respond to it with ecstatic admiration; others shudder in horror; still others – and I am one – come away with truly mixed feelings. Certainly, in a world gone cold from lack of human contact, movements like the Bruderhof have, at the very least, some important lessons to teach. Or can they be portents for the future of Western society? Evaluating the potential significance of the Bruderhof model must begin with a theme that has run implicitly through this book – the conflict between community and freedom.

## 1. *Freedom versus Community*

Modern Western man is the product of a half dozen generations that have rebelled against the restrictions of community (family, church, village) in search of freedom. The desire for freedom has not disappeared in the present generation, but many of its members have come to feel that they want to have their cake and eat it too. Those that have tried freedom by itself and found it too lonely have started creeping tentatively back to warm their hands a bit at the tribal campfire. Herman Schmalenbach has suggested that this natural enough desire for the best of both worlds is technically impossible. He argues that modern man really hungers for communion, rather than community, and that if he ever found true community he would not be able to tolerate it:

> To the peasant, emotionality is to be avoided because it gives psychic

processes too much autonomy. Often a peasant is considered sparse and dour in his emotional expressions. He is even said to lack feeling for nature. On the other hand, people argue that he not so much lacks feeling as words for its expression. Actually, peasants probably do 'have' extraordinarily few of these feelings by way of conscious experience. This is not because they do not have them at all, but because, being unconsciously *tied* both to community and to nature, emotional experiences do not articulate a peasant's relations to the world around him.

It is really strange that given these facts one should think of community as something both represented among peasants and based on feeling. This simply constitutes a sentimentalizing of peasantry. Urban people are prone to such distortions. They reflect the restlessness of the person who lives his life in urban society. Actually they are an expression of a desire for communion. Such a desire tends to combine a wish for belongingness with a high valuation of peasantry, of community, and of nature. In itself it does not, of course, constitute community . . . instead, it confuses community with communion.[111]

Communion, then, might be viewed as a way of reconciling the values of freedom and community. But communion, based as it is on feelings, which are unstable, is not a viable form. The Bruderhof itself gives evidence for this in the facts that emotional orientations were purged from the community after the Sannerz (communion) period, and that emotional outbursts still constitute one of the community's biggest problems. Of course, it is possible to choose this alternative merely by sacrificing a third important human value: stability. As we shall see, many hippies have done just this. Always holding on to freedom, they gratefully accept communion experiences when and where they occur, just as freely passing on when the communion cup has been drained. But even hippies, with increasing age or the birth of children, begin to think about the prospects of incorporating the value of stability as well.

The problem might be left at this impasse, except for one curious fact: alienated Western man does not feel that he really possesses community, but the members of the Bruderhof feel that they really possess freedom. We must consider then whether there is more than one kind of freedom and, if there is, whether all of them are equally incompatible with community. Whatever else he may possess, the Bruderhof member emphatically does not have the freedom of individualism. We must consider the possibility that the problem stems from confusing individualism with freedom.

James S. Coleman has called individualism in Western society 'one of the most important long-term secular trends since the Middle Ages'. As with any social trend, in being carried to an extreme it has given rise to a need for its antithesis. Coleman says:

> The 'problem of youth' in many countries today, and particularly in the United States, seems to me to be a problem of *egoisme*, in Durkheim's sense, a problem of too-great individualism, of the absence of a collective identity to which to bind oneself. The popularity of the euphoric drugs appears to me to be an attempt at escaping from this ... I think the magnetism of Kennedy lay in the fact that he offered a basis for collective identity and for sacrifice of the self in a larger cause.[112]

Individualism is the form in which Western man has sought his freedom. But it seems undeniable that community, which means bonds, obligations, and mutual interdependence, is fundamentally incompatible with individualism. There are, of course, other units that can experience freedom besides the individual. A chain gang, escaped from its guards, is free to go wherever it chooses, as long as the men all move in tandem. But we are too close in time to the slogans of fascism and Nazism to be anything but dubious of any brand of freedom whose ultimate referent is not the individual.

Modern Western society has only faint memories of an individual freedom which is not individualistic – echoes from feudal society and the monastic tradition. But the concept is very much alive in other cultures. The Pueblo Indians of New Mexico are an example. Frank Waters formulates it in a novel about a Pueblo Indian educated at a white school, who is caught between two worlds. His friend, a Pueblo traditionalist, gives him advice:

> You see, it is like this. I am mortal body and I am immortal spirit; they are one. Now on this earth I am imprisoned for a little while in

my mortal body. This gives me no discomfort; I have learned its needs and limitations and how to supersede them.

Now I, in this mortal body, am imprisoned also in a form of life – that of my tribe, my pueblo, my people. Nor does this give me discomfort; I have learned its needs and limitations also and how to supersede them. For as my body blends into my tribe, my pueblo, so this greater form blends into the world without – the earth, the skies, the sun, moon, stars, and the spirits of all . . . .

Now if I quarreled with my body, my spirit would not be free. Now if I quarreled with my greater body, my spirit would not be free. But by existing harmoniously in each, I am free to escape them for my greatest need – to become one, formless and without bounds, inseparable from the one flowing stream of all life . . . .

Now you, my friend, have your mortal body also, and are at peace with it. You too have a greater body, your form of life. It is not mine, for our old ways you reject; nor is it the Government's, the white man's, for you reject it also; but one you must have. Who knows which is best? They are all the same. All are merely shells of life. But they must be lived within harmoniously to be free. For only when there is no sense of imprisonment in form is the substance of spirit able to overflow and become one with the flowing stream of all life, everlasting, formless and without bounds.[113]

The problem of finding a way to reconcile freedom and community has become urgent in the most advanced Western nations (the United States, England, Germany) – the post-industrial societies. The most dramatic manifestation of this problem has been the revolt of youth. But underlying causes for the urgency can be found in the collapse of three of our basic institutions: the city, the neighborhood, and the family.

## 2. *Post-industrial Society*

For a long time, mankind's greatest concern was with getting enough of the material necessities to stay alive. Most of the world is still preoccupied with this problem but, during the last two hundred years, it has been solved, at least in principle, by the industrial revolution. The industrial revolution is really a series of revolutions: the bureaucratic organization of labor, the introduction of power machinery, and the successive development of mass production, automation, and cybernation. In no nation on earth has this revolution been completed, but in some nations (particularly in Western Europe and North America) it is far enough along so that the production of material goods has ceased to be the major problem.

Such nations have been called post-industrial societies. The United States is one. Although there is a great deal of poverty in the United States, this is the result of social, cultural, and political problems, not lack of economic capacity. Many of these social, cultural and political problems are themselves the result of disruptions brought about by the industrial revolution. These disruptions have affected every level of life and have led to what Maurice Stein has called, 'the eclipse of community.'[114]

Under ideal circumstances a sense of community can be found on three different levels. A man has pride in the achievements of his city. He is involved in the affairs of his neighborhood. He is nourished by the love of his family. At all of these levels, he encounters restrictions on his freedom. Post-industrial man has gained an unprecedented degree of freedom, but he has lost his sense of community on all three of these levels.

In America today, about 70 per cent of the population lives in areas designated as urban, and this figure is steadily increasing. Yet few people can be found who speak with pride of their cities. On the contrary, a mood of despair prevails. The largest cities, such as New York, seem to exist in a state of constant crisis, from which nobody has even suggested a credible plan of escape.

Every social order needs legitimation – reasons why people feel they ought to cooperate with, or at least tolerate, the system. But just when society in general, and post-industrial societies in particular, are commiting themselves to a basically urban way of life, the legitimacy of the city itself has come under serious question. People have been living in cities for about five and a half millennia.[115] For most of that time, the legitimation of the city was political. People felt the need for mutual protection. This function was primary on the American frontier even in fairly recent times. The city had walls. The city was a fortress.

The rise of the modern state made the need for communities to protect themselves obsolete. But, at the same time, it created a new legitimacy based on economic interdependence.[116] People of all ages and social classes could see clearly that their social environment was a system of interlocking economic functions. The industrial revolution created a great deal of inequality, and cities bred many types of rebellion. But the rebellion was, with few exceptions, against the rebels' place in the system, not against the system itself.

Norton Long has given an interesting picture of the city or town during the industrial period:

> The local community can be usefully conceptualized as an ecology of games. In the territorial system a variety of games goes on: banking, newspaper publishing, contracting, manufacturing, etc. The games give structures, goals, roles, strategies, tactics, and publics to the players. Players in each game make use of players in the others for their particular purposes. A banker uses the politician, the newspaperman, or the contractor in his game and is, in turn, used by them in theirs. The interaction of the games produces unintended but systematically functional results for the ecology. An over-all top leadership and social game provide a vague set of commonly shared values that promotes co-operation in the system though it does not provide a government.[117]

Although Long's model neglects the importance of power and of external influences, it nevertheless gives the flavour of the industrial city. The walls have come down. The fortress has been replaced by the sprawling playground.

During the 1920s and 1930s, the influential Chicago School of Sociology gave a convincing account of this type of city as a harbinger of freedom. Lewis Wirth, a member of this school, wrote:

> ... The city has thus historically been the melting-pot of faces, peoples, and cultures, and a most favorable breeding-ground of new biological and cultural hybrids. It has not only tolerated but rewarded individual differences. It has brought together people from the ends of the earth *because* they are different and thus useful to one another, rather than because they are homogeneous and like-minded . . . .
> Similarly, persons of homogeneous status and needs unwittingly

drift into, consciously select, or are forced by circumstances into, the same area. The different parts of the city thus acquired specialized functions. The city consequently tends to resemble a mosaic of social worlds in which the transition from one to the other is abrupt. The juxtaposition of divergent personalities and modes of life tends to produce a relativistic perspective and a sense of toleration of differences which may be regarded as prerequisites for rationality and which lead toward the secularization of life.[118]

Cities of today still conduct themselves as if they were ecologically functional game networks. But it is difficult to see the economic necessity of, say, New York City in the post-industrial age. The extreme population density of industrial-age cities was due largely to the concentrative logic of steam power.[119] But the logic of electricity is decentralization. Industries that are mobile enough thus tend more and more to move away from cities, leaving behind the characteristic urban problems of a decaying downtown and a dwindling tax base.

At the same time, as Marshall McLuhan has shown, electricity provides instant long-range communication; the automobile and the airplane provide instant long-range mobility. Post-industrial Americans come to consider their entire region, nation, or even continent the 'local ecology of games'. Loyalty to the primary community breaks down as people are freed from the economic necessity of living in one particular place, and begin to choose homes on the basis of cultural, climatic, or other considerations.

The democratic system itself is in danger of breaking down under these cirumstances, at least locally. Coleman has shown that democracy is a system very well suited for an ecology of games. Representative assemblies are actually meetings where the diverse but interlocking interests of various constituencies can be discussed by the constituent representatives, where bargains can be made, and where compromises and alliances can be agreed upon. Coleman's work on local fluoridation controversies has indicated that this process does not work as well in communities without complex networks of interlocking interests. There is much more likely to be bitter community polarization, and the losing side is more likely to bear a permanent grudge.

Cities like Los Angeles, whose population exhibits a high rate of geographical mobility and relatively little economic inter-dependence, even try to substitute bureaucracy for democracy in the governing process. The top bureaucrats are still *chosen* democratically, but, increasingly, the democratic *process* of bargaining and horsetrading is eschewed as irrational or even condemned as corrupt. At the same time, the crime rate, always dependent on the proportion of rootless in the population, soars in such cities. Los Angeles has one of the highest crime rates in the nation.[120]

Under these circumstances, people respond according to their means. Those who can afford to, flee, either to the suburbs or, increasingly, to walled, guarded, and privately maintained sub-communities within the city itself (a regression to the age of the fortress town). It's heartbreaking to see the lengths to which people will go to protect their stereo equipment. Those who know that they will never be able to escape resign themselves or rebel. But there is a novel strategy to rebellion in the post-industrial city. Consciously or unconsciously, the rebel senses that there is no longer any good reason for the city's existence. He seeks, not to restructure it, but to bring it to a standstill or burn it down. More and more people feel that this would improve their lives.

Not only the city as a whole, but the neighborhood as well, has disintegrated as a source of community. I am using the term neighborhood in a very inexact sense to cover a variety of small geographic clusterings of people. What I say about the neighborhood will in general hold true for the suburb, the small town, and the village.

For many people, the neighborhood or home town has given way to the community of interest. With the automobile and the telephone, it is probably easier for people of common interests to find one another, and spend time together, than ever before in history. Such communities of interest are a kind of intentional community, but they fall short of satisfying the human need for communal relationships. For one thing, an individual character-istically belongs, not to one, but to a number of different com-munities of interest. Since relationships between members of such interest groups tend to be segmental and transitory, their members tend to avoid becoming deeply dependent on one another. Another problem stems from the fact that communities of interest often have no physical center or boundaries. Spread out all over a city or even a region, this sort of community lacks any sense of permanence beyond the motivations of individual members. Under such circumstances, one would not expect to find the kind of friendship or belonging that comes from the sharing of pains and pleasures over a long period of time. One frequently does find in them the lonely, confused, and silently desperate – those for whom the major problem seems to be finding some way to order their lives, that is, to rid themselves of some of the surplus freedom with which their senses have been overwhelmed.

The neighborhood cannot compete with the community of interest. Here as nowhere else we see the dilemma of freedom versus community. There was certainly much that was stultifying about the neighborhood, home-town, and village life of previous generations. Privacy and the opportunity to develop individual differences were hard to achieve. The psychological deficiencies characteristic of traditional societies – superstition, narrowness, and intolerance – were common. It would be difficult to wish for the return of such communities.

Yet here is the paradox: for all their narrowness these were real communities, while communities of interest are not. Although it would be unrealistic to expect a suburban couple interested in Balkan folk dancing to play bridge with their next-door neighbors on Wednesday nights instead of driving fifty miles to be with a folk-dance group, it is important to realize that a sense of integration of life is lost by their failure to do so. (This sense of integration would be difficult to achieve in a suburb in any case because of the separation of work and leisure.) The Bruderhof illustrates that there is a particular joy and satisfaction inherent in sharing all of life's activities with the same group of people – working with them, playing with them, raising children with them, and making decisions with them. It is questionable whether this joy and satisfaction is worth sacrificing for the freedom to pursue one's particular interests.

Denied community at the level of the city and the neighbor-hood, post-industrial man can still turn to his family. He may, if he is lucky, be able to find love in his family, but he won't be able to find community. There aren't enough people. Gary Snyder writes:

The modern American family is the smallest and most barren family that has ever existed. Each newly-married couple moves to a new house or apartment – no uncles or grandmothers come to live with them. There are seldom more than two or three children. The children live with their peers and leave home early. Many have never had the least sense of family.

I remember sitting down to Christmas dinner eighteen years ago in a communal house in Portland, Oregon, with about twelve others my own age, all of whom had no place they wished to go home to. That house was my first discovery of harmony and community with fellow beings. This has been the experience of hundreds of thousands of men and women all over America since the end of World War II. Hence the talk about the growth of a 'new society'. But more; these gatherings have been people spending time with each other – talking, delving, making love. Because of the sheer amount of time 'wasted' together (without TV) they know each other better than most Americans know their own family. Add to this the mind-opening and personality-revealing effects of grass and acid, and it becomes possible to predict the emergence of groups who live by mutual illumination – have seen themselves as of one mind and one flesh . . . .[121]

Snyder's vision of intentional community is that of the tribe (a huge extended family). He wants the vanished extended family to be recreated, only this time on the basis of fellowship rather than kinship.

This is easier said than done. A closer look at the American family indicates that it is not merely barren, but positively destructive of community, and destructive of community-building potential in the children that it rears. In order to see how this is so, we must first take a brief look at the American family in cross-cultural perspective.

Anthropologist William Stephens, looking at America as one society among hundreds, both primitive and advanced, throughout the world, concludes that the American family is a very odd duck:

From time to time, throughout this book, I have referred to the peculiarities of American family customs: the fact that we sometimes give deference to our females, that we allow free courtship and mate choice, that we have practically nothing in the way of patterned kin behavior, that American husbands and wives do not observe public avoidance customs, that the American nuclear family tends to be isolated from larger kin groupings, and so forth. Child rearing is another one of those areas in which the United States is rather deviant. In regard to a number of child rearing issues, it seems that practically the whole world 'does it one way', whereas we 'do it another way'.[122]

According to Stephens, there is some evidence that the severity of childhood socialization is associated with the complexity of a culture's economy. For instance, he observes that among primitive societies, kingdoms, which generally have more complex systems of economic production and distribution than do non-kingdoms, also are stricter in child rearing, particularly in the area of sex restrictions. Stephens makes the following remarks about American child-rearing, cautioning that there is some doubt about the validity of the data:

How do we in the United States compare with the rest of the world, vis-à-vis severity of socialization? It looks as if we are rather harsh parents . . . . For oral training, America was rated somewhat more severe than average. For toilet training, America and the Tanala of Madagascar were rated the most severe. For sex training, we ranked more severe than about three fourths of the sample. For severity of independence training, we are about average . . . . For socialization of aggression we rated more severe than average. Finally, as far as over-all severity of socialization is concerned: the Dobuans were rated next more severe, and forty-four other societies were rated less severe . . . .

. . . in the more simple and clear-cut area of mere body contact with the mother – being carried by her, lying next to her, feeling her skin, sucking at her breast – the American infant is undoubtedly 'deprived' compared with infants in most other societies.

For one thing, in most societies the infant sleeps next to its mother for several years after birth. In forty-five of sixty-four societies . . . the nursing infant customarily sleeps by its mother's side . . . .[123]

Stephens does not mention another significant area in which the American family (or, to be more accurate, the post-industrial

Western family) is unusual. In almost all societies the family functions economically as a unit of production; in America it is merely a unit of consumption. Far fewer children are born in the average American family than in families in almost all less advanced societies. But these few children experience a childhood which, for sheer length, is unmatched by anything in the world. Due to the increasing length of education, it has become common to defer the two traditional indicators of entrance into adulthood, marriage and employment, until well into the twenties. Other societies, such as Ireland, which defer marriage even longer than does the United States, at least confer vocational adulthood at a very early age.

Stephens goes on to speak about the most important way in which the post-industrial family is unique: its almost total isolation from a surrounding kinship network. Here the same factors that helped to destroy the city, ease of mobility and preoccupation with individualism, have helped to create a dangerously vulnerable family situation. The slightest jar of fate – death, an illness, sometimes even an argument – seem capable of shattering it. The child characteristically grows up insecure, lonely, and emotionally overheated. Stephens says:

Here we come to an area in which our society is strikingly deviant. In all the societies in my ethnographic notes, with the lone exception of the Copper Eskimo, the people ordinarily live within residential kin groups that are larger than the nuclear family. A married couple lives either with or near the husband's kin . . . or they live with or near the wife's kin . . . .

Our society is unusual for the relatively high frequency of isolated nuclear households; because the nuclear family is usually isolated from other kin, the job of caring for the young children is left largely in the hands of the mother . . . . Talcott Parsons points out that the isolated nuclear family, as opposed to larger kin-groupings, constitutes a small, 'tight,' social-interaction system. It is an all-your-eggs-in-one-basket situation. Mother – and how mother feels – is very important, because she is the only mother you have; there are no surrogate mothers in the form of aunts, grandmothers, or older cousins. When mother becomes angry or estranged, there is no place to go, no one else to turn to.[124]

It is not surprising that this family situation breeds certain anti-communal character traits. Prolonged adolescence has, at least until recently, implied a high degree of sexual repression. The need to continuously defer gratification to a future time, for education, for marriage, or for independence, tends to create an alienation from here-and-now reality, a skill at going out of contact with the world and retreating inward. This leads to the numbness to stimuli which we have already seen is an important survival technique in the post-industrial city.

Deferred gratification also makes a man vulnerable to manipulation by external authorities. The more one has sacrificed for the sake of some future reward, the more one is vulnerable to threats that this future reward will be taken away. It also encourages people to think of their lives in terms of careers. They are then haunted by the fear of getting bad marks on their 'permanent records' which, they are taught in school, will follow them through life.

The manipulatable child is also made manipulative through another quirk of the post-industrial family. Stephens' argument is that kinship isolation, neolocality, and relatively small families result in a 'tight' family with a high degree of emotional involvement. But we have also seen that the isolated nuclear family is quite unstable and thus breeds emotional insecurity. It is plausible that this combination fosters the need for continual reaffirmation of love which is so characteristic of our society, and probably has helped to sustain the romantic love myth as well. But this need for love continually reaffirmed naturally creates a need to manipulate others.

Society, as we have defined it, is based on reciprocity, and the city of industrial society was an ecology of games. The post-industrial family rears good game players for the industrial age. This is a cultural lag. But community is based, not on reciprocity, but on the feeling of belonging together. In our society this feeling can no longer be based on kinship or ancient territorial proximity. Both of these are too dependent upon the accident of birth to be satisfying to members of a free and mobile society. Two alternatives are the folk nationalism engendered by fascism or the global brotherhood based on something like Eberhard

Arnold's cosmic perspective or Gary Snyder's 'mutual illumination'. To use Martin Buber's term, community requires an I-thou perspective, that people see each other as subjects rather than as objects. This non-manipulative, immediately involved attitude is the antithesis of the game perspective engendered by the American family.

Ironically, some of the same factors which make it difficult for the post-industrial child to enter into communal relationships also create in him an unusually strong need for community. Everyone desires a sense of immortality through membership in some collectivity whose span is greater than the normal human lifetime. The extended family is just such an immortal unit. A single death, which ordinarily disrupts a nuclear family completely, has little effect on the solidarity of the extended family. Furthermore, there is a progression of generations. Under normal circumstances, by the time the grandparents have all died off, the parents have already become grandparents themselves, and so on, endlessly.

If a member of an extended family were deprived of community on the level of neighborhood and city, he could withdraw into his family for solace. In fact, this is what Confucius advised the wise man to do during times of trouble in ancient China. But the post-industrial man has no such consolation. This cool, detached, sensually and sexually dull, manipulating, and manipulative individual earnestly desires community and involvement. But of what sort of community and involvement is such a person capable? Only that of the herd, that of the mass, which is that of nationalism. The nationalistic frenzies of various modern states may be partly explained by this need. I think we are going to begin to find that Nazism is not an isolated political phenomenon confined to a particular historical epoch, but actually a characteristic aberration in the transition from industrial to post-industrial society.

The hippie movement may be seen as a revolt against every aspect of this personality complex. Hippies emphasize sensual and sexual awareness, living in and for the present rather than the future, spontaneity, treatment of people as ends rather than as means to ends, and desire for community on the level of the primary group rather than the nation-state. This may explain why the need for tribalism is a major theme of hippie life and literature.

## 3. *The Hippie Response*

I estimate that there are currently about a thousand rural hippie communes in North America, and at least twice that many urban communes. I have personally visited close to a hundred of these in the last five years. In 1965, there were probably not a hundred on the entire face of the continent. Most intentional communities existing at that time were relics of a previous era – groupings of religious fundamentalists, utopian socialists, or Quaker conscientious objectors. Today, only five years later, America is in the midst of a flowering of communitarian experiment unequalled in its history, even at the time of the great utopian movements of the Owenites and the Fourierists in the early nineteenth century. These five years have been years of rapid change for American society. From the point of view of the communitarian movement, the most significant change of the past five years has been the exposure of society to the widespread use of psychedelic drugs.

Of course, drugs alone cannot account for the rise of the hippie and communitarian movements. Many theories have been advanced tracing connexions to such things as the breakdown of the modern family, the insecurity of the nuclear age, widespread exposure to electronic devices such as T.V. and the computer, progressive education, etc., etc. Such writers as Marshall McLuhan, Gary Snyder, and Buckminster Fuller are probably right in speaking of a general trend toward retribalization in our society. And this trend would probably have occurred eventually even without the spread of drug use. In attributing the rise of the present-day communitarian movement to the use of drugs, I am therefore speaking not of an ultimate cause but of an immediate cause – a 'triggering mechanism'.

There are two major ways in which drug use triggered the

development of communes. One was through the institution of the *crash pad*. The other was through the fostering of the psychological experience of *communion*. Crash pads are simply dwelling units, usually urban but occasionally rural, in which a varying number of people live and cooperate in obtaining the necessities of life. Crash pads have generally attracted young and drifting people of both sexes – teenage runaways, drop outs, and those whose primary life concerns have become drug-inspired mystical, emotional, or artistic pursuits, and who, therefore, have reduced economic functions to a minimum. A crash pad may be distinguished from a true commune by the totally utilitarian attitude of the members toward its structure. Although the residents of a crash pad may become very attached to one another, each individual (or couple) remains primarily concerned with his own 'trip', and the collectivity is valued only as a means to the furthering of basically individualistic ends.

The crash pad is significant for two reasons. The first is that, for the overwhelming majority of hippies who eventually become involved in communal living, crash pad experiences have provided the first taste of this sort of life. In some cases, whole crash pads have actually made the transition and become true communes. In other cases, subgroups of crash pad populations have 'discovered their tribe' and gone on to found communes. But in the majority of relevant cases, it has simply been that crash pad living has whetted an individual's desire for something deeper, and started him out on a search which eventually led him to life in a commune. The second reason for the significance of the crash pad to this study is that, unfortunately, the popular conception of what communal living is like has largely been formed through the observation of crash pads. For this reason, mention of communes conjures up visions of glassy-eyed kids staring off into space, of sexual promiscuity and group marriage, and of almost total lack of economic enterprise. Anyone familiar with contemporary communes knows how absurd this picture is, but most communes are very difficult to become familiar with. They tend to be closed, secretive, and inconspicuous, whereas crash pads tend to be just the opposite. Naturally, therefore, journalistic coverage of communal living has tended to draw its material from observation of crash pads rather than communes.

Drugs have influenced the formation of communes indirectly through the proliferation of crash pads. But drugs have also had an important direct role in the development of communes through the fostering of experiences of communion. Very often, in reconstructing the history of a particular commune, one finds repeated reference to a mystical event which occurred early in the group's life together. Often this takes the form of a group acid trip. Sometimes drugs are not involved at all but, even in these cases, images and ideas from the drug culture are heavily drawn upon.

What is this mystical, semi-mythical event? It is the shared realization that this group of people 'belongs together', 'is together', is a true family, brotherhood, or tribe. This experience, often accompanied by personal ego-loss and a melting (or exploding) absorption into a communal ego is, of course, a commonly reported psychedelic vision even among those not communally oriented, and is often, as in the Bruderhof, part of a non-drug-induced religious experience.

In a certain sense, drugs can provide a functional equivalent to religious experience, at least in the early stages of the life of the commune. The communion experience evokes a style of life together very similar to that of the Bruderhof in its communion stage at Sannerz. Drug experiences may even carry the group further, to a stage analogous to that experienced by the Bruderhof at Rhön, which I have called charismatic community. At this stage, Eberhard Arnold was able, through the contagion of his cosmic perspective, to transform the communal *eros* into *agape*, thus leading the group to a form of true community, which was, however, still dependent upon him. Psychedelic drugs, by dulling the intensity of direct emotional contact while at the same time inducing a cosmic perspective, can sometimes transform the erotic emotionality of a commune into *agape*. The members stop thinking, 'You are my brother because I love you,' and start thinking, 'I love you because you are my brother.' This is true community, but just as at the Bruderhof Rhön stage, it is extremely unstable because dependent on an external force.

The commune movement can be understood in part as a reaction against the city and the family. Urban people, from teenagers to men and women in their forties and fifties, become disgusted with city living but feel that they lack the skills and resources to make the transition to rural life alone. At the same time, communion experiences have given them insight into the positive values of community living. Having been made aware, through such experiences, of the spiritual and emotional poverty of the nuclear families in which most of them were raised, they are reluctant to settle down to a conventional life and start their own nuclear families. Perhaps, through the ferment of the movement, coming together in crash pads, at meetings, or even through advertisements, a group of people discover that they are a tribe. Their next problem is to gain access to some land and move out of the city.

The geographical areas in which communes are densely clustered (New England, New Mexico, Southern Oregon, Northern California) have in common the availability of relatively cheap arable land which nevertheless does not lend itself to use by huge mechanized commercial farming enterprises. As the small independent farmer is squeezed out of business, those of his holdings which cannot, for topographical reasons, be incorporated into large agricultural industries, are snapped up by communitarians. The land is obtained in various ways. Sometimes it is owned by one of the members, who decides to allow others to live there, perhaps retaining formal ownership, perhaps relinquishing it to a board of trustees. Sometimes a rich patron buys land for a commune. Sometimes the founding members themselves save up enough money for a down payment on a piece of land before they drop out. Some communes find ways to obtain the use of land without buying it – by squatting, camping out, establishing mining or homesteading claims on some of the still available public land, or even by renting.

The commune that forms on this land is almost always very loosely structured at first. There is a shared relief at being out of the city. It is common to find members of such communes boasting about how long it has been since they were last in a city. The number of people in a commune varies; some have only six or eight members, others over a hundred. Many of the more accessible ones seem to stabilize around a population of about twenty-five adults. Often there is a rapid turnover of the peripherally involved around a small stable nucleus, as at Sannerz. Also as at Sannerz, there tend to be many visitors. Rather than the formal surrendering of all private property that is the rule at the Bruderhof, there is an informal pooling of resources. Reacting against the fragmentation and abstractness of the urban economy, commune members try to get into cooperative primary occupations such as building, crafts, and gardening.

The garden is the economic focus of most communes. As yet, few communes have been able to set up viable craft enterprises or other businesses, although many are trying to do so. Communes typically have intensely cultivated and, on the whole, amazingly successful gardens which yield huge quantities of many different varieties of vegetables, melons, fruit, berries, and grains. Garden produce provides the nucleus of the commune's daily food supply. Through canning, drying, and other means of storage, home-grown food is available year round.

Typically, when a commune is first set up, nobody knows anything about farm skills. Armed with how-to-do-it books and government pamphlets, the communitarians proceed in the best traditions of frontier pragmatism, making many mistakes while learning. By the second or third year, they will have become seasoned agriculturists who can command the respect of, and talk on equal terms with, the neighboring farm population, and even teach them something about organic methods of farming.

Hunting and gathering activities often supplement garden cultivation. Gary Snyder writes:

A few of us are literally hunters and gatherers, playfully studying the old techniques of acorn flour, seaweed-gathering, yucca-fiber, rabbit snaring, and bow hunting.[125]

A commune member sometimes disappears for a day, arriving home around evening laden with small game, berries, mushrooms, or edible roots. This a form of communal recreation which also provides important supplements to what might otherwise prove a monotonous diet. In this one respect at least, taking psychedelic drugs is a definite aid to the communal economy, helping to provide both the frame of mind and the sensitivity to small details in nature necessary for such projects.

When additional money or supplies are needed by the commune, various members will venture to nearby towns and neighboring farms in search of wage labor. In the larger communes, a source of income not to be neglected derives from the steady influx of visitors and new members. Dropping out of urban society, they bring with them clothing, staple foods, luxury items, and cash.

None of this would be a sufficient economic basis for community, if the life style did not involve the radical reduction of what is considered necessary. A pioneer willingness to tolerate what most of us would consider a near-subsistence and highly monotonous diet, to make do with few luxuries or labor-saving devices, to wear only second-hand or homemade clothing, enable this peculiar economic system to work within the American economy of abundance. The pioneer simplicity of living is accompanied by pioneer self-reliance and diversification of skills. Much of the activity of commune members involves the cultivation of such skills as carpentry, plumbing, mechanics, and canning. A wide range of commune-oriented publications (of which the *Whole Earth Catalogue*[126] and the *Green Revolution*[127] are the most notable) offer practical advice on how communitarians with little or no money can make much of what they need and want out of materials at hand. The rudiments of a distinctive communitarian technology have emerged, of which geodesic dome architecture, organic gardening, and homeopathic medicine are examples.

Freedom is a much more central value in the contemporary commune than in the Bruderhof. The communes cherish the joy of brotherhood, but do not focus their lives completely on it. Three motivations seem about equally important in the early careers of commune members: escape from the city, reconstitution of the extended family, and the opportunity to be free. An emphasis on freedom creates a form of communal organization which is different in certain respects from that of the Bruderhof. Members come and go as they choose with little or no rancor or guilt. Nobody would think of asking anybody else to make a permanent commitment to the life. Commune members generally work hard, but the choice of hours and tasks is strictly voluntary, as is the pooling of money and resources. The predominant philosophy is a type of anarchism.

Communitarian anarchism, strictly speaking, is not pure anarchism, but a blend of anarchism and antinomianism. Anarchism can be defined as the belief that the individual is capable of regulating himself in the absence of any external authority, and the belief that there is no such thing as good authority, that authority by definition is subversive. Antinomianism, on the other hand, is the belief that, through grace or enlightenment, one is freed from the constraints of moral law.

The anarchist strain has little or nothing to do with the classical anarchism of the nineteenth century or the political and philosophical anarchist thinking of today. It is a naïve anarchism, a *sui generis* response to specific conditions of post-industrial society. In part, it is a rebellion against the phony freedom of this society, a freedom which encourages the mind to explore and challenge without limits, but prevents people from following up their thoughts with the appropriate actions.

A curious element of this anarchism is the inability or unwillingness to distinguish between authoritarianism and authoritativeness. When I visited a number of communes in the company of a highly experienced organic farmer, we found that many commune members resented and would not accept his advice on quite elementary but serious mistakes they were making in their first attempts at vegetable gardening. They accepted and loved this man as a person, but mistrusted any knowledge not gained through their own trial and error. Some communes have had to suffer epidemics of hepatitis or dysentery because of a stubborn unwillingness to adopt fundamental health precautions that had not grown out of their own experience.

It would be difficult to trace the roots of this attitude that authority, in and of itself, is evil. Certainly it has a lot to do with the erosion of the traditional sources of civic and church authority in post-industrial society. It is common for young people to grow up without a single model of good authority. Nowadays, when people speak of 'the authorities' they are generally referring to the police or the national government, neither very dear to the hearts of young communitarians. Respect for scientific authority went poof at Alamogordo.

The peculiar form of the American family also contributes to this attitude. The ability to distinguish between good and bad authority requires the ability to establish a critical distance from the authority. This is difficult to do in the isolated nuclear family, where the two parents serve simultaneously as the major sources of authority and the major sources of love. It is too psychologically threatening to be critical in such a relationship one is driven either to totally accept or to totally rebel. This problem is compounded by an unfortunate interpretation of modern educational psychology whereby authority tries to mask itself as encouragement to the child to be self-motivated in directions which the parent or teacher think proper. Many children 'feel through' this technique, even if they do not see through it, and come away with the suspicion that all authority is inherently sneaky. Finally, in the American family as a unit of consumption rather than a unit of production there is little reason why the parents should have more authority than the children. Certainly the factors which market researchers have shown to determine the typical housewife's choices among products in a supermarket are in no significant way superior to the factors which motivate five-year-old children.

Antinomianism, the other strain of communitarian anarchism, has been a recurrent theme in Western history. Nathan Adler says:

The Gnostics believed that through their spiritual exercises they achieved union with the Holy Ghost and sin was no longer possible for them. They were therefore absolved of obligation to the moral law....
Recurrent generations of 'flower children', the 'innocent', the

'guileless', the 'pure in heart', who do not speak with the forked tongues of the adult world and its Establishment, arise in ages of anxiety and transition. Burned at the stake by the Dominicans, impaled on Turkish swords, the Gnostic movement returns in new cults with new names. The underground stream runs and rises in occult rites and Kabbalah, in witchcraft, and in its secular form as a Romantic movement.[128]

The antinomian strain in communes, in most cases, comes from the psychedelic experience. The individual 'sees' that moral codes are games, that all morality is relative and arbitrary, and that the ultimate force behind all morality is not authority but love. Intuition is very important in the commune. Love is seen as an active force, holding things together and, in so far as a member is judged, it will not generally be so much by his actions as by his vibrations. Adler says:

The antinomian fears diffusion and depersonalization . . . .

In this situation, and with such needs, the physical, the visceral, and the concrete are of greater moment than the abstract, the generalized and the cognitive. The antinomian personality values most the immediate and the vivid, the uninhibited and the outrageous. Feeling, texture, touch, warmth become more important than central modes which are more likely to make for a discrete self differentiated from objects. Visual modes are manipulated and distorted by drugs and by fasting so that the discrete components melt, merge and fuse.[129]

Neither anarchism nor antinomianism alone provide a sufficient basis for the communitarian life style. Anarchism does not prepare one for the strong feelings and unconscious energy released by the collective behavior experience. Pure antinomianism tends to the decadent; it does not foster the tough pragmatic frontier spirit which is so necessary for the creation of a new life style. Antinomianism is fit for ringing out the old; anarchism for ringing in the new. Together they blend to create a golden age in the commune – for a little while.

Most communes start out with no restrictions on behavior. Everyone is allowed to do his own thing at all time. It is expected that the gentleness, love, and compassion engendered by mystical drug experiences (or in other ways) will prove adequate substitutes for the moral and legal constraints which all other societies have found necessary. The initial experiences are often encouraging and exhilarating. This first stage is one of discovering that many of the previously accepted boundary safeguards of our society are in fact unnecessary. In the cases of some taboos generally accepted in our society, this merely means that their reasons for being are not discernible in terms of the immediate negative consequences of breaking them. Pooling all money and sharing one another sexually are examples of such attempts at boundary erasing. After a while, however, the strains inherent in such situations begin to reassert themselves. Work may slow down, jealousies may arise, or people may start spending more and more time away from the commune. At the same time, as the commune grows older, it may begin to give its attention to complex tasks such as starting a school, expanding housing facilities, or developing a business enterprise. Increased strain on one hand, and more complex tasks on the other, eventually lead most communes to abandon their absolute anarchism in favor of some more restricted alternative.

Ephemeral as it is, the brief golden age of complete anarchism on a commune is inspiring to experience. To me it seems a brief foretaste of how the human race may someday be able to live. Visiting a commune early in its history, one often feels that a new age has already dawned for mankind. Superhuman labors are accomplished with no apparent strain. Money is simply kept in a pot to which anyone can go and take what he needs. Mothers, fathers, and childless people cooperate in taking care of children, resulting in liberation for both parent and child. Portents of later conflicts are visible, but usually not disturbing. One can sense a mild tension between parents and non-parents, and between those who are thinking of the commune as a long-range home and those who are living there from moment to moment.

The first cracks in the tranquil pattern often center around the sense of family. The basic conflict between freedom and community, between anarchism and tribalism, manifests itself here. This is illustrated in an incident that happened at Dawn commune. (All names of communes in this chapter are fictitious.) Dawn commune began when its founding members shared an ineffable spiritual experience which made them feel that they belonged together. A new couple arrived at the commune around a month later. There was little or no opposition to their joining. Most members, as anarchists, felt that membership was open to anyone who cared to come. But the new couple could not fit in. They had not shared the communion experience, and so, in a sense beyond anyone's control, they were not a part of the family. They were also unwilling or unable to think of themselves as part of the family and they soon left. At other communes, when this same problem has occurred under different circumstances, the original family has sometimes been capable of broadening its conception of 'family' to include certain, but not all, prospective members.

As time passes, the strains become more severe. Perhaps the commune has received some publicity in the media and is now overrun with visitors; perhaps there are sexual jealousies; perhaps somebody has stopped working or somebody else has been inspired to guide the group in a certain direction. People leave, new people take their place, and after a while the original members may start to feel that 'their' commune is changing in an undesirable direction. A power struggle similar to the great crisis of the Bruderhof may occur.

For many communes, the initial communion experience serves as a talisman against discord as long as it lasts. But such communion experiences, especially if drug-induced, tend to fade over time, and periodic attempts to revive the spirit with group acid, mescaline, or peyote trips usually have, at best, mixed success. Legalism then enters the life. One evening, the members of Dawn commune were just finishing dinner. They took their meals seated on two long benches at either side of a long table. A couple who had formerly been in the commune suddenly came into the house and politely asked those seated at one side of the table to stand up. Then they calmly picked up one of the benches and, before the unbelieving eyes of the commune members, carried it out of the house, loaded it onto their truck, and drove away. These two people had constructed the bench, and therefore felt entitled to it. At the time the bench was built, everyone had been working on the principle of 'from each according to his ability, to each according to his need'. But since this had never been made explicit, there was nothing the commune could do.

Overpopulation is another common problem in communes. Many communes maintain an open-door policy in accord with their anarchist philosophy. But after the strenuous pioneering phase of the community's history is over, and certain amenities have been established, the commune may find itself overrun with a parasitical breed of city hippies too immature to pull their own weight in an unstructured community. When this happens, often there is a split among the old membership, between those who have faith in the transforming powers of anarchism and those who want to kick the loafers out.

Most contemporary communes eventually find themselves stumped by this basic dilemma – the conflict between freedom and community. They do not want to give up either anarchism or the warm sense of family. The Bruderhof experience teaches that this type of family feeling is possible if the self dies and is reborn. Many communes recognize this in speaking of the necessity of ego transcendence. But the old self – the grasping, jealous, isolated ego – refuses to die of itself, and few commune members have the determination or the faith to kill it.

Unwilling to undergo a complete transformation of self, most commune members, nevertheless, eventually conclude that some modification of absolute anarchism is necessary if the commune is not to dissolve in chaos. The modifications attempted fall into three broad categories. One is segmentation either of the commune itself into a number of smaller 'families' or sub-communes, or of the life into communal, cooperative, and individualistic areas. A second type of modification can be called contractual anarchism. The community members make agreements with one another and then expect them to be kept. The third type of modification can be called consensual anarchism. The community actively seeks to find solutions satisfactory to everyone, refusing to override even a one-person minority.

Freedom Ranch, one of the earliest and longest-lasting of contemporary communes, illustrates both varieties of segmentation. This community was deliberately set up as an experiment in anarchism. Its two hundred acres of land are held in trust for the community by a nonprofit corporation whose articles of incorporation specifically state that anyone may come and live there and that no one may be forced to leave for any reason. Many different kinds of people settle at Freedom Ranch. Some are hermits, loners, or individual families desiring to live in relative isolation; others are intensely gregarious communitarians. Some are energetic and highly competent at farm skills; others are totally lost outside an urban environment. Some are altruistic, others parasites. As a result of this diversity, Freedom Ranch has generally had a small central community centered around the main house, a couple of peripheral communities composed of two or three families, and a number of other residents only marginally associated with any of these sub-communities. Periodic attempts to bring the entire group together on some basis have all failed. Land maintenance and care of animals are communal activities at Freedom Ranch. Gardening and building are cooperative enterprises (private voluntary arrangements in which each person agrees to take on specific responsibilities). Finances and child care fall into the domain of individual concern. Meal preparation is generally a communal function but, during the annual summer invasion of city hippies, has often temporarily passed into the cooperative or the individual sphere.

Homestead Community was originally set up on a basis identical to that of Freedom Ranch (anybody can come, nobody can be made to leave) except that the land remained in the legal ownership of one individual. This one individual was committed not only to permitting anyone to stay, but also to making everyone welcome. Problems similar to those at Freedom Ranch developed and, in addition, there was violence, over-crowding, drunkenness, and conflicts with neighbors and the authorities (both health and police). No limitation on anarchy was ever attempted on the original site of Homestead Community. But another large parcel of land was opened up on a similar basis, and gradually most of the serious and competent communitarians moved there. The second site was deliberately built with no communal kitchen and no communal shelters. Thus, those not capable or willing to provide their own food and shelter were effectively screened out of the community, without compromising the ideal of total anarchism. Much voluntary cooperation is engaged in at Homestead, as at Freedom Ranch. It might be argued that those groups which rely upon segmentation exclusively are not really communities at all. But the need to screen out incompetents and the need to compromise between tribalism and individualism are problems faced by all communes.

Dry Creek Community is an example of a commune that felt it necessary to employ segmentation in only one area of life – that of privacy of domicile. The Dry Creek people found it relatively easy to work communally, to pool all economic resources, and to have meals and other communal functions together. But all members felt a need for a place where they could retreat from the rest of the community. As a result, Dry Creek gave high priority to the building of individual shelters, allowing farming and other communal activities to be relatively neglected.

Segmentation seems to work well in communities that have no common goal beyond living together. As communes take on more complex goals, the need for more complex forms of integration soon becomes apparent. It is not enough to eliminate those aspects of communal living in which harmony does not occur spontaneously. A certain amount of harmony and coordination must be maintained constantly, somehow, without infringing upon the freedom of the individual. Toward this end, some communities have modified their initial absolute anarchism into what may be called contractual anarchism. Basic anarchism assumes that men are responsible in intention and responsible in action. Contractual anarchism makes only the first of these assumptions. Thus it permits freedom in entering into contracts, but it demands that contracts, once entered into, be carried out.

Sylvan Hills is an example of a commune employed in a type of contractual anarchism. It consists of around twenty people on forty acres of land, who engage in commercial crafts and manufacturing as well as farming. Certain jobs need to be done on a regular basis. Lists are posted describing these jobs. There is no compulsion for anyone to sign up for any particular job or any particular number of hours (although great social pressure would be brought upon anyone who did no or very little work). Once signed up for the job, however, the person is expected to do it with no excuses. If he protests curtailment of freedom, he will be told that he freely entered into the contract, and that next time he should not sign up for a job he does not wish to do.

Another commune known as Astar attempted a similar system. But their organizational structure was a good deal more complex than that of Sylvan Hills (manufacturing, printing, and running a large ranch), and it was soon discovered that the same methods didn't work. A few people had an overview of the community and thus assumed their fair share of the responsibility, but most members simply couldn't grasp the totality of the communal operation. This led to certain people giving orders, with consequent hard feelings and rebelliousness. So another innovation was adopted. On a rotating basis, everyone was made dictator of the community for a week. During this time, the dictator had the responsibility of bearing in mind all work that had to be done, and assigning jobs to each person. It was felt that, after serving a week as dictator, each person would have an overview of what needed to be done and a sense of his fair share. The commune could then revert to straight contractural anarchism. This never occurred because the commune disintegrated in the middle of the experiment. The approach was nevertheless an interesting one.

The most extensive use of contract is made by Mandala Commune. Mandala also exhibits a most ingenious use of segmentation, dividing its year into two six-month seasons. During the summer, Mandala functions as a highly structured commune, relying heavily on the institution of contract. Mandala has never tried to be an anarchistic commune. Many of its members have come to it with previous experiences in less structured communes which have disillusioned them with anarchism. The prospective member must agree to the commune's basic contract as soon as he arrives. This contract requires him to work a forty-hour week, attend communal meetings twice a day, abstain from drugs and certain foods, and abide by the communal bylaws. Other contracts may subsequently be made. The entire commune may contract to keep silent for a day. Or an individual may make a contract, with another person or with the group as a whole, to abstain from smoking, or lose weight, or keep his temper. This heavy reliance on contract places many restraints on the individual during the summer season. But, during the winter season, much of the structure is abandoned, and Mandala becomes a commune very similar to Homestead. This is a use of segmentation that solves the problem of freedom versus community by emphasizing each for half the year. It also assures that only competent, self-reliant individuals will be able to live at Mandala, since they have to be responsible for their own support for half of each year. In a similar vein, I have often thought that the Bruderhof could solve many of its problems by insisting that every member take a sabbatical leave every few years and support himself for a while in the outside world, without being under the stigma of exclusion. This would prove to both the community and himself that he was a member because he wanted to be, not because he needed to be. At Mandala, members return to structured community each spring with a sense of freshness and expectation which the Bruderhof is able to achieve only through periodic crises.

The most widely used means of normative structuring is the search for consensus. Communes carry out this search in meetings similar to the Bruderhof's Brotherhood meetings or Quaker business meetings. The usual procedure, as in the Bruderhof, is for the members to discuss a matter thoroughly until everyone is agreed on a course of action. If unanimity cannot be reached, the matter is tabled. I know of no commune that makes its decisions by majority vote. I have seen several instances, however, of commune members unanimously agreeing to abide by the will of the majority on a single particularly urgent problem.

The search for consensus does not compromise a position of anarchism, because a single veto is enough to prevent any decision from being made. As with contractual anarchism, once a decision is made, everyone is expected to abide by it. This procedure might be called consensual anarchism. I have seen a number of cases in which one or more members of a commune refused to attend or, attending, refused to cooperate with meetings for decision making. These absolute anarchists felt that, even with the guarantee of veto power, the pressure of 'public opinion' at meetings was so strong that individual freedom was dangerously compromised. At Dawn Commune, one member went so far, for a while, as to deliberately veto every decision that was proposed, on the theory that the commune did not have the right to make decisions.

The occurrence of such decision-making meetings is one of the most universal elements of contemporary communes. I observed them in Earth Mother Community, in Hobbit Hole, in Geodesic Village, in Dawn, in Dry Creek, in Astar, and in Mandala. In all of these communities, the form was virtually the same: everyone sat around in a circle; there was a moment of silence to begin, and then the discussion. These discussions were remarkable for the ability of the participants really to listen to one another. At Hobbit Hole the tone was combative; at Geodesic Village, urbane and witty; and at Mandala, psychoanalytic and spiritual. But in all of them the process was essentially the same: deeper and deeper probing into meanings and motivations until a common ground was found. An extremely important latent function of such meetings was the fostering of communal solidarity. It was often noticed and reported that the more difficult the decision was to make, the closer together the discussion brought the community members. Only at one commune did I see a meeting which had the opposite effect – it demonstrated that there was not any real underlying consensus among the members, and that therefore the community was doomed to failure.

Decision-making meetings are not the only places in community life in which the search for consensus is carried on. This search is a continuing process which sometimes is suddenly manifested in a single dramatic act. Riverside is a community of around fifty people. In its early days, it was basically a segmental community, but always a good deal more structured and communal than Freedom Ranch or Homestead. With only eight acres of land, the members lived quite close together, so a great measure of consensus was needed despite the absence of any communal industry. Once I saw some Riverside members gathered in the dining room listening to records. The record player volume was up very high. A girl came in from the kitchen and turned down the volume. Some people grumbled but nobody said anything and the girl went back to the kitchen. Five minutes later the volume was up high again. The girl came back in and the whole pattern was repeated. Five minutes later, again the volume was turned way up. This time the girl came in with a knife and cut the wire. Without a single word being spoken consensus was reached. Nobody in the community questioned the right either of the listeners to turn up the volume or the girl to cut the wire. Each had been 'doing his own thing'. But the girl had registered the intensity of her feelings by her act, and when, a while later, the record player was repaired, the volume was kept low.

Despite incidents like this, Riverside Community was never able to achieve a degree of consensus satisfying to its members while located on its original site. Eventually two major groups branched off from Riverside, and the rest of the community disintegrated. One of the groups formed a spiritual community, led by a charismatic leader who imposed a degree of consensus from above. The other formed a wilderness community, high in the mountains, where it was possible only for the most hardy and woods-wise to survive.

The various techniques that I have discussed can only be described as moderately successful. Seven of the eleven communes mentioned have disintegrated (Sylvan Hills, Dawn, Hobbit Hole, Astar, Dry Creek, Homestead, and Riverside) with an average life span of slightly less than two years. An eighth, Geodesic Village, still exists, but all of its original members have left under duress. A wave of publicity in the mass media brought a sudden onslaught of visitors to Geodesic Village. Some of these visitors decided to stay. They soon outnumbered the original members and a consensus on a conception of community soon emerged which was very different from anything the founders had envisioned or could happily live with.

Segmentalized communes generally last the longest. They are

based on a quite rational strategy of not forcing community, but letting it happen only in those areas of life in which it occurs naturally, letting it grow organically. People whose main objectives are living in the country and having congenial neighbors can be content in a segmental commune. But those who desire a strong sense of family, or who want to commune to do something (start a school, become economically self-sufficient, promote a political or religious doctrine) usually find segmental communes unsatisfactory.

Communes based on contractual anarchism or consensual anarchism, or – what is most common – some mixture of the two, encounter a fundamental problem. These techniques are very practical modifications of absolute anarchism to meet the reality demands of communal living. But both still adhere to the fundamental anarchist assumption that men, as they are, can regulate themselves, love each other, and live together harmoniously, if only placed in the proper environment. Evidence from the Bruderhof indicates that this is not true, that people carry the remnants of the old society within themselves, and that these old selves must be left behind for community to be possible. Evidence from communitarian history and from contemporary communes seems to bear this out. I watched the Hobbit Hole Commune, which practiced both contractual and consensual anarchism very well, disintegrate before my eyes. None of the members wanted this to happen, but strong jealousies and hatreds rose up which went far deeper than anything that could be dealt with through contract. The search for consensus might have reached the root of the problems, but, under stress, each person was too concerned with guarding his own right of veto to help search for the higher unity that always lies beyond apparent discord.

As the golden age of the communion experience fades, anarchism becomes more than ineffectual; it becomes oppressive. It can even become a means of exploitation. Anarchy without mutual concern favors the tyranny of the strong over the weak, and the tyranny of the least committed over the most committed. At Army Surplus, a now defunct urban commune of the early hippie era, the strong and competent males lorded it over the weaker males and the females. Life was not very pleasant at Army Surplus without these men around to fix things, eject unwanted visitors, gather food, and score dope. In the early days, and during the occasional recurrent periods of communion, they performed these services freely and graciously. But during times of discord one became aware of an implicit threat – that if things did not go in a way which was pleasing to these members, they might withdraw from active participation in the commune, or even leave. It is significant that the men at Army Surplus were generally anarchists, while the women were democrats. The women, especially those with children, were more committed to the commune and were less free to leave it. They felt more willing to abide by the will of the majority, even if opposed to it, as long as some common decisions could be made. The men, freer to leave when things got bad, were less willing to so bind themselves. There is a type of Gresham's Law which operates in anarchist communes, whereby the less committed gradually drive out the more committed. An example of this was seen at Earth Mother Commune, located in an area with severe winters. Serious communitarians, especially those with families, foresaw the need to weatherproof buildings and accumulate a supply of firewood. But they were unable to get any cooperation on these projects from those whose commitment did not go beyond the summer, and thus were forced to leave and seek community elsewhere.

Many communes eventually reach some sort of compromise between anarchism and the need for structure. But a few do a surprising flip from anarchism to authoritarianism instead and place themselves under the power of some charismatic leader. This dramatic reversal cannot be explained entirely by the need for structure. It very likely has something to do with the dangers inherent in releasing feelings which has been long repressed.

Psychedelic drug experiences and other experiences of communion liberate great quantities of feelings from the unconscious. Many people are not prepared to handle this energy. A few fall victim to uncontrollable violent or self-destructive urges, but most merely panic and seek some way of regaining rational control. Situations occur which would be ludicrous if they were not so sad. After heroic efforts to break away from the city, find a tribe, and build community, the communitarian panics at simple manifestations of the very community he is seeking: 'I'm so freaked out. I feel like you people are all inside my head and I'm inside yours.' Experiences which are commonplace to many primitive people are totally alien to him. He reacts in terror, often resorting to mystification in an attempt to regain mastery rather than admitting that he doesn't understand. Most communes lack an interpretive framework like that of the Bruderhof with which to explain such phenomena in terms of commonly shared beliefs. In desperation, the communitarian may give blind support to a guru and adopt an ascetic Eastern discipline of enlightenment. The guru may become the commune's charismatic leader. If so, he will fulfil a dual function: making 'mystical' experiences of communion comprehensible and restraining the commune members from what many of them unconsciously fear most, their own unbridled freedom

With or without a charismatic leader, those communes that have survived the conflict between freedom and family have become increasingly aware of the need for an interpretive framework, both to explain collective experiences and to give the commune a vocabulary and a common set of values. Much spiritual search, often eclectic, is associated with the movement. Some communes have taken up a Christian mythos, although it seems extremely doubtful that this will ever become widespread in America. Interest in Oriental religions is much more common. Although these emphasize ego-loss, I see little in them to support the idea of community. However, I am told that this is a blind spot of mine. Concern with native American Indian culture and religion seems to me to be the most likely path for Americans to true community. If it happens this way, tribes will develop in which *agapic* brotherhood is traced, not through God the Father, but through earth the mother.

## 4. *The Bruderhof as a Model*

In the light of the problems that we have been discussing, what can we say about the relevance of the Bruderhof model to post-industrial society? It seems very doubtful that the Bruderhof could ever be a widespread model in the naïve sense of wide-scale adoption *in toto*. Nevertheless, there are important lessons to be learned from the Bruderhof experience, both for the communitarian movement and for the larger society.

One use of the Bruderhof as a model for the communitarian movement is in demonstrating some of the hidden costs of tribalization. To the cynical, the fate of contemporary communes is always the same old story – young idealists starting out in a burst of enthusiasm to create a better world, and ending, sadder but wiser, with their dreams in ruins. The Bruderhof is a counter example, but one that shows that the observations of the cynic contain a germ of truth.

The only reason it is not possible to create a new society out of the materials of the old is that people will not release their death grip on the old. The story that one hears from communes that have disintegrated is always the same. Emotional garbage which had been thought buried safely, deep beneath the ground, comes seeping into the communal drinking water with poisonous results. Two lessons might be drawn from this – one, that men are basically evil and incapable of living together harmoniously, or the other, drawing support from the Bruderhof model, that the costs of commune formation are greater than has generally been anticipated. The Bruderhof would say that the cost is nothing less than the death of the old self, to make room for the birth of the new.

The Bruderhof model also has something to teach society as a whole about the nature and function of the collective behavior experience. Collective behavior, like fire, can be a valuable tool of society if it is properly understood and respected. Emile Durkheim points out the curious fact that primitive people seem to have a better understanding of the importance of this phenomenon than we do, sometimes even sacrificing the functions of their precarious economies to engage in the rituals of collective behavior.[130] Western culture has tended to treat this phenomenon at best as a curiosity, at worst as a dangerous aberration. It has either been unaware of the existence of the unconscious or felt that it was inherently an uncontrollable and malignant force. The Bruderhof, through its controlled utilization of the collective behavior experience, has demonstrated that it need be neither.

If the hippie movement illustrates some of the problems of premature release of unconscious forces, the larger society shows the problems resulting from their over-long repression. A half century after Freud, there has still been no evolution of institutions in Western societies to take into account that the unconscious even exists. The school system is still largely predicated on the concept of man as a rational actor and the child as a blank slate. Cities and towns, as we have seen, have essentially disqualified themselves as possible objects of civic pride (a valuable collective behavior experience), resulting in a dangerously absurd need, on the part of many people, to vent this pride at the level of the nation state.

One result of our widespread cultural ignorance and fear of the collective behavior function is that our society lacks institutions through which mutually manipulative behavior can be temporarily abandoned. Other societies have found it important to have fiestas, saturnalia, and carnivals to provide for periodic psychic regression, release of energy, and renewal. In our own society, Christmas is supposed to serve this function but it has gotten curiously mixed with economic functions. Occasional fads and panics carry some of the weight. Among the middle class, encounter groups have tried to satisfy this need. Perhaps it also helps to explain the character of contemporary college rebellions. One need not discount the serious purpose of these rebellions to notice that the form they often take – mass frenzy, which dies down as suddenly and rapidly as it flared up – serves the important residual function of providing young people with much needed collective behavior experiences.

Societies that ignore the need for the collective behavior experience run the risk of exploding. War abroad and fascism at home provide supreme opportunities for the venting of unconscious energy. We may someday find that adequately channeled collective behavior experience is as essential for the mental health of society as getting a good night's sleep with a good quota of dreams is for the mental health of the individual.

Another value of the Bruderhof model to the larger society is that it illustrates that joy and economic productiveness are not necessarily incompatible. A basic assumption of Western culture that needs to be challenged is that cold-hearted people bring home the most bacon. This may have been true during the developmental phase of our economy, but the needs and circumstances of the post-industrial era are quite different. Many traditional objections to the intentional community as a type of organization thus need to be re-examined. Theodore Caplow discusses some of these traditional objections to what he calls 'utopian communities':

What are the disadvantages of utopia? Why, in the face of repeated demonstrations that segments of society are perfectible, is there so little interest in perfectionism? . . . .

The first disadvantage is that of scale. A utopia cannot be very large, if its members are not to have competing affiliations. The utopian formula is applicable only to small settlements, although these may combine into larger federations . . . .

Another drawback is that the time and energy spent by the utopian organization on its own maintenance is disproportionate to its resources. The rituals, the convocations, the ceremonies, the long indoctrination, the punishment of minor deviations, the conservation of obsolete methods and ideas, are all very costly . . . .

Aside from the direct costs of internal maintenance, utopian organizations tend to be inefficient because achievement is not stressed. The problem of maintaining integration and voluntarism at very high levels takes precedence over problems related to achievement. Utopian experiments in urban factories have been short-lived and rather pathetic.

A utopian organization needs an overwhelming incentive. It is misleading to discuss our utopias in terms of structure alone. Their members are animated by a powerful faith – in perfectionism, in the mystical body of Christ, in Zionism, in the Moravian Creed. They subordinate themselves to the organization for the sake of a goal that takes precedence over any other . . . .[131]

Let us consider these objections, one by one.

It is certainly true that smallness of scale is essential to the communitarian model. Caplow points out that the only way of surmounting this difficulty is to establish federations of small colonies. But elements of post-industrial technology begin to make such federations feasible. There is a decentralist logic to the widespread use of electricity as a means of energy. Electrical devices such as the telephone and the television provide for easy instantaneous communications linkups. This naturally leads to a situation in which people begin to spread themselves out more evenly over the available land surface, and in which these people can easily link up in any conceivable combination for easy communication. In chapter two I spoke of how the Bruderhof horrified its more traditional Hutterian associates by running up enormous long-distance phone bills each month. The Bruderhof had learned about the value of this innovation, while the Hutterians had not. This is not to suggest that the world of the future might be comprised of millions of communes all linked together by the wires of A.T.&T., but only that such communes, or institutions very much like them, may involve a larger proportion of the population than is involved at the present time.

Caplow's second objection is to the amount of time and energy needed by intentional communities to maintain their infra-structures. The Bruderhof model certainly bears this out, but it also demonstrates that this time and energy is a major source of gratification to the members, and cannot be considered 'wasted' except from the narrowest cost-accounting perspective. In post-industrial societies, necessary labor for survival commands very little of the average person's time and energy. This labor must, of course, always be given first priority in the design of any social system, but, beyond that, it is a matter of taste whether it is preferable to devote oneself to the economic pursuit of various luxuries and to 'leisure time' activities, or to 'the rituals, the convocations, the ceremonies, the long indoctrination', etc. of communal life.

The same factors bear on the third of Caplow's objections, that of low economic efficiency. We have seen that the Bruderhof factory does operate at a low level of efficiency but with a high level of quality control. Again it seems a matter of choice whether to strive for an economy of maximum efficiency and huge surpluses, or for an economy of greater craftsmanship.

On the final point, the need for an overwhelming altruistic incentive, Caplow is simply incorrect. We have seen that the Bruderhof provides an immediate and very personal incentive, one that 'costs' the community nothing because it is inherent in the collective life of the group itself. If people desire community, they need only restructure their own lives and perspectives. There is no need for an incentive to be provided for them.

I believe that the chief difficulty for a wider application of the Bruderhof model is none of those discussed by Caplow, but lies in the fact that the collective behavior experience and the re-socialization process, both of which are essential to the model, put individuals in touch with very intense and often long buried primal feelings, often with disastrous results. The discussion of the Bruderhof's crisis indicates some of the dangers, many of which appear in the hippie movement in connexion with the use of psychedelic drugs. In both cases, people are put in contact with very deep and very real feelings which they are not equipped, or only partially equipped, to handle, and which they must therefore obscure in a cloud of mystification.

Neither community nor society, unmixed, seem responsive to the needs of modern man. In traditional community, people are in touch with their basic feelings but enslaved to them through ignorance and superstition. The transformation to society is a long process of liberation through understanding. However, in the course of this liberation, contact with the feeling basis of life itself somehow gets lost. Intentional community, at least as exemplified by the Bruderhof, re-establishes contact with feeling life and, because man is still not capable of dealing with it, re-

enslaves him. Since it is not normally possible to erase knowledge, this re-enslavement is accomplished not through ignorance
and superstition but through mystification and distortion.

There is a need, not for a simple return to community, but for a
return and a new liberation. A liberation is needed in which the
mind is used, not to insulate people from their feelings, but to
give them an understanding of how to preserve them while living
in and meeting the challenges of the world. In this sense, communitarianism seems a highly promising evolutionary and
experimental movement.

It may be that there is no possible solution to the problems
posed by the conflct between community and freedom. I may be
accused of naïve optimism in assuming that there is. But, of
course, no one really knows. Intentional community is essentially
a search, an adventure, and can be valued in and of itself, regardless of whether it is ultimately successful. The most famous
intentional community in American history, Brook Farm, was a
failure. Years later, Nathaniel Hawthorne, who was one of the
early participants, and who could hardly be called an optimistic
character, reminisced in a novel about the experience:

The better life! Possibly, it would hardly look so, now; it is enough
if it looked so then. The greatest obstacle to being heroic is the doubt
whether one may not be going to prove one's self a fool; the truest
heroism is, to resist the doubt; the profoundest wisdom, to know when
it ought to be resisted, and when to be obeyed.

Yet, after all, let us acknowledge it wiser, if not more sagacious, to
follow out one's day-dream to its natural consummation, although if
the vision has been worth the having, it is certain never to be consum-
mated otherwise than by failure. And what of that? Its airiest fragments, impalpable as they may be, will possess a value that lurks not in
the most ponderous realities of any practicable scheme. They are not
the rubbish of the mind. Whatever else I may repent of, therefore, let
it be reckoned neither among my sins nor follies that I once had faith
and force enough to form generous hopes of the world's destiny –
yes! – and to do what in me lay for their accomplishment; even to the
extent of quitting a warm fireside, flinging away a freshly-lighted cigar,
and travelling far beyond the strike of city clocks, through a drifting
snow-storm.[132]

# *Appendix A* □ NOVITIATE AND BAPTISM VOWS

## QUESTIONS FOR ACCEPTANCE INTO THE NOVITIATE 1964

1. Are you certain that this way of brotherly community, based on a firm faith in God and Christ, is the way to which God has called you?

2. Are you ready to put yourself completely and utterly at the disposal of the Church-Community of Christ to the end of your life – and with yourself, all your faculties and the whole strength of your body and soul, as well as you entire property, both that which you now possess and that which you may later inherit or earn?

3. Are you ready to accept every reproof (where this is justified) and vice versa, to reprove others if you sense within our community life something which should be clearer or more fittingly bespeak the Will of God, or if you should feel that something should be abolished or set aside?

4. Are you firmly decided to remain loyal and true, bound with us in mutual service as brothers and sisters, so that our love may be more complete in the building of the Church-Community, in the outreach to men, and in the proclamation of the Gospel?

5. Are you ready, then, to surrender yourself completely and to bind yourself unreservedly to God, Christ and the brothers?

[An earlier form has a sixth question:

Are you ready to be used in whatever place the Church-Community needs you, be it Germany, England, Uruguay, Paraguay or whatever country where there are Bruderhof Communities or wherever you may be sent?]

## BAPTISM, 1964

Baptism is the sign that we are humble before Christ and that we dedicate ourselves to Him. We confess ourselves to Him. All human greatness is refuted. *He is the Head.* He is the Master. He is the King, and we give ourselves in faith to Him.

Let us consider together what one must do to join the Church of Christ.

1. The Church of Christ is the Community of the believing, the people of God, who do and have abstained from sinful life. Into this community we are brought through true submission – (that is, into the spiritual Ark of Noah, in which we can be preserved).

2. It is not a human deed, but an act of God. Just as Mary through faith and the Holy Spirit conceived Christ when she placed her will in God's and said, 'Here am I, a servant of the Lord. Be it unto me according to Thy words.' Thus we must also conceive Christ in faith – then He will begin and complete His work in us.

3. Let each be mindful that the Church has the key and power to loose and to bind, even as Christ has commanded to put away the vicious and to receive the contrite, that it should also be binding in heaven according to the words of Christ (Matthew XVI).

4. That each should count the cost first that will come, but one is not to counsel with flesh and blood. For they that would enter the service of God must be prepared for tribulation for the sake of the truth and the faith, and to die for Christ's sake, if it be the will of God, be it by fire, water or the sword. For now we have the house and shelter, but we know not what will be the morrow. Therefore, no one should join for the sake of the prosperous days. He who will not be steadfast with all the Godly, to suffer the evil as well as the good, and accept all as good whatever the Lord may direct, let him remain away. We desire to persuade no man with smooth words. It is not a matter of human compulsion or necessity, for God wants voluntary service. Whoever cannot

render that cheerfully and with hearty pleasure, let him remain in his former station.

5. Let no one undertake to join the church for the sake of another – the wife for the sake of the husband, or the husband for the wife, or the children for the sake of their parents – that would be vain and building upon the sand, having no permanency, but who would build upon rock tries to please God alone. For each must bear his burden upon that day.

6. One must submit to and follow brotherly admonition, address and punishment – also practice the same and apply the same with respect to others in the house of God, so that no one may partake of another's sins.

7. One should submit himself to obedience to God and His Church, and not be obstinate, or do only his own desire, but permit himself to be guided for the good and necessity of the Church whithersoever it be known to be right.

8. That no one shall have any private possession any more – for one who gives and surrenders himself to the Lord and His Church with all that he has and is able to do, as it was in the original apostolic church when no one said of his possessions that they were his, but all things were common to them. This we regard as the safest way and the most perfect foundation – of this we are also well assured in our hearts.

9. This we now plainly state to everyone beforehand, so that we may be under no obligations to return anything to anyone afterwards. Therefore, if anyone should undertake to join and later feel it impossible to remain and wish to have his goods returned, let him now stay away, keep his own, and leave us in peace. We are not anxious for money and possessions, but desire Godly hearts.

10. Whoever has wrong dealings that are punishable in the world, be it that he is owing men or that he has defrauded them – or if anyone has involved himself in matters of marriage or is engaged to be married, he should first straighten these matters out. For if anyone should conceal any of these things from us, and should in the meantime have himself baptised and we should learn of these matters afterwards, such a one we should be com-

pelled to excommunicate as one who came into the Church improperly and by falsehood. Therefore, let each one be truly warned.

## *Questions:*

1. Do you recognize the teaching of Jesus as set forth in the Gospels and by the Apostles to be the truth and the true foundation of life, and do you acknowledge the Church-Community as being the living expression of this truth in the world today?

2. Do you believe in God, the Father, the Son, Jesus Christ and the Holy Spirit, and will you confess to this?

3. Do you desire that the Church pray that God may forgive the sins which you have committed?

4. Do you desire to give yourself unreservedly to God in the bond of baptism?

© 1971 by Plough Publishing House

This is not a comparative study. There are frequent references to the Hutterians, whose influence on the Bruderhof has been enormous, and occasional mention is made of other communitarian experiments. But the reader who wishes to place the Bruderhof in full comparative perspective must be referred to a number of excellent monographic accounts of other intentional communities, listed in the bibliography appendix.

My experience is that it is very difficult to merge good comparative sociology and good ethnographic sociology. The several excellent comparative studies that I have read (notably John Humphrey Noyes and Rosabeth Kantor) could not at all have prepared me for my experiences in encountering the Bruderhof. The comparative approach to sociology, being excessively concerned with the common denominators of things, often misses their flavor and overlooks their importance. Studies of intentional communities in general have suffered through excessive concern with external forms and insensitivity to inner meanings. The main thing I have to offer in this book about the Bruderhof is an account of what I saw and heard and how I was moved by it.

One ex-Brother criticized preoccupation with the specific patterns of Bruderhof life by citing an analogy. 'Suppose,' he said, 'you saw a man standing up straight and tall wearing clothes in which the creases were also straight and well-ironed. You might as well explain the man's posture by his clothing, as explain the Bruderhof by its external forms.' Almost all previous writings on intentional communities have fallen into this error of fascination with form and technique. Of course, it is important for a community's life to have some form. But this can, and often does, vary tremendously over time, and especially from one successful community to another. All of these forms, however, derive from essentially similar means of maintaining commitment and order.

This study was begun in 1965. I had visited a dozen or so intentional communities in the eastern part of the United States, of which the Bruderhof seemed by far the most interesting. I made arrangements for my wife and myself to visit the Woodcrest colony for a long stay beginning in August. They did not like the idea of a sociological study, but they said that I could come since I also had a personal interest in the community and a desire to understand the life from inside instead of merely analyzing it from without. This was certainly correct. On my part, I assured them that I would conduct no 'surveys' while I was there, do everything possible to fit into the life, and remain open to their Christian message as well. The arrangement was that we would be treated the same as any other guests. That is, we would both work full time in whatever departments of labor we were assigned to, and we would receive free room and board from the community. I asked if we could come for several months, leaving the exact date of departure open. They said that we should come for a month and, at the end of that time, see how we and they both felt about a longer visit.

Before going to the Bruderhof, I spoke to several ex-members of the community. It became clear, from conversations with them, that, in order to get an accurate picture of Bruderhof life, I would have to conduct extensive interviews with ex-members as well as visit the community myself. One reason for this is that a great deal of information in the Bruderhof is kept secret. For instance, Brotherhood meetings are closed to all but full members of the community. I decided to put this off until after our stay at Woodcrest was over.

We stayed at Woodcrest from 11 August 1965 to 5 December 1965, except for two short trips back to Baltimore. Relations with the Bruderhof during almost all of this time were excellent. Toward the end of our stay, the Bruderhof was plunged into one of its periodic crises. Our original intention was to spend two weeks in each of the other two American *hofs* but, because of the crisis, we were not allowed to do this. During our stay at Woodcrest we tried to behave as much as possible like any other residents. I worked in the toy shop, and my wife was shifted around to the various women's work departments. We both kept extensive journals, recording our experience with no attempt, at this point, at analysis or interpretation. While at Woodcrest we were also able to speak informally with many of the members about their own backgrounds and reasons for joining the community. We were also given access to the Bruderhof archives which contain much written material about the Bruderhof community. Minutes of meetings, however, were off limits.

After leaving the Bruderhof, I conducted twenty in depth tape-recorded interviews with ex-Bruderhof members. These averaged approximately four hours in length, the shortest being two hours and the longest over eleven hours. I treated the interviewees mostly as informants rather than as respondents. I followed the format, as much as possible, of a completely unstructured interview, allowing the informant to talk about what he thought was significant. This, I believe, results in greater validity than if the data had been elicited in response to my question. I did, however, guide the interviews by general topic. And some of the time I asked quite specific questions.

In choosing informants, I tried for a great diversity of standpoints. I spoke to *sabras*, to people who had been brought to the Bruderhof, as children, when their parents joined, long-term visitors, novices, full members, and former members of the power hierarchy (Servants of the Word, Witness Brothers, etc.). I spoke with some who had been members in Paraguay and some who had been members in the United States.

## *Appendix C* □ BIBLIOGRAPHY

This bibliography has been divided into three sections. The first lists works dealing with the Bruderhof; the second, general works on intentional communities; the third, all other works. In the case of the first two sections, there is a slight amount of overlap and double listing. Two abbreviations are used: AJS stands for *American Journal of Sociology*, and ASR stands for *American Sociological Review*.

## *I. Bibliography of Works Pertaining to the Bruderhof*

1. Arnold, Eberhard. *Love and Marriage in the Spirit.* Rifton, New York: Plough Publications, 1965.
2. Arnold, Eberhard, *et al. When the Time Was Fulfilled.* Rifton, New York: Plough Publications, 1965.
3. Arnold, E.C.H. 'Eberhard Arnold'. *Mennonite Quarterly Review*, XXVI (1951), 219–21.
4. —. 'Education for Altruism in the Society of Brothers in Paraguay.' *Forms and Techniques of Altruistic and Spiritual Growth*, ed. P.Sorokin. Boston: Beacon Press, 1954.
5. —. 'The Society of Brothers.' *The Mennonite Encyclopedia*, vol. 4, 1126–7.
6. Arnold, Emmy. *Torches Together.* Rifton, New York: Plough Publications, 1963.
7. Armytage, W.H.G. 'Wheathill Bruderhof 1942–58.' *American Journal of Economy*, XVIII (1959), 285–94.
8. Becker, Howard. *German Youth: Bond or Free.* New York: Oxford University Press, 1946.
9. Benepe, Jagna W. 'An Analysis of the Growth and Stability of the Bruderhof Movement.' Unpublished M.A. thesis, Hunter College, 1957.

10. Clement, Jane T. 'Brotherhood is a Way of Life.' *Smith Alumni Quarterly*, Smith College, 1961.

11. Freier, Kolka. 'Housewarming at the Woodcrest Bruderhof.' *Cooperative Living*, VI (1954), 1, 4–5.

12. Fretz, J.W. *Pilgrims in Paraguay*. Scottdale, Pa.: Herald Press, 1953.

13. Hack, Hendrik. 'Primavera, A Communal Settlement of Immigrants in Paraguay.' *Amsterdam Dept. of Cultural and Physical Anthropology*, Royal Tropical Institute, 1958.

14. Hall, Francis. 'Revival of Christian Community.' *Christian Century*, Vol. XXXIV (1957), 1253–5.

15. Hazelton, Philip. 'On Being a Second-Generation Bruder.' *This Magazine is About Schools* (Toronto), IV, 2 (Spring, 1970), 11–41.

16. Lejune, R. *Christoph Blumhardt and His Message*. Rifton, New York: Plough Publications, 1963.

17. Marchant, Will. 'The Bruderhof Communities.' *Cooperative Living*, 1952.

18. Rhoads, Grace. 'Community in the Wilderness.' *Fellowship*, XVIII (1952), 7, 1–5, 32.

19. Rideman, Peter. *Account of Our Religion*. Rifton, New York: Plough Publications, 1965.

20. Society of Brothers. *Living Together*. Farmington, Pennsylvania: Plough Publications, 1958.

21. *Children in Community*. Rifton, New York: Plough Publications, 1963.

22. *Eberhard Arnold*. Rifton, New York: Plough Publications, 1964.

23. *The Plough: The Quarterly of the Bruderhof Communities*. Bromdon, England: Plough Publications, 1953–60.

24. 'Society of Brothers.' *Time Magazine*, LXX, 29 July (1957), 48.

## *II. General Bibliography of Works on Intentional Communities*

No attempt has been made to provide an exhaustive bibliography of these works. Those listed here will serve to provide a thorough introduction to the subject of intentional communities in general. For communities in America which existed before 1830, Bestor's *Backwoods Utopias* provides the definitive bibliography. For more recent material, there is no comparable bibliographic work. The nearest equivalent, published in 1942, is Eaton and Katz's *Research Guide on Cooperative Group Farming.*

25. Albertson, Ralph. 'A Survey of Mutualistic Communities in America.' *Iowa Journal of History and Politics*, XXXIV (October, 1936), 375–445.

26. Alyea, Paul E. & Blanche R. *Fairhope 1894–1954*. University of Alabama Press, 1956.

27. Andrews, E. *The People Called Shakers*. New York: Dover Press, 1953.

28. Armytage, W.H.G. *Heavens Below*. London: Routlege & Kegan Paul, 1961.

29. Baldwin, Monica. *I Leap Over the Wall*. New York: Rinehart, 1950.

30. Ballou, Adin. *History of Hopedale Community*. Thompson and Hill, 1897.

31. Belov, Pedor. *The History of a Soviet Collective Farm*. New York: Praeger, 1955.

32. Bennett, John W. *Hutterian Brethren: The Agricultural Economy and Social Organization of a Communal People*. Stanford: Stanford University Press, 1967.

33. Bernard, L.J. *Origins of American Sociology*. New York: Thomas Y. Cromwell, 1943.

34. Bestor, A.E., Jr. *Backwoods Utopias: The Sectarian and Owenite Phases of Communitarian Socialism in America, 1663–1829.* Philadelphia: University of Pennsylvania Press, 1950.

35. Bettelheim, Bruno. *The Children of the Dream: Communal Childrearing and American Education*. New York: The Macmillan Company, 1969.

36. Bishop, Claire. *All Things Common*. New York: Harper & Row, 1950.

37. Bloesch, D. *Centers of Christian Renewal*. Philadelphia: United Church Press, 1964.

38. Buber, Martin. *Paths in Utopia*. Boston: Beacon Press, 1949.

39. Bushee, Frederick A. 'Communistic Societies in the United States.' *Political Science Quarterly*, XX (December, 1905), 625–64.

40. Calverton, V.F. *Where Angels Dared to Tread*. Indianapolis: Bobbs-Merrill, 1941.

41. Carden, Maren Lockwood. *Oneida: Utopian Community to Modern Corporation*. Baltimore: Johns Hopkins University Press, 1969.

42. Clark, Bertha W. 'The Hutterian Communities.' *J. of Political Economy*, XXXII (1924), 357–74, 468–86.

43. Clark, E.T. *The Small Sects in America*. Gloucester, Massachusetts: Peter Smith, 1949.

44. Conkin, Paul K. *Two Paths to Utopia*. Lincoln, Nebraska: University of Nebraska Press, 1964.

45. Deets, L.E. 'The Origin of Conflict in the Hutterische Communities.' *Publications of the American Sociological Society*, XXV (1931), 125–35.

46. Diamond, Sigmund. 'From Organization to Society: Virginia in the 17th Century.' *AJS*, LXIII (1958), 5.

47. Ditzion, S. *Marriage, Morals, and Sex in America*. New York: Bookman Associates, 1953.

48. Doll, Eugene. 'Social and Economic Organization in Two Pennsylvania German Religious Communites.' *AJS*, LVII (1951), 168–77.

49. Doyle, Leonard J., trans. *St. Benedict's Rule for Monasteries*. St John's Abbey, Collegeville, Minnesota: The Liturgical Press, 1948.

50. Eaton, Joseph and Katz, S. *Research Guide on Cooperative Farming*. New York: H.W. Wilson, 1942.

51. Eaton, Joseph. 'Controlled Acculturation: A Survival Technique of the Hutterites.' *ASR*, XVII (1952), 331–40.

52. Eaton, Joseph and Weil, Robert. *Culture and Mental Disorder: A Comparative Study of the Hutterites and Other Populations*. New York: Free Press, 1955.

53. Etzioni, Amitai. 'Solidaric Work-Groups in Collective Settlements.' *Human Organization*, XVI (1957), 2–6.

54. —.'Functional Differentiation of Elites.' *AJS*, LXIV (1959), 476–87.

55. Gide, Charles. *Communist and Cooperative Colonies*. New York: Thomas P. Crowell, 1928.

56. Hawthorne, Nathaniel. *The Blithedale Romance*. New York: Norton Press, 1852.

57. Kriyananda. *Cooperative Communites: How to Start Them and Why*. San Francisco: Ananda Publications, 1968.

58. Hennacy, Ammon. *The Book of Ammon*. Salt Lake City: published by the author, 1964.

59. Hinds, W. *American Communities*. New York: Corinth Books, 1961.

60. Hine, R.V. *California's Utopian Colonies*. San Marino: Huntington Library 1961.

61. Holloway, Mark. *Heavens on Earth*. New York: Dover Press, 1951.

62. Hostetler, John A. *Amish Society*. Baltimore: Johns Hopkins University Press, 1963.
63. Infield, Henrik. 'Social Control in a Cooperative Society.' *Sociometry*, August, 1942.
64. —. *Cooperative Communities at Work*. New York: Dryden Press, 1945.
65. —. *The American Intentional Community*. Glen Gardner, New Jersey: Libertarian Press, 1955.
66. Infield, Henrik and Maier, J. *Cooperative Group Living*. New York: Henry Koosis, 1950.
67. Kaplan, Bert, *et al. Personality in a Communal Society*. University of Kansas Press, 1956.
68. Kramer, Wendell B. 'Criteria for the Intentional Community.' Unpublished Ph.D. thesis, New York University School of Education, 1955.
69. Lipscomb, Winifred. 'Status and Structure of the Family in Idealistic Communities.' Unpublished Ph.D. thesis, University of North Carolina, 1947.
70. Lockwood, George B. *The New Harmony Movement*. New York: Appleton Press, 1905.
71. Loomis, Mildred. *Go Ahead and Live*. New York: Philosophical Library, 1965.
72. MacIver Robert. 'Social Cohesion in the Utopian Communities.' *Society: A Textbook in Sociology*. New York: Farrar & Rinehart, 1937, 347–51.
73. Mikkelson, Michael. 'A Religious Communistic Settlement in Henry County, Illinois.' Unpublished M.A. thesis, Johns Hopins University, 1892.
74. Morgan, Arthur. *The Small Community*. New York: Harper & Row, 1942.
75. —. *Nowhere Was Somewhere*. Chapel Hill: University of North Carolina Press, 1946.
76. Nordhoff, Charles. *Communistic Societies of the United States*. New York: Dover Press, 1875.
77. Noyes, J.H. *History of American Socialisms*. New York: Hillary Press, 1870.
78. Noyes, Pierrepont. *My Father's House*. New York: Farrer & Rinehart, 1937.
79. Parker, Robert A. *A Yankee Saint: J.H. Noyes and the Oneida Community*. New York: Putnam, 1935.
80. Peters, Victor J. *All Things Common: The Hutterites of Manitoba*. Minneapolis: University of Minnesota Press, 1965.

81. Persons, Stow, ed. *Socialism and American Life*. Princeton University Press, 1952.

82. Poll, Solomon. *The Hassidic Community of Williamsburg*. New York: Free Press, 1962.

83. Randall, E.O. *History of the Zoar Society*. Columbus, Ohio: Fred J. Heer, 1899.

84. Rideman, Peter. *Account of our Religion*. 1565. Translation by K. Hasenberg. London: Hodder & Stoughton (1950).

85. Rosenfield, Eva. 'Social Stratification in a "Classless" Society.' *ASR*, XVI (1951), 766–74.

86. Schmalenbach, Herman. 'The Sociological Category of Communion.' Talcott Parsons *et al.*, ed., *Theories of Society*, I, New York: Free Press, 1961.

87. Shaw, A. *Icaria*. New York: Putnam Press, 1884.

88. Skinner, B.F. *Walden Two*. New York: The Macmillan Company, 1948.

89. Spiro, M. *Kibbutz: Venture in Utopia*. New York: Schocken Press, 1956.

90. —. *Children of the Kibbutz*. New York: Schocken Press, 1958.

91. Sugihara, Yoshie & Plath, David W. *Sensei and His People: The Building of a Japanese Commune*. Berkeley: University of California Press, 1969.

92. Swift, L. *Brook Farm*. New York: Corinth Press, 1900 (1961).

93. Tyler, Alice. *Freedom's Ferment*. Minneapolis: University of Minnesota Press, 1944.

94. Vallier, Ivan A. 'Production Imperatives in Communal Systems.' Unpublished Ph.D. thesis, Harvard University, 1959.

95. Wesson, Robert. *Soviet Communes*. Rutgers University Press, 1963.

96. Whitney, Norman. *Experiments in Community*. Wallingford, Pennsylvania: Pendle Hill, 1966.

97. Williams, Julia. 'An Analytical Tabulation of the North American Utopian Communities by Type, Longevity, and Location.' Unpublished M.A. thesis, University of South Dakota, 1939.

98. Wooster, Ernest. *Communities of the Past and Present*. New Llano, Louisiana: Llano Cooperative Colony Press, 1924.

99. Yablonsky, Lewis. *Synanon: The Tunnel Back*. New York: The Macmillan Company, 1965.

100. —. *The Hippie Trip*. New York: Pegasus Press, 1968.

101. Yambura, Barbara & Bodine, Eunice. *A Change and a Parting*. Almes: Iowa University Press, 1960.

## III. Bibliography of Materials not on the Subject of Intentional Community

The materials listed in this section, although not directly related to the subject of intentional community, have been of aid to me in formulating the ideas presented in this book. I was especially influenced by the essay by Herman Schmalenbach in writing chapter two. Robert Lifton's book was an important influence on chapter six. The Elsworth Baker and Gary Snyder entries were important to me in the writing of chapter seven.

102. Adler, Nathan. 'The Antinomian Personality: A Typological Construct.' Address given at the University of California Medical Center, November 1, 1967.

103. Almond, G. *The Appeals of Communism.* Princeton: Princeton University Press, 1954.

104. Arensberg, Conrad. 'The Community Study Method.' *AJS*, LX: 11 (1954), 109–24.

105.     'The Community as an Object and Sample.' *Amer. Anthro.*, LXIII: 2, Part 1 (1961).

106. Baker, Elsworth F. *Man in the Trap: The Causes of Blocked Sexual Energy.* New York: The Macmillan Company, 1967.

107. Barnard, Chester. *The Functions of the Executive.* Harvard University Press, 1938.

108. Banfield, Edward. *The Moral Basis of a Backward Society.* Glencoe: Free Press, 1958.

109. Bettelheim, Bruno. *The Informed Heart.* Glencoe: Free Press, 1960.

110. Bion, W. R. *Experiences in Groups.* New York: Basic Books, 1959.

111. Brown, J. A. C. *Techniques of Persuasion: From Propaganda to Brainwashing.* Baltimore: Penguin Books, 1963.

112. Caplow, T. *Principles of Organization.* New York: Harcourt Brace & World, 1964.

113. Chafee, G. 'Isolated Religious Sects as an Object for Research.' *AJS*, XXXV (1958), 618–30.

114. Collin, Rodney. *The Theory of Celestial Influence.* London: Stuart & Watkins Ltd, 1968.

115. Durkheim, Emile. 'On Mechanical and Organic Solidarity.' Talcott Parsons, *et al.*, ed. *Theories of Society*, I, New York: Free Press, 1961.

116. —. *Suicide.* Glencoe: Free Press, 1951.

117.     *The Elementary Forms of Religious Life.* New York: Free Press, 1965.

118. Faris, Robert. *Handbook of Modern Sociology*. Chicago: Rand McNally, 1964.
119. Festinger, Leon, *et al. Social Pressures in Informal Groups*. Stanford: Stanford University Press, 1950.
120. *When Prophecy Fails*. New York: Harper, 1956.
121. Friedrich, C., ed. *Community. Nomos, The Yearbook of the American Society of Political and Legal Philosophy*, II, New York: Liberal Arts Press, 1959.
122. Fuller, Buckminster. *Operations Manual For Spaceship Earth*. Carbondale: Southern Illinois University Press, 1969.
123. Goffman, Erving. *Asylums*. New York: Anchor Press, 1961.
124. Gustaitis, Rasa. *Turning On*. New York: The Macmillan Company, 1969.
125. Hesse, Herman. *Journey to the East*. New York: Noonday Press, 1956.
126. Hoffer, Eric. *The True Believer*. New York: New American Library, 1951.
127. Johnson, Benton. 'On Church and Sect.' *A S R*, XXXVIII:4 (1963), 539–49.
128. Jones, Maxwell. *The Therapeutic Community*. New York: Basic Books, 1965.
129. Kogon, Eugen. *The Theory and Practice of Hell*. New York: Berkeley Books, 1950.
130. Le Bon, Gustave, *The Crowd*. London: Ernest Benn Ltd, 1896 (20th print 1952).
131. Lee, Alfred M. *Principles of Sociology*. New York: Barnes & Noble, 1946.
132. Lewin, Bertram. 'The Psychoanalysis of Elation.' *Psychoanalytic Quarterly* (New York), LXI.
133. Lifton, Robert. *Thought Reform and the Psychology of Totalism*. New York: Norton, 1961.
134. Maslow, Abraham. *Religions, Values, and Peak Experiences*. Columbus: Ohio State University Press, 1964.
135. Marx, Karl. *The Communist Manifesto*. Beer, Samuel H., ed. New York: Appleton-Century-Crofts, 1848.
136. McLaughlin, Barry. *Studies in Social Movements: A Social Psychological Perspective*. New York: Free Press, 1969.
137. McLuhan, Marshall. *War and Peace in a Global Village*. New York: Bantam Books, 1968.
138. Mead, Margaret. *Cooperation and Competition Among Primitive Peoples*. Boston: Beacon Press, 1937.

139. Parsons, T. and Bales, R. *Family Socialization and Interaction Process*. Glencoe: Free Press, 1955.

140. Rand, Christopher. *Los Angeles: The Ultimate City*. New York: Oxford University Press, 1967.

141. Schmalenbach, Herman. 'The Sociological Categories of Communion.' Talcott Parsons, *et al.*, ed., *Theories of Society*, I. New York: Free Press, 1961.

142. Simmel, Georg. *Conflict and the Web of Group Affiliations*. Glencoe: Free Press, 1955.

143. Smelser, Neil. *Theory of Collective Behavior*. New York: Free Press, 1962.

144. Snyder, Gary. *Earth House Hold*. New York: New Directions, 1969.

145. Sorel, Georges. *Reflections on Violence*. T.E. Hulme, trans. New York: Peter Smith Publications, 1941.

146. Sorokin, P. *Explorations in Altruistic Love and Behavior*. Boston: Beacon Press, 1950.

147. Stein, Maurice. *The Eclipse of Community*. New York: Harper & Row, 1959.

148. Steiner, Jean-Francois. *Treblinka*. New York: New American Library, 1967.

149. Stephens, William N. *The Family in Cross-Cultural Perspective*. New York: Holt, Rinehart & Winston, 1963.

150. Theobald, Robert. *An Alternative Future for America, II*. Chicago: Swallow Press, 1970.

151. Thrupp, Sylvia, ed. *Millenial Dreams in Action*. The Hague: Mouton & Co., 1962.

152. Toch, Hans. *The Social Psychology of Social Movements*. Indianapolis: Bobbs-Merrill, 1965.

153. Tonnies, F. *Community and Society*. C. Loomis, trans. East Lansing: Michigan State Press, 1957.

154. Troeltsh, J. *The Social Teachings of the Christian Churches*. New York: The Macmillan Company, 1931.

155. Turner, R. and Killian, L. *Collective Behavior*. Englewood Cliffs, New Jersey: Prentice Hall, 1957.

156. Warren, Roland, ed. *Perspectives on the American Community*. Chicago: Rand McNally, 1966.

157. Waters, Frank. *The Man Who Killed the Deer: A Novel of Pueblo Indian Life*. Chicago: Swallow Press, 1942.

(At the time of this writing we are looking forward to the publication of Rosabeth Moss Kanter's, *Utopia: A Study of Comparative Organization*.)

# ☐ NOTES

## Introduction

1. A.E. Bestor, Jr., *Backwoods Utopias: The Sectarian and Owenite Phases of Communitarian Socialism in America, 1653–1829*, 3 f.
2. Karl Marx, *Communist Manifesto*, 38.

## Chapter One

3. Georges Sorel, *Reflections on Violence*.
4. R. Lejune, *Christoph Blumhardt and His Message*.
5. G. Almond, *The Appeals of Communism*.
6. Matthew 5:14–16, (King James version).
7. Rasa Gustaitis, *Turning On*, 167.
8. Emmy Arnold, *Torches Together*, 159–60.
9. Erving Goffman, *Asylums*.
10. Mircea Eliade, *The Myth of the Eternal Return*.
11. Gustaitis, 168.
12. Mark 14:33–37.
13. Emmy Arnold, 55.
14. Emmy Arnold, 57.
15. Society of Brothers, ed., *Eberhard Arnold*, 23.
16. Emile Durkheim, *The Elementary Forms of Religious Life*, 23.
17. These ideas are taken from the writings of Bronislaw Malinowski.

## Chapter Two

18. F. Tënnies, *Community and Society*.
19. Herman Schmalenbach, 'The Sociological Category of Communion,' 334.

20. Schmalenbach.
21. Schmalenbach, 335 *f.*
22. Emmy Arnold, *Torches Together*, 12.
23. Emmy Arnold, 15.
24. 'The Emperor's New Clothes,' unpublished college term paper, by an ex-Bruderhof member.
25. Emmy Arnold, 27.
26. Emmy Arnold, 37.
27. Emmy Arnold, 36.
28. Emmy Arnold, 34.
29. 'The Emperor's New Clothes.'
30. Emmy Arnold, 63.
31. Emmy Arnold, 52 *f.*
32. Emmy Arnold, 65.
33. Emmy Arnold, 46 *f.*
34. Schmalenbach, 337.
35. Emmy Arnold, 194.
36. Emmy Arnold, 121.
37. Emmy Arnold, 123.
38. Emmy Arnold, 123.
39. Victor J. Peters, *All Things Common: The Hutterites of Manitoba*, 174 *f.*
40. Emmy Arnold, 147 *f.*
41. 'The Emperor's New Clothes.'
42. Emmy Arnold, 123.
43. Emmy Arnold, 126.
44. Emmy Arnold, 207 *f.*
45. 'The Emperor's New Clothes.'
46. Norman Whitney, *Experiments in Community*, 34 *f.*
47. Hendrik Hack, 'Primavera, A Communal Settlement of Immigrants in Paraguay,' 4.
48. J. W. Fretz, *Pilgrims in Paraguay*, 59.
49. Fretz, 59.
50. Hack, 6.
51. Article by a Bruderhof member.
52. Victor J. Peters, 176.
53. 'The Emperor's New Clothes.'
54. Jagna W. Benepe, 'An Analysis of the Growth and Stability of the Bruderhof Movement,' 51.
55. Hack, 12.
56. 'The Emperor's New Clothes.'

57. Victor J. Peters (an earlier version of the manuscript).
58. G. Almond, *The Appeals of Communism.*

## *Chapter Three*

59. Eberhard Arnold, *Love and Marriage in the Spirit,* 115.
60. Eberhard Arnold, 64 *ff.*
61. Eberhard Arnold, 28–32.
62. *Community Playthings Toy Catalogue,* 1955.
63. Don Peters, 'Men and Their Work,' *Plough* IV–3, 1956, 73–8.
64. Other communal societies, such as the kibbutzim, praise good work highly. See M. Spiro, *Kibbutz: Venture in Utopia.*
65. A catalogue is available from Plough Publishing Company, Society of Brothers, Rifton, New York.
66. Stan Ehrlich, 'Is This Escape?' *Plough,* IV–I, 1956, 3–6.

## *Chapter Four*

67. Herbert Blumer, 'Collective Behavior,' in Alfred M. Lee's *Principles of Sociology,* 170 *f.*
68. Ralph Turner and L. Killian, *Collective Behavior,* 1.
69. 'The Emperor's New Clothes.'
70. Eberhard Arnold, *Love and Marriage in the Spirit,* 236–7.
71. Bertram Lewin, 'The Psychoanalysis of Elation,' 12.
72. Lewin, 14.
73. Lewin, 166.
74. Lewin, 218.
75. Emile Durkheim, 'On Mechanical and Organic Solidarity.'
76. Maren Lockwood Carden, *Oneida: Utopian Community to Modern Corporation,* 58.
77. Georg Simmel, *Conflict and the Web of Group Affiliations,* 140.
78. Eberhard Arnold, 126 *f.*

## *Chapter Five*

79. T. Caplow, *Principles of Organization,* 314.
80. Matthew 18:15–18. (King James version).
81. Peter Rideman, *Account of Our Religion,* 131 *f.*

82. Robert Lifton, *Thought Reform and the Psychology of Totalism*, 65 *f*.
83. Erving Goffman, *Asylums*.
84. Robert Friedman, 'Living in a Society of Brothers', *Fellowship*, July 1965.
85. Joseph Eaton, 'Controlled Acculturation.'

## *Chapter Six*

86. Letter from a novice, 1953.
87. Other nationalities had representation at other *hofs* however.
88. Robert Lifton, *Thought Reform and the Psychology of Totalism*, 66.
89. Erving Goffman, *Asylums*.
90. Lifton, 67 *f*.
91. Lifton, 68.
92. Lifton, 69.
93. Lifton, 487.
94. Bruno Bettelheim, *The Informed Heart*.
95. Lifton, 73.
96. Lifton, 74.
97. Lifton, 75.
98. See, for instance, Lewis Yablonsky, *Synanon: The Tunnel Back*.
99. Lifton, 78.
100. Lifton, 78–9.
101. Rodney Collin, *The Theory of Celestial Influence*, 322 *f*.
102. Lifton, 66.
103. Philip Hazelton, 'On Being a Second-Generation Bruder,' 41.
104. Hazelton, 31 *f*.
105. Society of Brothers, *Children in Community*, 88.
106. Hazelton, 35.
107. *Children in Community*, 95.
108. Note the analogy to inmate-staff relationships as described in Erving Goffman, *Asylums*.
109. Emile Durkheim, *Suicide*, 24 *f*.
110. *Hazelton*, 37 *f*, 41.

## *Chapter Seven*

111. Herman Schmalenbach, 'The Sociological Category of Communion,' 13.
112. James S. Coleman, personal correspondence.

113. Frank Waters, *The Man Who Killed the Deer: A Novel of Pueblo Indian Life*, 76 *f.*

114. Maurice Stein, *The Eclipse of Community*.

115. Gideon Sjoberg, 'The Origin and Evolution of Cities,' in Patrick Gleason, ed., *America Changing*, 91.

116. Sjoberg, 81.

117. Norton Long, 'The Local Community as an Ecology of Games,' in Roland Warren, ed., *Perspectives on the American Community*, abstract of the article which appeared in an earlier version.

118. Lewis Wirth, 'Urbanization as a Way of Life,' in Roland Warren, ed., 49.

119. Wirth, 51.

120 Christopher Rand, *Los Angeles: The Ultimate City*, 131 *f.*, 163 *f.*

121. Gary Snyder, *Earth House Hold*, 110 *f.*

122. William N. Stephens, *The Family in Cross-Cultural Perspective*, 347 *f.*

123. Stephens, 360, 370 *f.*

124. Stephens, 366.

125. Snyder, 111.

126. *Whole Earth Catalog*, Portola Institute, 558 Santa Cruz Ave, Menlo Park, California.

127. *Green Revolution*, Route 1, Box 129, Freeland, Maryland,

128. Nathan Adler, 'The Antinomian Personality: A Typological Construct,' 10, 13.

129. Adler, 22.

130. Emile Durkheim, *The Elementary Forms of Religious Life*.

131. T. Caplow, *Principles of Organization*, 315 *f.*

132. Nathaniel Hawthorne, *The Blithedale Romance*, 38 *f.*